REGIONAL CULTURES IN AMERICAN ROCK 'N' ROLL

AN ANTHOLOGY

EDITED BY: **DAVID STUART**   **SCOTT ANDERSON**

cognella™
San Diego, CA

Bassim Hamadeh, CEO and Publisher
Christopher Foster, General Vice President
Michael Simpson, Vice President of Acquisitions
Jessica Knott, Managing Editor
Kevin Fahey, Cognella Marketing Manager
Jess Busch, Senior Graphic Designer
Jamie Giganti, Project Editor
Brian Fahey, Licensing Associate

First published in the United States of America in 2013 by Cognella, Inc.

Printed in the United States of America

ISBN: 978-1-935551-61-4 (pbk) / 978-1-62131-449-3 (br)

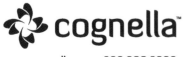

www.cognella.com 800.200.3908

♪ Contents

 # Preface

Regional Cultures in American Rock 'n' Roll: An Anthology

Audience

Regional Cultures in American Rock 'n' Roll: An Anthology has been created as an additional supplementary text to accompany a standard course textbook for a semester or quarter-length introductory history of rock 'n' roll. It has been produced for the student who has no specialized knowledge of music. Because of the cultural/historical slant of its articles, the book is also well suited for inclusion in a course on popular American culture.

Approach

Like Janus, the Roman mythological god of gates and doors, beginnings and endings, art both reflects the society that produces it and anticipates future changes. Rock 'n' roll is no exception. Rock, however, focuses more intently on its chosen demographic: the youth audience. Additionally, as rock 'n' roll became a major player in popular culture in the late 1960s, it began to splinter into categories, genres, and subgenres as the star-maker machinery behind popular songs began to hear within rock the sweet sounds of the cash register. In the 1950s and early '60s most writers and critics had dismissed rock 'n' roll as a fad, but the huge baby boomer demographic flocked to buy the music and it became a dominant force in popular culture. With the publication of *Rolling Stone* magazine in 1967 with critic Ralph J. Gleason and gonzo journalist Hunter S. Thompson, both the press and audiences began to take this type of popular music more seriously. Other gifted and insightful writers such as Greil Marcus, Charlie Gillette, Lester Bangs, and Dave Marsh soon followed, giving a serious, critical voice to this music. A later generation of writers, including Peter Guralnick, Mikal Gilmore, Robert Christgau, and Jim De Rogatis, has continued the tradition into the twenty-first century.

American "rock 'n' roll" includes many genres or categories that share a style or common musical language. Additionally, nonmusical criteria such as cultural and/or geographical origin also define genres. Three major regional cultural centers represented by their respective song forms and styles proved crucial to the development of a popular music style that is now assimilated and practiced throughout the world. *Regional Cultures in American Rock 'n' Roll: An Anthology* will begin with these important regional influences as rock 'n' roll emerges in the mid to late 1940s: Memphis and Nashville in Tennessee, and Tin Pan Alley in New York. Archetypical styles are the blues from Memphis, country from Nashville, and "American popular music" from Tin Pan Alley. Classic characteristics of these archetypical styles form the three basic formats of rock songs: 12-bar blues (blues), AABA/32-bar pop (pop), and verse-and-refrain/verse-chorus (country). These forms (or a variation or combination) are evident in nearly every rock song.

As these three elemental forms began to combine and recombine in the late 1940s and early '50s, they coalesced as jump blues, rockabilly, and rhythm and blues (R&B). Through the next five decades, the ongoing combinations and permutations of basic forms and styles resulted in a list of genres that continues to grow. Below are some of the current "genres" used to describe contemporary "rock" music:

> Jump blues, rhythm and blues, rockabilly, rock, country music, electronic music, electronic dance music, electronica, melodic music, reggae, dub and related forms, punk music, new wave, folk rock, country rock, hip hop/rap, contemporary African music, fusion/jazz rock, art rock, prog rock, high-energy, house, dream house, acid house, garage, chicago, acid jazz, disco house, tribal house, progressive house, techno/techno-house, trance, jungle/drum n bass, happy hardcore, sexcore, energy alternative, ambient—not to mention, **pop**

Categorizing music genres provides a method for tracing musical threads through history. It also makes it easier for individuals to find artists that they enjoy.

Labeling music into genres and subgenres, however, can often be both contrived and confusing to the listener, for artists are always experimenting, and newly emerging styles may incorporate features of multiple genres. Such labeling can sometimes be negative because pigeonholing particular musicians into a single genre can be ill-founded; artists often include a variety of genres over time or even within a single piece. Also, a particular genre category could scare away prospective fans who may be prejudiced against a particular label.

Because rock 'n' roll is an important part of popular culture, many believe that the categorization of music into genres is based more on commercial and marketing motives than musical criteria. This is common with online music sellers that show us "customers who purchased (or downloaded) 'X' CD also purchased 'Y' CD." Or witness the vast number of websites such as Pandora.com that allow the listener to search and create lists of artists with "similar" music.

Many of these old styles are reintroduced and marketed as "new styles" by the movers and shakers of popular culture seeking the "next great thing." The biblical verse from Ecclesiastes 1:9, "What has been will be again, what has been done will be done again;

there is nothing new under the sun," might be a good description of the popular music industry.

Content and Organization

The anthology consists of five parts:

Part I — Rock's Roots and How We Got Electric
Part II — Rock Rises from American Song Traditions: The Blues, Folk/Country and Popular Song
Part III — Styles Splinter and Classic Rock Emerges
Part IV — Rediscovering the American Voice: The Singer/Songwriter
Part V — Back to the Basics: Rock Returns to the Garage

Each of these five parts contains writings by critics and scholars, some contemporary to the artists and music discussed, and some offering perspective from years later. Each of the parts will have a short introduction setting the stage for the excerpts covered.

Acknowledgments

The authors wish to thank Karol Crosbie for invaluable editing and helpful suggestions, Meredith Stuart for her creative cover design, and Al Grisanti, Jennifer Bowen, Brent Hannify, and Amy Wiltbank at Cognella Academic Publishing for editorial assistance. We would especially like to thank the former and current students of the History of Rock 'n' Roll courses at Iowa State University and the University of Nebraska, Lincoln, for their enthusiasm for America's popular music. Their energy and input have inspired this text.

♪ Part I

Rock's Roots and How We Got Electric

Many of the of the techniques and styles that coalesced into rock 'n' roll were characteristic of earlier traditions that included regional blues, jazz, folk, country music and the popular song. As popular music recording exploded in the late 1940s and through mid-'50s, recording studios in Memphis, Nashville, and New York City attracted regional performers of these styles. As the big band faded out following World War II and music by smaller, amplified groups became more popular, new styles such as rockabilly, jump blues and rhythm and blues (R&B) combined with elements of blues, jazz, and country to form the new hybrid known as rock 'n' roll.

Technology drives nearly all genres of rock 'n' roll. The development of the electric guitar in the 1930s and electric bass in the 1950s allowed fewer musicians to produce bigger, louder sounds. Vocal amplification allowed singers to work with amplified guitars, basses, and drums. Blues and country artists in the 1940s and '50s were among the first to take advantage of these instruments as they moved into juke joints and bars to bring their music to larger audiences.

There is no question about which came first when it comes to rock and rock criticism—the music predates critical analysis by more than a decade. Once rock criticism took off, radio disc jockeys became early advocates. In America, there were many writers, but in England, writer Charlie Gillett stood out in a less crowded scene. *The Sound of the City* was the culmination of Gillett's master's degree thesis and writing that he had done during the rise of rock 'n' roll in England in the '60s. The book was a detailed primer about how early-source rhythm and blues became rock 'n' roll. Gillett's attention to detail, including his coverage of obscure record labels, was legendary.

The excerpt in this anthology traces pop music back to the roots of its sound and its industry. The overview encompasses country music, including hillbilly, country and western and the music of the Grand Ole Opry. It traces the beginning of the youth culture that grew out of the affluence of post–World War II America and the attempts of adult listeners to explain the popularity of this new music. The late-night sound that Alan Freed cultivated in Cleveland suddenly became the "sound of young America"—a term that would be appropriated by Berry Gordy Jr. in Detroit at the end of the '50s as the slogan of Motown Records. Gillett explains how the pop music industry was able to make money from the hybrid music called rock 'n' roll. A new licensing agency, Broadcast Music Incorporated (BMI), was created. Music was now made for adolescents rather than exclusively for adults. The world would never be the same.

Cincinnati is rarely the first city that comes to mind when one considers the early days of rhythm and blues or rock 'n' roll. Certainly Cleveland belongs in that conversation, and perhaps even New York because of the influence of Alan Freed. But Cincinnati? Jim Miller, original editor of *The Rolling Stone Illustrated History of Rock 'n' roll* and the principal consultant to the 1995 Warner TV/Time Life Home Video *History of Rock and Roll,* and for 10 years pop music critic for *Newsweek* argues for Cincinnati's early-day status. Wynonie Harris' version of the rhythm and blues cum rock 'n' roll song *Good Rockin' Tonight* was recorded in Cincinnati—perhaps the beginning of the music that would become rock 'n' roll. As Miller notes, "Nobody noticed…the music we call rock 'n' roll hadn't yet been named much less invented."

This is how it begins. Small storms gather. Black singers and groups begin to make inroads with white audiences primarily through cover versions of songs initially popularized by white artists. It all leads us to the South—to Memphis and New Orleans and then, north to Chicago and Detroit. The geographical roots of 'rock 'n' roll are often obscure and include Omaha, Neb. (Roy Brown's birthplace), and Kansas City, where the music flourished before becoming rock 'n' roll. The birth of rock 'n' roll has been romanticized and simplified in movies, books, stories and songs. But, in fact, its story is filled with failed or muted attempts that eventually led to the breakthrough. It was worth the wait.

Monica M. Smith, an exhibition program manager at the Lemelson Center for the Study of Invention and Innovation at the Smithsonian Institution, traces the rise of the electric guitar from the Rickenbacker "frying-pan" of the 1930s through the developments of Leo Fender and Les Paul to the myriad of models such as Junior Brown's "guit-steel" and the Flying V. Smith traces the evolution of the electric guitar beginning with big-band guitarist Charlie Christian, who used the instrument to step out in front of the band and play some of the first-ever guitar solos. She traces its evolution through the first decades of rock and makes an excellent case for the instrument becoming the tail-that-wags-the-dog: "At first the electric guitar just wanted to be heard, but it ended up taking over popular music and revolutionizing society."

Good Rockin' Tonight

December 28, 1947

By James Miller

As epochal events go, it was modest, unimpressive—and, at the time, all but ignored. The site was a nondescript recording studio in Cincinnati, Ohio. The occasion was a recording session for a company unknown to most Americans, King. The agent of change was a singer named Wynonie Harris, thirty-two years old, also practically unknown. In most respects, there was nothing noteworthy about the setting, the singer, or his songs. But one of the songs Harris sang on December 28, 1947, "Good Rockin' Tonight," would become a best-selling hit, played on jukeboxes and aired on radio stations across black America. And by popularizing the word "rock," Harris' recording would herald a new era in American popular culture.

Nobody noticed. In December of 1947, the music we now call "rock and roll" hadn't yet been named, much less invented. When Harris sang his pathbreaking song, he was simply doing what he had done for years, practicing a time-honored craft he had mastered in an old-fashioned way, through trial and error, learning how to make music that would lift listeners up, put people into motion, and let them dance the night away.

"Hence the dance hall as temple," the novelist and critic Albert Murray has written: "Hence all the ceremonially deliberate drag steps and shaking and grinding movements during, say, the old downhome Saturday Night Function, and all the sacramental strutting and swinging along with all the elegant stomping. … And hence in consequence the fundamental function of the blues musician (also known as the jazz musician), the most obvious as well as the most pragmatic mission of whose performance is not only to drive the blues away and hold them at bay at least for the time being, but also to evoke an ambiance of Dionysian revelry."

In the way that Wynonie Harris had lived his life, and made his music, his objective was plain and simple: it was revelry, the more "Dionysian" the better. At the time he recorded "Good Rockin' Tonight," he was already a minor legend. Renowned for his fast living and hard drinking, he'd been playing Saturday Night Functions from coast to coast since the mid-Forties, building up a reputation as one of the wildest black showmen of his day. Photographs show a coffee-colored Clark Gable, debonair, cocky, a gleam in his eyes, the promise of pleasure on his lips.

A generation later, Harris would have become a pinup for kids, a pop culture icon, just like Michael Jackson or Prince, two of his spiritual heirs. But in 1947, he was, by comparison, a nobody—an anonymous journeyman. In those days, there were few magazines devoted to pop music, no TV shows about it (television was still in its infancy), and little mainstream media coverage of Negro stars like Wynonie Harris.[1] Despite the widespread popularity in America of black dance music and of certain black entertainers, such as Louis Armstrong, the Mills Brothers, and the Ink Spots, patterns of social segregation cut deep. Inhabiting a common culture, whites and blacks still lived largely in worlds apart.

Harris had first achieved fame in the world of black music with Lucky Millinder, who led one of Harlem's hottest dance bands. After scoring a vocal hit with the Millinder band in 1945—it was a good-natured blues novelty, "Who Threw the Whiskey in the Well?"— Harris went solo, recording for several different small labels, and selling just enough copies to sustain his career.

His session for King after Christmas in 1947 hardly promised anything out of the ordinary. As was customary in those days, the session was scheduled to last three hours and produce three or four usable takes of three or four new songs. The band consisted of seasoned musicians, most of them jazzmen like Oran "Hot Lips" Page, an alumnus of Count Basie's renowned Kansas City band. As usual, the label's A & R man (for "artists and repertoire") had selected the songs for the band to play. The tunes ran the gamut. One was a risqué novelty, long since forgotten, called "Lollipop Mama." Another tune, "I Believe I'll Fall in Love," was even less distinguished. Songs like this—and the fare was typical—did not give a singer much to work with. Still, if luck was with him—if Harris caught the right feeling, if his band hit a relaxed rhythmic groove—even the most hackneyed of songs might let a blues musician fulfill his fundamental function, making music of sufficient energy and earthiness to provoke an outburst of emotion that carried listeners away.

The composer of "Good Rockin' Tonight" was a young singer named Roy Brown, a native of New Orleans and a fan of Wynonie Harris. Legend has it that Brown, inspired by hearing Harris in person, wrote the song on a paper bag and offered it to "Mister Blues" (his nickname) backstage. When Harris refused the gift, Brown sang the song himself at his first recording session. Brown's version was selling well in the South, and so came to

---

[1] I should explain the racial terms used in the book. "Colored" and "Negro" were terms in common usage in America well into the Sixties, when "black" became preferred in many contexts, just as "African-American" is often preferred today. All of these terms appear at various points in this text, as the historical context dictates.

the attention of Harris' new A&R man at King, Henry Glover, a big band veteran charged with finding fresh "repertoire" for his "artists."

The song's rhythmic style was apt. This was the heyday, in black popular music, of a relaxed kind of boogie-woogie—the musical backbone of "Good Rockin' Tonight." Almost offhandedly, Harris and his combo transformed the song into a celebration of everything dance music can be: an incantation, an escape, an irrepressibly joyous expression of sheer physical existence.

They took Brown's song at an easy lope. The band was loose, Harris in rare form. A sax riffed, a piano pumped, and Harris shouted: "Have you heard the news? There's good rockin' tonight!"

Five months later, the news was out. By June of 1948, Harris' record was spinning on jukeboxes from coast to coast. The era of "good rockin'" had arrived.

Or so it would later seem. To chronicle the past is to search for some place to start, some more or less arbitrary moment to begin: and more than one historian of rock has thought to open his story with "Good Rockin' Tonight." Not that experts can agree. In 1992, an account of fifty pioneering rock and roll recordings demonstrated the intractability of the question posed by the book's title, *What Was the First Rock 'n Roll Record?*

Questions of historical priority scarcely preoccupied Wynonie Harris. Born in 1915 in Omaha, Nebraska, he had honed his talents in the Midwest, performing as a buck dancer, a drummer, a singer, touring with carnivals, doing vaudeville, entertaining at minstrel shows, covering a territory that ran from the Dakotas in the north to Oklahoma in the south.

The undisputed cultural capital of this territory was Kansas City. And it was in Kansas City that Wynonie Harris first heard Joe Turner—and first found his true calling. "He went crazy over the big blues shouter," Preston Love, one of Harris' lifelong friends later recalled. "He thought the blues was a way of life—an only life, and he patterned himself as a singer after Joe Turner."

In the 1930s, when Harris first visited Kansas City, Joe Turner was tending bar, bouncing bums, and singing the blues at a club called the Sunset—the kind of place that later rock and roll stars could only dream about. Located at Twelfth and Woodlawn, the club was surrounded by dozens of other saloons, promising an endless supply of whiskey, women, and song. Tricks were two dollars an orgasm, marijuana three sticks for a quarter. In these days, Kansas City was a mecca for white revelers and black musicians, attracting one of the greatest concentrations of jazz talent in history: Count Basie, Lester Young, Ben Webster, Buck Clayton, Andy Kirk, Mary Lou Williams, Jay McShann, Charlie Parker—the list goes on. Every night after hours, musicians like this converged on the Sunset to blow the blues away, in the process refining the jazz form called swing—dance music with a sleek pulse, bursting with energy and brimming with riffs: short fusillades of melodic ostinato, repeated, developed, elaborated,, repeated again, reinforcing the music's rhythmic thrust, cutting through the air like the night train to Memphis.

The Sunset was a tiny place, roughly twelve feet wide and sixty feet deep, a "black and tan" with a bandstand at one end and a rope down the middle to separate the black patrons from the whites (or "tans"), who in the Thirties were numerous—this, after all, was the heyday of swing, the style of popular music preferred by most Americans, white and black. The Sunset's house pianist in these years was Pete Johnson, the best in the city, a boogie-woogie virtuoso with a rock-steady sense of time that sent patrons flocking to the dance floor. A primitive amplification system piped the music into the darkened streets, allowing Johnson's partner, Big Joe, to "call his children home," summoning customers inside. Turner served drinks and sang at the same time. He handed down the bleakest of lyrics—"you may be beautiful, but you gonna die someday"—with unswerving author- ity and infectious good humor. Sometimes, as Turner later recalled, "we'd start playing around three in the morning. The bossman would set up pitchers of corn-likker, and we'd rock"—which gives an idea of one thing that Wynonie-Harris may have had in mind when he sang about "good rockin'" ten years later.

The world had changed in the interim. Kansas City's wonder years were over. But the city's riffing style of swing lived on, not least in the music of Wynonie Harris.

A tall, handsome man from a racially mixed background (one of his wives would later claim that his father had been an American Indian by the name of Blue Jay), Harris was dapper and slim, with striking eyes of bluish green and a pencil-thin mustache—a far cry from Joe Turner, who was a blues version of Paul Bunyan. During World War II, Harris, like Turner, had joined the great black migration of these years to the West Coast, where work could be found in wartime factories running round the clock. Both men ended up in Los Angeles, where they regularly performed together, sometimes staging a friendly "cutting" session, as if to summon the memory of times past at the Sunset.

In 1947, Harris and Turner recorded a series of duets, including a boisterous "Battle of the Blues" that nicely illustrates the difference in their styles. Swapping boasts about their sexual prowess, Turner as usual sounds earthy, offhand, almost absentmindedly lustful—a force of nature, untamed and sublime. Harris by contrast is dogged, strident, strenuously energetic.

He made a career out of bellowing off-color novelties, drinking songs, and raucous blues. "I Want My Fanny Brown" was one jukebox favorite, "I Like My Baby's Pudding" another. Dumb double en-tendres didn't faze him. A prototypical "rock" singer, he at- tacked the most inane of lyrics with melodramatic gusto.

The 1940s was a time of change in the music that most Americans listened to. In mainstream pop, the big bands were being replaced by crooners like Vaughn Monroe and Perry Como. In the world of jazz, dance music was out, bebop was in, turning the art of improvisation into a form as demanding as anything heard in European concert halls. As jazz ceased to be a truly popular music, even among blacks, the so-called race charts published by the music trade magazine *Billboard*—charts meant to document the recorded music black Americans preferred to hear—registered a historic shift: the hot new style was jump, a simplified and superheated version of old-fashioned swing, often boogie-woogie based, usually played by a small combo of piano, bass, and drums, with saxophone and trumpet.

From its streamlined riffs to the genre's very name, jump owed a large debt to the Kansas City scene of the 1930s. Count Basie had shown the way with "One O'Clock Jump." But the genre's greatest postwar exponent was the singer and saxophonist Louis Jordan, a native of Arkansas later based in New York City and Los Angeles. In a string of popular recordings that began in 1942, and included four million-sellers ("G.I. Jive," "Caldonia," "Choo Choo Ch'Boogie," and "Saturday Night Fish Fry"), Jordan perfected a propulsive, boogie-woogie-based style of swing, animated by a clownish stage manner he had inherited from Louis Armstrong, Fats Waller, and Cab Calloway. At the height of Jordan's career, between 1944 and 1946, his recordings were as popular with whites as with blacks. One of his biggest hits, "G.I. Jive," actually topped the normally lily-white "folk" (or country-western) chart in 1944, becoming the first recording in history to top simultaneously all three *Billboard* charts (pop, race, and folk). Despite his huge white following, Jordan was un-apologetically black. Before him, the black stars most popular with white listeners, such as Louis Armstrong, the Mills Brothers, and the Ink Spots, had hurdled America's racial divide by singing Tin Pan Alley material. Jordan took a different tack, singing songs filled with images from ghetto life ("Saturday Night Fish Fry," for example, recounts a police raid on a block party). And though his flair for comedy took the sting out of his lyrics, and sometimes brought Jordan to the brink of self-parody, he was a committed entertainer, a peerless bandleader—and for any up-and-coming jump blues star, the man to beat.

For one striking moment—in the studio that December day in 1947—Wynonie Harris did just that. Like Jordan's classic hits, Harris' "Good Rockin' Tonight" swings effortlessly. An epitome of the jump genre, the record opens with a growling trumpet fanfare. The bass player doubles the pianist's pumping left hand, and hand-clapping reinforces the drummer's backbeat. Knocking out a perfect boogie beat, the group hews to a formula, but the formula is tried and true: ten years later, it would be all but impossible to locate five musicians able to animate the same simple riffs with such style and elan. Harris himself was in rare form. Uncommonly subdued, he sings with blithe artistry. Apart from a feverish sax solo, the song glides by.

Harris' recording turned into one of the biggest race hits of 1948: in June, it topped *Billboard* magazine's weekly lists of both Most-Played Juke Box Race Records and Best Selling Retail Race Records. Its popularity triggered a small boom in race records that highlighted the word "rock." In the months that followed, there was Joe Lutcher's "Rockin' Boogie," the tenor saxophonist Wild Bill Moore's "We're Gonna Rock, We're Gonna Roll," vocalist Roy Brown's "Rockin' at Midnight," Jimmy Preston's "Rock the Joint," and yet another Wild Bill Moore disc, this one with the pithy and prophetic title "Rock and Roll."

Prophetic or not, these records at first changed little in the music most Americans listened to, or in the culture that most Americans inhabited. Distributed primarily on jukeboxes located in Negro clubs and bars, none of these pioneering "rock" records reached the larger white audience—not even Wynonie Harris' exuberant version of "Good Rockin' Tonight."

The primary problem was not the color of the musicians' skins—Louis Jordan after all played a virtually identical brand of music. The problem was the word "rock." As the record's A&R man, Henry Glover, later explained, "we were restricted with our possibilities of promoting this song because it was considered filth"—and though "filth" was acceptable on a ghetto jukebox, it was not acceptable on most radio shows: "They had a definition in those days of the word 'rock,' meaning the sex act, rather than having it known as 'a good time,' as they did later."

In the late 1940s, Glover was a talent and song scout for King. A label founded in 1943, King was owned and operated by Syd Nathan, a Cincinnati record retailer. Priding himself on his prowess as a salesman, Nathan had made a small fortune by "selling records in a location that nobody could sell a record in," as he told his sales staff in 1951—"it was like trying to sell a grand piano out in the desert. But we done business because we knew how to do business."

Nathan had started up King by recording hillbilly artists, and quickly made his mark in the folk field. Branching into race music, Nathan in 1946 hired Glover, a former trumpeter and arranger in Lucky Millinder's big band, and one of the first black men in the postwar record business to be given any creative clout. It was Glover's job to help his label's artists by finding songs, booking studios, hiring musicians, and supervising the recording sessions. Like Nathan, Glover "knew how to do business." One of the first artists he signed and supervised for Nathan was Bullmoose Jackson, a popular baritone who would produce naughty novelties and lugubrious ballads for King starting in 1946.

The commercial success of labels like King in these years was symptomatic of a number of concurrent changes in the American music industry. As cheap and improved record players came on the market after World War II, retail sales of recordings grew rapidly, particularly in the areas of country music and rhythm and blues. Registering the change, Billboard in May 1948 augmented its old charts listing jukebox favorites with two new charts listing the week's best-selling retail recordings of race and folk music. The new popular interest in both black and country music grew out of the wartime experience of a large number of Americans: thanks to the regional and racial mixing that had occurred in the armed forces, and also thanks to the heterogeneous musical fare piped round the world on armed forces radio programs and V-Discs, a generation had been exposed to a range of musical styles far wider than anything heard on the live variety shows broadcast by America's national radio networks in the 1930s. At the same time, the country's established labels, faced with a shortage of shellac during the war, had sharply cut back their involvement in musical genres they deemed marginal. The reluctance of the major labels to meet a growing demand left the field wide open for independent entrepreneurs like Syd Nathan.

The postwar independent record business was risky and brawling—but Syd Nathan was a pugnacious entrepreneur. As an associate later recalled, he was a "short, round, rough, gruff man with a nose like Porky Pig and two Coca-Cola bottles for eyeglasses." He smoked cigars, growled hoarsely, and governed his record label like a modern-day fiefdom, barking out orders to underlings. He turned King into one of the few vertically integrated operations in the music business. He owned his own studio, he owned the plant that stamped his records, and he owned the press that printed King's record jackets. He also drove hard bargains, offering his race and folk artists a flat fee to record, and taking care to purchase the copyright on virtually every song that his label issued. The most lucrative aspect of the music business is song publishing: whoever owns the publishing rights to a piece of music is in a position to make money every time the sheet music or a recording of the song is sold, and virtually every time the music is performed live, or a recording of it is broadcast. Trying to maximize his profits, Nathan became a virtuoso at imaginatively exploiting his catalogue of songs, having his folk acts record race songs that he owned, and vice versa: one of Wynonie Harris' biggest hits was a remake of an earlier country hit for King, Hank Penny's "Bloodshot Eyes." Cheerfully philistine by temperament, Nathan took special pride in making money from smutty songs no other label would touch, churning out off-color records with titles like "I Want a Bowlegged Woman," the notorious "Work With Me Annie," and its equally notorious sequel, "Annie Had a Baby."

"The first thing you learn is that everyone is a liar," Syd Nathan once snapped to an inquiring reporter: "The only thing that matters is the song. Buy the song, own the song, but remember, no matter what anyone tells you, they are liars until they have convinced you they are telling the truth."

Nathan's vulgarity was legendary—but in Wynonie Harris, he met his match. In 1947, Nathan and an associate journeyed to New York City to talk Harris into signing with King. As Nathan told the story a few years later, they found Mister Blues "in a backstreet dingy hotel in Harlem. And when we knocked on the door, he says 'come in,' and there were three gals in the room with him. All naked. So one of them opened her mouth, and he threw her out in the hall without any clothes on. … So we sat there talking to this drunk, stupid individual—and if he were here I'd tell it to him (he's got a little more sense since then)—till six o'clock in the morning." As the sun rose in the east, Harris signed with King.

"Good Rockin' Tonight" was the first in a series of best-sellers that Harris recorded for Nathan's label. The consistent popularity of his recordings for King over the next five years made him wealthy and famous.

"As a statement of fact, clean of any attempt to brag about it, I'm the highest-paid blues singer in the business," Harris boasted in 1954 (just as his star was starting to fade). "I'm a $1,500 a week man. Most of the other fellows sing for $50 to $75 a night. I don't. That is why I'm no Broadway star. The crooners star on the Great White Way and get swamped with Coca-Cola-drinking bobby-soxers and other 'jail bait.' I star in Georgia, Texas, Alabama, Tennessee and Missouri and get those who have money to buy stronger stuff and my records to play while they drink it. I like to sing to women with meat on their bones and that long, green stuff in their pockets. You find them mostly down south. As a matter of fact, I like all kinds of women, regardless of what color they are or what size and shape they may have. Just so long as they're breathing, that's me!"

Such vainglory was a sign of "good rockin'" to come. For Wynonie Harris and those who would follow in his footsteps, from Chuck Berry to Mick Jagger to Prince, the new music would, in time, become what Big Joe Turner's blues had been at the Sunset in Kansas City—"a way of life," a free life, an "only life." Organized, like jump, around the single-minded pursuit of simple musical pleasures, rock, too, would hold out the promise of wealth, of fame, of physical gratification without measure or limit. And all for a song!

October 29, 1949: Red Hot and Blue

The sun had set and the radio was rocking. The deejay's patter was manic, his voice a blur, his words a jumble. "Get your bald-headed nanny goat runnin' through the front door," the man said breathlessly, jamming together syllables and words and sentences without pause, as if without punctuation, "tell 'em Phillips sencha down there from *Red Hot 'n' Blue* the next fifteen minutes of *Red Hot 'n' Blue* is comin' to ya through the courtesy of that good Old Amigo Flour we're gonna play the next record for LeAnn Sandwich for Erma King Annie L. Sandwich for Cathy for W.J. Johnson also for Yumma Black for Ernie Black for Porter for Ruby Young I believe it is a call for Monroe Williams and the title is 'Say you ever get booted' here's a record that's gettin' hot man 'Booted' by Roscoe Gordon!"

A drum rolled. A raspy voice shouted out, "Jack, man! Have you ever been booted?"

A chorus shouted back. "Did you say booted?"

"Yeah, man. Booted!"

A piano shuffled into a boogie beat—and another hour of the Dewey Phillips show began on radio station WHBQ in Memphis, Tennessee.

Phillips first aired his show on October 29, 1949, filling a forty-five-minute slot from 10:15 until 11:00 at night. But within weeks, Phillips was on the air from 9:00 till midnight, hawking flour, spinning records—and changing, forever, the way white people would hear black music.

Memphis in 1949 was a boomtown. It was also a bastion of segregation, with separate (and unequal) parks, schools, and restaurants.

♪ The Sound Begins

By Charlie Gillett

In tracing the history of rock and roll, it is useful to distinguish *rock 'n' roll*—the particular kind of music to which the term was first applied—both from *rock and roll* the music that has been classified as such since rock 'n' roll petered out around 1958—and from *rock,* which describes post-1964 derivations of rock 'n' roll.

It is surprisingly difficult to say when rock 'n' roll "started." The term had been in use in blues songs to describe lovemaking long before it came to signify a dance beat. By 1948 it was being used in a number of songs to suggest both lovemaking and dancing—in "Good Rockin' Tonight" (recorded by Roy Brown) and in "Rock All Night Long" (the Ravens, and many others). In 1951 Gunter Lee Carr recorded a straight dance song, "We're Gonna Rock," dropping the sexual implication, and a year later Alan Freed, the disc jockey who was to rise to fame on rock 'n' roll, named his radio show "Moondog's Rock and Roll Party." But as a kind of music, rock 'n' roll did not make its impact on the national popular music market until 1953, when "Crazy Man Crazy," a recording by Bill Haley and His Comets, became the first rock 'n' roll song to make the best-selling lists on *Billboard's* national chart.

By the early fifties, the interrelated institutions of major music publishers, record companies, and radio networks, which between them constituted the effective source of power in the popular music industry, were all threatened by rock 'n' roll's writer performers and the businessmen who helped them find their audience.

I

Publishers had dominated the popular music industry since the years before music was recorded. Sales of sheet music to amateur and professional musicians were then the major source of revenue in the industry. The introduction of records did not immediately change this: the early inventors of sound recording were more interested in the spoken word than in music, and more in classical or serious music than in popular music. Thus, well into this century, live performances of songs were more important to the publishers than were the firms that recorded them.

In the early years of the century, the most important source of new live songs was vaudeville and music halls, and many publishers had their offices close to the 27th Street vaudeville theatres in Manhattan, an area that became known as "Tin Pan Alley." When stage musicals began replacing vaudeville in its role of introducing new songs, publishers began moving uptown. By the end of the 1930s "Tin Pan Alley" was the area in the forties and lower fifties close to Broadway.

The record companies took their cues from the publishers, and up to the end of the thirties the vast majority of recorded music were "show tunes," or sounded like show tunes. They ranged from the witty comments of Cole Porter on love and society, through the elegant ballads of Hoagy Carmichael and Lorenz Hart, to the nonsense novelties of numerous long-forgotten writers. Occasionally there were writers like George Gershwin, with aspirations to make popular music as complicated as classical music.

Towards the end of the thirties, Tin Pan Alley and its show tunes were challenged briefly and in an indirect way by the sudden trend to the orchestral "name" bands, whose "swing" music was a derivation of the Kansas City jazz style developed by various black bands in the late twenties and early thirties. So far as we can tell from record sales, the spirit of these bands brought a welcome change from the bland temper of the lighthearted show tunes. The record industry revived from a depression which had seen sales slump from $106,000,000 in 1921 to a little over 5 per cent of that, $6,000,000, in 1933. By 1939, with the big bands, the figures had recovered to $44,000,000.

Records by the bands dominated the best-selling lists from 1937 to 1941. During this period band recordings accounted for twenty-nine of the forty-three records that sold over a million copies each.[1] The publishing houses were affected because the repertoires of the swing bands consisted mainly of original material written by band members, or compositions by the black band leaders (Count Basie, Jay McShann, and others) whose musical style was often imitated, or familiar songs given new arrangements, and so the houses had a hard time introducing new songs.

But they came into demand again from 1942 to 1945, as the vocalists with the bands began to gain more prominence. The shift from the bandleader to the singer was begun by the bandleaders themselves, who competed with one another by featuring their increasingly famous singers. The strategy soon backfired. While Glenn Miller's reputation always exceeded that of his singer, Tex Beneke, Frank Sinatra in particular began to attract more attention than the bandleaders he sang with (who included Tommy Dorsey and Harry James). The singers, in any case, depended on the publishing houses for their songs.

Since 1912 songwriters and publishers had protected their interests through ASCAP—the American Society of Composers, Authors and Publishers-who licensed performance rights to broadcasting outlets, primarily radio; in 1941 an association of radio stations set up a rival licensing organisation, BMI—Broadcast Music Incorporated—who represented many previously ignored writers and publishers (hillbilly, race, ethnic and foreign) whose business boomed during an **ASCAP** boycott on radio broadcasts in 1941.

The band vocalists, having re-established the need for new songs, were supplied with novelty songs and sing-along ballads. Perhaps the appeal of this material lay in its ability to relieve wartime tension, but even after the end of the war these songs continued to proliferate, in the company of growing numbers of the kind of sentimental and melodramatic ballads that were still in sway ten years later.'

The singers of this kind of material were all influenced to some extent by the creator of the modern ballad style, Bing Crosby, whose light tenor, in its flexibility, gentle humour, and easy charm, was ideally suited to the needs of Tin Pan Alley material. Crosby had begun his career in vaudeville, where he developed the technique of singing quickly and wittily. Then, as a vocalist with Paul Whiteman, he had learned the techniques of singing with a megaphone (necessary before the days of electrical amplification if the singer was to make himself heard above the orchestra). The megaphone produced a curious deadpan and emotionless manner of expression, which was to form the basis of the "crooning" style that developed after microphones and electrical amplification were introduced.

Two distinct kinds of crooning were developed, one the smooth, "soft," emotionally relaxed style of Perry Como, the other the more angular-toned, "hard," involved style of Frank Sinatra. The soft style was best suited to sing-along novelty songs and sentimental ballads, while the hard style was better for more melodramatic songs. But singers of either style were expected by their record companies to handle all kinds of songs.

Hardly any vocalists wrote their own material, and their "creativity" was measured in their ability to improvise phrasing and impart meaning on Tin Pan Alley songs. The leading virtuosos were Billie Holiday, dry and bitter; Ella Fitzgerald, sweet and warm; Louis Armstrong, and Fats Waller, both gruff-voiced and humorous. But most so-called jazz singers were crooners whose ambitions outran their imaginations.

The most original of the ex-band vocalists was the hard crooner Frank Sinatra, who rejected the style of singing that encouraged the audience to sing along with him, and instead took risks with melodies, improvising his own timing of phrases by stretching some syllables and cutting others. The effect was a personal style that gave specific meaning even to songs that had been written as conventional "general" love songs.

Sinatra's style involved audiences in his singing—and in him—as no previous singer had done, and stimulated devotion comparable to that previously aroused only by film stars like Rudolph Valentino. The audiences willingly confused Sinatra's image with his private self, amplifying the character promoted by the singer's public relations staff and the press. Perhaps largely as a result of Sinatra's popularity, a singer's image became as important to his style and its effectiveness as the words of a song. Audiences expected singers to project themselves (or what was publicly known of their selves), and each listener wanted to feel as if the singer were singing to her (or for him, if the listener was male).

With this intense level of audience involvement in the singer's stage personality, the physical appearance of the singer became important. The conventional dark and handsome stereotype of the American romantic hero favoured the dark-complexioned singers of Italian descent who suddenly dominated the hit parades. Tony Martin, Al Martino, the Ames Brothers, the Four Aces, Dean Martin, Tony Bennett, Vic Damone, Sinatra, Como, and Frankie Laine were a few of the most successful, all of them helped at a crucial stage in their careers by night-club owners of Italian descent who were glad to feature them.

In terms of audience involvement, Frankie Laine, whose style was drawn from the western ballad style, from Al Jolson, and from Vaughn Monroe, inspired a following even more vociferous than Sinatra's with a series of unprecedented melodramatic epics of love and fury, including "That's My Desire" and "Jezebel." And in 1951, involvement rose to a new peak when another singer, for once not of Italian descent, inspired furores at airports, hotels, and backstage theatre doors—Johnnie Ray. In contrast to his predecessors, Ray lacked smoothness, precision of phrasing, or vocal control; instead, he introduced passionate involvement into his performance, allowing sighs, sobs, and gasps to become part of the sound relayed by the amplifiers. News of his style horrified observers across the Atlantic. The columnist Laurie Henshaw wrote in the British *Melody Maker* (February 9, 1952):

> Johnnie Ray, a 25-year-old Oregon-born vocalist, has jumped from the $90 to $2,000 bracket by hitting on the excruciating formula of virtually breaking into tears while singing a song.
>
> According to a U.S. report, "his stentorian sobbing sometimes so unhinges him that he has to rush offstage to compose himself. That this uninhibited and tasteless showmanship registers with American audiences is indicated that [sic], within eight weeks of issue, Johnnie's tearful version of "Little White Cloud That Cried" shot past the 1,000,000-sales mark.
>
> If an artist has to descend to this level to capture the masses, then the outlook for popular music is bleak indeed.

However bleak the future, the present was barren enough. Even Johnnie Ray was hardly as remarkable as the enthusiasm of his supporters, or the distaste of his decriers, would suggest. Only in comparison with the generally emotionless music of the times, to which Ray, like Laine, were exceptions, could the silly and sentimental "Cloud" have attracted anybody's interest.

II

Six major recording companies dominated the popular music market. All had their own distributing systems, which enabled them to ensure that each of their records would get to retailers in every regional market. Each of them had their own A&R staff—the Artist and

Repertoire men who decided what singers to use and what records to issue. Independent record companies, in contrast, relied on a loose network of independent regional distributors, and had to persuade each one in turn to distribute their products. The independents specialized mainly in ethnic folk music and in rhythm and blues, and before 1953 they were of little significance in the popular-music market; of one hundred and sixty-three records that each sold over a million copies from 1946 to 1952, all but five were recorded by one of the six major companies.[2]

Of the major companies, two, Columbia and Victor, had survived from the early days of recording at the end of the last century. A third, Decca, had been founded as the American branch of British Decca in 1932, and like its rivals was based in New York. In 1942 the first major West Coast firm, Capitol, was established in Hollywood, and in 1946 the film corporation MGM set up a record-producing department, again in the film capital. In 1946 the Mercury Corporation was established in Chicago.

During the twenties, the big record companies had been challenged by a number of small independents, which had been particularly successful in the specialist markets of black music, especially the "race" market, as the Negro buyers of blues records were then classified. But the Great Crash at the end of the twenties undermined the independent companies, which either went bankrupt or were bought up by one of the majors.

By the end of the thirties, the major companies had a solid hold on the complete market for records, but during the war they yielded the specialist "race" and "new jazz" markets when forced to make economy cuts by the government ruling that customers must trade in an old record every time they bought a new one (so that the material could be melted down and used again). By the end of the war, a new generation of "indies" had established a firm hold on the "race" market, but the major labels had consolidated their grip on the "hillbilly" market, now becoming known as "country and western."

The term "country and western" was coined to escape the derogatory associations of "hillbilly," but the new phrase soon became as limiting as the one it had replaced. "Country" music was never literally played only by and for people who lived in rural areas, but represented that strain of pop music which presented "real" attitudes and situations in a "sincere" manner and with "traditional" musical accompaniment. Country music shared roots in gospel music with black music, and during the forties probably absorbed more elements of black music than were accepted into the mainstream pop of the time. Decca's "sacred" country singer Red Foley recorded gospel songs written in the thirties by the black composer Thomas Dorsey; Ernest Tubb, also with Decca, updated the white blues style of Jimmie Rodgers by introducing electrically-amplified guitar into what became known as a "honky tonk" style. For Columbia, both Roy Acuff and Bill Monroe showed black influences in their respective "Smokey Mountain" and "Blue Grass" styles, while the Delmore Brothers (for King, one of the few indie labels in the country market) and several others played what they called "hillbilly boogie." When Hank Williams emerged on the new MGM label in the late forties, he shook all these black-influenced country styles together, using as strong a beat as his recording supervisor Fred Rose would sanction.

As head of Acuff-Rose Music and A&R man for MGM's country division, Fred Rose was one of a coterie of businessmen who centralized the country and western industry in Nashville, Tennessee, a process which led to the virtual elimination of most of the "western" associations of the term "country and western," in particular the western swing of bands like Bob Wills and his Texas Playboys. As if hoping to deny the strain of black music implicit in most country styles, there was a virtual embargo on drums in Nashville recording sessions and, more relevant in this period, broadcasts on WSM's "Grand Ole Opry," the premier radio showcase for country music.

Radio was a more important outlet than records were for country music, and although the majority of country radio shows were at off-peak hours on low-wattage stations in small towns, they provided the framework for performers to develop their style, repertoire, and reputation which enabled the most determined to get exposure on one of the big live shows beamed across several states—"The Barn Dance" from WLS in Chicago, the "Midwestern Hayride" on WLW in Cincinnati, the "Big D Jamboree" on KRLD in Dallas, the "Louisiana Hayride" on KWKH in Shreveport, and the "Opry" on WSM. (The names of these shows recur in the life stories of every country artist, among which *Country Gentleman* by Chet Atkins is particularly well-told and evocative.)[3]

The influence of the "Opry" became increasingly apparent during the early fifties as firms based in Nashville outran rivals based elsewhere—talent booking agencies, publishers, recording studios, and the record companies themselves. Decca was the first company to set up a Nashville office, with Paul Cohen as head of A&R, and the other majors followed suit with Columbia appointing Don Law, Capitol setting up Ken Nelson, and RCA-Victor's Steve Sholes deputing Chet Atkins to oversee the Nashville office.

Most of the companies regarded "country and western" as a specialist music without pop appeal, but during the late forties and early fifties some of the pop A&R men began to exploit the BMI affiliation of most country publishers by recording pop covers of country songs; Mitch Miller was particularly adept, first at Mercury where he produced the enormous hit version of "Tennessee Waltz" by Patti Page, and then at Columbia where virtually every major artist on his roster had at least one million-selling version of a country song. This practice of covers benefitted the publishers, among whom the leaders were Nashville-based Acuff-Rose and two New York—based companies, Peer-Southern and Hill and Range; but most country artists were shut out of the pop charts, even the remarkable Hank Williams, whose songs proved universally adaptable. Among the few country artists who did occasionally cross over to the pop, most recorded for Capitol's West Coast A&R department, whose promotion team brought pop hits home as "novelty" records for Red Ingle and his Natural Seven, Tex Williams, Merle Travis, Tex Ritter, Hank Thompson and Tennessee Ernie Ford.

But still, for an audience that lived predominantly in cities and sought its entertainment in their centres, the music that came out of the radios and juke boxes was incongruous. And there was, as increasing numbers of people were coming to realize, a much more appropriate alternative—rhythm and blues—and here the main companies were far less successful in satisfying what at first seemed to be only another speciality audience.

III

According to a report on rhythm and blues in a special edition of *Billboard* (March, 1954), the "Negro market" did not exist in a national sense until the end of the Second World War. Until that time, so-called race records, produced primarily by independent companies, tended to be distributed within particular areas—the East Coast, the Midwest, the South, the Southwest, and the West Coast. In the sixties, these areas still constituted distinct markets in that there were particular singers whose sales depended mainly on the local audiences within them. But now it is relatively easy for a company to distribute records across the country if there is a demand, which is usually created by disc jockeys playing the records in different areas.[1]

During the ten years after the War, Los Angeles had the largest number of successful independent companies specializing in rhythm and blues. (On occasion, a few firms offered hillbilly or country and western catalogues.) The companies included Specialty, Aladdin, Modern, Swingtime, and Imperial. But across the country, similar types of record companies were established from humble beginnings in garages, store-rooms, and basements, with early distribution carried out by the owners from the trunks of their cars. King, in Cincinnati; Peacock, in Houston; Chess, in Chicago; Savoy, in Newark New Jersey; and Atlantic, in New York, were all founded between 1940 and 1950, a decade in which as many Negroes (one and a quarter million) left the South as had done so in the previous thirty years. By 1952 there were over one hundred independent companies in business (apart from many others which had failed to last), many of them specializing in rhythm and blues.[2]

In almost every respect, the sounds of rhythm and blues contradicted those of popular music. The vocal styles were harsh, the songs explicit, the dominant instruments—saxophone, piano, guitar, drums—were played loudly and with an emphatic dance rhythm, the production of the records was crude. The prevailing emotion was excitement.

Only some Negro records were of this type, but they were played often enough on some radio programmes to encourage the listeners who found these programmes to stay

---

[1] The man responsible for enabling greater mobility of distribution between regions was a Los Angeles distributor, Jack Gutshall, who established a national network in 1945.

[2] In a Billboard survey of the proliferation of independent companies (5 September, 1953), Bob Rolontz wrote: "there is a street in New York that is rarely visited by dealers, publishers, A&R men, and other distinguished members of the music fraternity. It has no plush restaurants, no uniformed elevator operators, and few Cadillacs. Pushcart peddlers still sell hot dogs and pop from their carts and on hot summer days no male wears a coat or tie. Yet it is, in a competitive sense, one of the most vital and stimulating avenues of the music business. The street is Tenth Avenue, and in the area bounded on the North by 56th Street and the South by 42nd Street are poured daily the hard work and boundless optimism of a score of indie labels, indie distributors, one-stops, and juke-box distributors. ... Over the years, the Tenth Avenue independent companies have furnished the larger firms with personnel, ideas and records to cover."

tuned. The other records played were similar to the music already familiar in the white market. But as the white listeners began to understand the different conventions by which black audiences judged their music, they came to appreciate the differences between the sing-along way white singers handled ballads, and the personal way black groups handled them.

The early and fullest impression on the new white audience of these stations was made by the dance blues—whose singers included Amos Milburn, Roy Brown, Fats Domino, and Lloyd Price—which provided a rhythm and excitement not available in white popular music. At first the number of white people interested in this music was not enough to have much effect on the sales of popular music. This portion of the audience probably consisted at first of college and a few—high school students who cultivated an "R & B cult" as most of their equivalents earlier (and even then) cultivated a jazz cult.

By a happy coincidence, we happen to have some observations of remarkable insight made by the sociologist David Riesman on the popular music audience in this period, which illuminate the character of the specialist audience. In an article, "Listening to Popular Music," Riesman noted that two groups could be identified: the majority audience, which accepted the range of choices offered by the music industry and made its selections from this range without considering anything outside it; and the minority audience, which he described with details that are relevant here.

> The minority group is small. It comprises the more active listeners, who are less interested in melody or tune than in arrangement or technical virtuosity. It has developed elaborate, even over-elaborate, standards of music listening; hence its music listening is combined with much animated discussion of technical points and perhaps occasional reference to trade journals such as *Metronome* and *Downbeat*. The group tends to dislike name bands, most vocalists (except Negro blues singers), and radio commercials.
>
> The rebelliousness of this minority group might be indicated in some of the following attitudes towards popular music: an insistence on rigorous standards of judgment and taste in a relativist culture; a preference for the uncommercialized, unadvertised small bands rather than name bands; the development of a private language and then a flight from it when the private language (the same is true of other aspects of private style) is taken over by the majority group; a profound resentment of the commercialization of radio and musicians. Dissident attitudes towards competition and cooperation in our culture might be represented in feelings about improvisation and small "combos"; an appreciation for idiosyncrasy of performance goes together with a dislike of "star" performers and an insistence that the improvisation be a group-generated phenomenon.
>
> There are still other ways in which the minority may use popular music to polarize itself from the majority group, and thereby from American popular culture generally: a sympathetic attitude or even preference for Negro musicians;

an egalitarian attitude towards the roles, in love and work, of the two sexes; a more international outlook, with or without awareness, for example, of French interest in American jazz; an identification with disadvantaged groups, not only Negroes, from which jazz springs, with or without a romantic cult of proletarianism; a dislike of romantic pseudo-sexuality in music, even without any articulate awareness of being exploited; similarly a reaction against the stylized body image and limitations of physical self-expression which "sweet" music and its lyrics are felt as conveying; a feeling that music is too important to serve as a backdrop for dancing, small talk, studying, and the like; a diffuse resentment of the image of the teenager provided by the mass media.

To carry matters beyond this descriptive suggestion of majority and minority patterns, requires an analysis of the social structure in which the teenager finds himself. When he listens to music, even if no one else is around, he listens in a context of imaginary "others"-his listening is indeed often an effort to establish connection with them. In general what he perceives in the mass media is framed by his perception of the peer-groups to which he belongs. These groups not only rate the tunes but select for their members in more subtle ways what is to be "heard" in each tune. It is the pressure of conformity with the group that invites and compels the individual to have recourse to the media both in order to learn from them what the group expects and to identify with the group by sharing a common focus for attention and talk.[4]

Riesman's observation that no matter what the majority chooses, there will be a minority choosing something different explains how popular music continues to change, no matter how good—or bad—the dominant types of music are at any particular period. And because the minority audience defines itself as being radical within the music audience, its taste is likely to favour, consciously or unconsciously, music with some element of social comment or criticism in it.

During the early fifties, young people like those described by Riesman turned in increasing numbers to rhythm and blues music, and to the radio stations that broadcast it. If the first listeners were those with relatively sophisticated standards for judging music, those that came later included many whose taste was more instinctive, who liked the dance beat or the thrilling effect of a hard-blown saxophone, people who may have found the rough voices of the singers a bit quaint and appealing as novelties.

It was this second group of listeners who provided the inspiration and audience for Alan Freed, who, with Bill Haley, played a crucial role in popularizing rhythm and blues under the name "rock 'n' roll."

Alan Freed was a disc jockey on an evening quality music programme in Cleveland, Ohio, when he was invited, sometime in 1952, to visit a downtown record store by the owner, Leo Mintz. Mintz was intrigued by the musical taste of some of the white adolescents who bought records at his store, and Freed was amazed by it. He watched the excited reaction of the youths who danced energetically as they listened to music that Freed had previously considered alien to their culture—rhythm and blues. He recalled (in the British *New Musical Express,* September 23, 1956):

> I heard the tenor saxophones of Red Prysock and Big Al Sears. I heard the blues-singing, piano-playing Ivory Joe Hunter. I wondered. I wondered for about a week. Then I went to the station manager and talked him into permitting me to follow my classical programme with a rock 'n' roll party.

At Mintz's suggestion, Freed introduced a euphemism for rhythm and blues by calling his show "Moondog's Rock 'n' Roll Party," which started in June, 1951. By March, 1952 Freed was convinced he had enough listeners to justify promoting a concert featuring some of the artists whose records he had been playing. "Moondog's Coronation Ball" was to be staged at the Cleveland Arena, capacity 10,000; but according to firemen's estimates more than 21,000 people showed up, mostly black, causing such a panic that the show had to be called off (as reported in the *Cleveland Press*). Abandoning the idea of holding mammoth dances, Freed persevered with reserved-seat shows, and climaxed his career in Cleveland in August, 1953 with a bill that featured the Buddy Johnson Orchestra, Joe Turner, Fats Domino, the Moonglows, the Harptones, the Drifters, Ella Johnson, Dakota Staton, and Red Prysock.

Freed's success among white audiences with Negro music was widely reported in *Billboard,* and in 1954 he was signed by a New York station, WINS, which he quickly established as New York's leading popular music station. He continued to champion the original Negro performers of songs which were "covered"—recorded by someone else-for the white market by the major companies, and in interviews he accused other disc jockeys of prejudice when they preferred to play the cover versions.

Once the new audience became apparent, juke-box distributors began putting rock 'n' roll records in juke boxes, which then provided a new channel of communication for white record buyers who did not yet tune in to the Negro radio stations. At the same time, in response to the new demand for uptempo dance tunes with a black beat from audiences at dance halls, a number of white groups were incorporating rhythm-and-blues-type material into the repertoires. It was with such a song, "Crazy Man Crazy," recorded for the independent Essex, that Bill Haley and His Comets made their first hit parade appearance in 1953 and pushed rock 'n' roll up another rung of popular attention.

By the end of 1953, at which point the Negro market comprised only 5.7 per cent of the total American record sales market, a number of people in the music industry were beginning to realize the potential of Negro music and styles for at least a segment of the white market. Decca took a chance and considerably outpaced its rival major companies by contracting Haley from Essex. At his first session with Decca, he recorded "Rock Around the Clock" and "Shake, Rattle and Roll," which between them were to transform throughout the world the conception of what popular music could be.

Haley's records were not straight copies of any particular black style or record. The singer's voice was unmistakably white, and the repetitive choral chants were a familiar part of many "swing" bands. In these respects the music was similar to a style known as "western swing" (and in particular a group called Bob Wills and His Texas Playboys). But the novel feature of Haley's style, its rhythm, was drawn from black music, although in Haley the rhythm dominated the arrangements much more than it did in Negro records. With Haley, every other beat was heavily accented by the singers and all the instrumentalists at the expense of the relatively flexible rhythms and complex harmonies of dance music records cut for the black audience.

"Shake, Rattle and Roll" was in the top ten for twelve weeks from September, 1954; "Rock Around the Clock" was in the list for nineteen weeks, including eight at the top, from May, 1955. By the summer of 1955, roughly two years after Haley's "Crazy Man Crazy," with most of the majors still moving uncertainly, the demand for records with an insistent dance beat was sufficient for three independently manufactured records to reach the top ten in record sales—"Seventeen" by Boyd Bennett (King), "Ain't That a Shame" by Pat Boone (Dot), and "Maybellene" by Chuck Berry (Chess), the last recorded by a black singer.

IV

The growth of rock 'n' roll cannot be separated from the emergence, since the Second World War, of a new phenomenon: the adolescent or youth culture. Since the War, adolescents have made a greater show of enjoying themselves than they ever did before. Their impact has been particularly sharp because there were so few facilities that easily accommodated their new attitudes, interests and increased wealth. Neither individual communities nor the mass communication industries anticipated the growth of adolescent culture, or responded quickly to it.

The initial reaction of society was generally disapproving, which served to reinforce whatever rebellious feelings existed among the adolescents, thereby contributing to an identity and a style which were fostered until, by the early fifties, adolescents really seemed to consider themselves a "new breed" of some kind. Among the creators of popular culture, this self-impression was fostered in particular by Hollywood, whose producers began to adjust their films to the realization that an increasing proportion of their audience were in their teens.

Apart from various films dealing with the general social life of adolescents (in family, school, and leisure situations), there were two pictures in the first half of the fifties that focused specifically on the generation conflicts of the time, *The Wild One* (1954) and *Rebel Without a Cause* (1955). With Marlon Brando and James Dean, respectively, these pictures provided figures with whom the new teenagers could identify, figures whose style of dress, speech, movement, facial expressions, and attitudes helped give shape and justification to unrealized feelings in the audience. The plot in both films was clumsy, artificial, and morally compromised, but the undercurrents of frustration and violence in each were sufficient to give the films credibility. The sullen defiance of Brando and the exploited integrity of Dean were simultaneously reflections of and models for large segments of the audience.

Cinema was at this time the epitome of "mass culture," drawing situations from the lives of its audience, ordering these situations to fit a dramatic plot, and then returning the packaged product to its source as entertainment. There was little real interchange between the producers and the customers; the customers, having no alternative source of films, could only choose from what was made available to them, and the producers measured their audience's taste almost entirely in terms of the way they spent money. The producers thus tended to put their own money into formulas that had already proved successful. New ideas were notoriously difficult to introduce into this arrangement.

Despite these rigidities, the film industry realized and responded to the needs of its audience faster than did the music industry. The film industry, for example, was prepared to accept Negro styles of speech into scripts much faster than ASCAP would allow these styles to infiltrate radio broadcasts: "Dig," "flip," "cat," "jive," "square," and the rest of be-bop talk all made their way on to the screen with apparently no strong opposition—although of course black people themselves weren't very often evident on the screen. So, while in the film the images and the script were telling a new story in new words, as in *The Wild One* and *Rebel Without a Cause,* the music on the sound track remained the big band music that the new young audience had already rejected. Their rejection became explicit in a third film, *Blackboard Jungle* (released in 1955, the same year as *Rebel Without a Cause),* which was a major factor in accelerating the popularity of rock 'n' roll.

Blackboard Jungle, adapted from the novel by Evan Hunter, was about a teacher's experience in a vocational high school in the Bronx. His students, of various national and racial origins, were near-delinquents whose threatened violence gave the plot most of its dramatic strength.

One of the main scenes in the novel, where the students came into open defiance and conflict with a teacher, described an attempt by a teacher to establish rapport with his class by playing records from his collection. He began with Bunny Berigan's "I Can't Get Started." The collective reaction of the class was: "So it's a guy singing. Does he stack up against Como? Where does he shine to Tony Bennett? Guys singing are a dime a dozen. … Ain't he got no stuff by The Hill-toppers?" The teacher tried again—Harry James, Will Bradley, Ray McKinley, Ella Mae Morse. The students grew more restless. "What the hell is this, a history lesson? Come on, let's have some music." Their impatience turned to violence, and they broke up the teacher's treasured collection, throwing the records across the classroom. The teacher broke down in tears.

The scene accurately expressed the dislocation between the cultures of two generations.

Hunter's book was published in 1954, and in the relatively short space of time between the date of publication and the release of the film late in 1955, the musical culture of the young had gone a step beyond the terms of the novel. In the film version (directed by Richard Brooks), it was the relentless rhythm of Bill Haley's "Rock Around the Clock" that emphasized the rejection of the relatively sophisticated "swing" of the jazz records played by the teacher. By late 1955, Tony Bennett and Perry Como were as obsolete as Bunny Berigan and Will Bradley, so far as the self-consciously youthful adolescents were concerned. The film version of *Blackboard Jungle* was a large success and a much discussed movie. What the presence in it of the music of Bill Haley, rather than of Tony Bennett and Perry Como, helped to establish in the minds of both adolescents and adults was the connection between rock 'n' roll and teenage rebellion.[5]

V

Both large segments of the general public and the music industry establishment looked upon the growing popularity of rock 'n' roll with uneasiness. There were three main grounds for mistrust and complaint: the rock 'n' roll songs had too much sexuality (or, if not that, vulgarity), that the attitudes in them seemed to defy authority, and that the singers either were Negroes or sounded like Negroes. This last change was a matter of most open concern in the South.

Some of the general attitudes towards rock 'n' roll were perhaps represented in the comments of the syndicated television critic John Crosby, who on most matters represented a civilized and sophisticated point of view. To Crosby, Elvis Presley, who was soon to begin his amazing rise to popularity, was an "unspeakably untalented and vulgar young entertainer." Crosby asked: "Where do you go from Elvis Presley, short of obscenity—which is against the law?"

The most extreme and bizarre expressions of antagonism towards rock 'n' roll tended to take place in the South. In April 1956, the *New York Times* reported several attempts by white southern church groups to have rock 'n' roll suppressed. The whole movement towards rock 'n' roll, the church groups revealed, was part of a plot by the NAACP to corrupt white southern youth.

A well-publicized outbreak of southern antagonism occurred in Birmingham, Alabama, where it was directed, ironically, at the non-rock 'n' roll singer, Nat "King" Cole. The incident was reported by Nat Hentoff as follows in the British music paper *New Musical Express* (April 13, 1956):

> One of the world's most talented and respected singing stars, Nat "King" Cole, was the victim of a vicious attack by a gang of six men at Birmingham (Alabama), during his performance at a concert on Tuesday.
>
> His assailants rushed down the aisles during his second number and clambered over the footlights. They knocked Nat down with such force that he hit his head and back on the piano stool, and they then dragged him into the auditorium.

Police rushed from the wings and were just in time to prevent the singer from being badly beaten up. They arrested six men, one of whom is a director of the White Citizen's Council—a group which has been endeavouring to boycott "bop and Negro music" and are supporters of segregation of white and coloured people. The audience—numbering oyer 3,000—was all white.

In the music industry, the feelings of antagonism were mixed with and reinforced by economic considerations.

ASCAP, the association of the "establishment" publishers, maintained such a restrictive attitude on the use of their material that many smaller publishers, who handled most of the songs recorded by the independent companies, joined a rival organization, Broadcast Music Incorporated (BMI). ASCAP did everything it could to prevent the major radio networks from playing BMI material—which necessarily meant most rock 'n' roll songs. The association's greatest triumph was getting Johnnie Ray's "Such a Night" banned from the airwaves on the grounds of sexual suggestiveness.

Although Ray's version was for a major company, Columbia, the song was originally recorded for the independent Atlantic, by Clyde McPhatter and the Drifters early in 1954, and was registered with BMI. A typical "rhythm and blues" love song of the period, "Such a "Night" recalled a recent evening's experience of the singer:

> *It was a night, ooh,*
> Ooh, what a night it was. …
> The moon was bright,
> *Ooh how bright it was, …*
> Just the thought of her kiss
> Sets me afire,
> I reminisce,
> And I'm filled with desire.
>
> I gave my heart to her
> In sweet surrender,
> *How well I remember,*
> *I'll always remember. …*
> Came the dawn
> And my heart and my love and the night were gone.
> But I know I'll never forget
> Her kiss in the moonlight,
> Ooh, such a kiss,
> Such a night.

McPhatter was so intense about the memory of the experience that the audience often found the performance funny. The singer slightly overdid the ecstasy, feigning innocence of the humour in the situation yet somehow also communicating the sense that he was aware of his own ridiculousness.

Because of the intensity of McPhatter's style, and the success of the record in the Negro market, the producer in charge of Johnnie Ray's repertoire at Columbia thought that the song would be suitable for Ray, who had not managed in three years to repeat the huge success in 1951 of "Cry." In contrast to McPhatter, Ray showed no awareness of the essential humour of "Such a Night," and recorded the song straight in his usual dramatic style. In April, 1954, soon after its release, the record appeared in *Billboard's* list of the twenty records most played by disc jockeys. But during the next week, largely through the efforts of ASCAP, the radio networks agreed that the song was offensive to good taste, and the record was banned from the airwaves, which effectively ended its sales potential in the United States. Meanwhile, in the United Kingdom the record held second place in the best-seller list throughout the summer (kept from the top by Doris Day's "Secret Love").

Billy Rose, a senior member of ASCAP, was quoted in *Variety:* "Not only are most of the BMI songs junk, but in many cases they are obscene junk, pretty much on a level with dirty comic magazines."[6] In general and as usual, the case against accusations of obscenity is hard to argue for, since a listener's interpretation, different from one person to another, is the final arbiter. Many of the songs that Rose would have classified as obscene were enjoyed as funny records by the Negro audience.

Nonetheless, to combat the accusations, the composers of rock 'n' roll songs were obliged to amend words originally written for the Negro audience. One of the most popular records in the Negro market in 1954 was "Work With Me, Annie," by Hank Ballard and the Midnighters (Federal). Written by Ballard, the song made crude double use of the expression "work," as the singer implored:

> *Work With Me, Annie* [four times]
> *Let's get it while the gitting is good.*

The next lines were unambiguous:

> Annie, please don't cheat,
> Give me all my meat.

In this form the song was an easy target for critics of BMI's rhythm and blues songs, and a modified version, closely following the original's tune and arrangement, was recorded by Etta James as "Wallflower" (Modern). Written by the singer and Johnny Otis, the song provided the reply to "Henry" (Ballard) by challenging his ability to dance (and, by implication, his sexual prowess). The opening chant was changed to:

Roll with me, Henry [five times]
You better roll it while the rollin' is on.

In the last verse, the singer challenged Henry, while Henry—Richard Berry on the record—wailed his willingness to do as she asked:

Well, I ain't teasin'   talk to me. baby
You better stop your freezin' all right, mama
If you want romancin'   OK, sugar
You better learn some dancin' mm, mm

Although the song was more respectable than "Work With Me, Annie," it still was not considered suitable for the general public—that is, the white audience. When Mercury recorded a version by Georgia Gibbs, the song was retitled "Dance With Me, Henry," and the opening lines were unequivocally about dancing:

Dance with me, Henry [four times]
Let's dance while the music rolls on.

Although the Gibbs version was spirited compared to most records made for the white market, it lost the sense of dialogue and communal feeling that the other versions had.

A similar destruction of feeling took place when Bill Haley transcribed "Shake, Rattle and Roll." The song was first recorded by Joe Turner for Atlantic, whose version was very popular in the Negro market in 1954. As written by Charles. Calhoun, the song begins, in effect, in bed:

Get out of that bed,
And wash your hands, [twice]

Get into the kitchen,
Make some noise with the pots and pans.

Well you wear low dresses,
The sun comes shinin' through, [twice]

I can't believe my eyes,
That all of this belongs to you.

As transcribed by Haley the song begins more vaguely and more decorously:

Get out in that kitchen,
And rattle those pots and pans, [twice]

Roll my breakfast
'Cause I'm a hungry man.

You wear those dresses,
Your hair done up so nice, [twice]

You look so warm,
But your heart is cold as ice.

One verse of the Calhoun/Turner original is missing entirely from the Haley version:

I said over the hill,
And way down underneath, [twice]
You make me roll my eyes,
And then you make me grit my teeth.

Haley, commenting on the charges of obscenity, insisted:

We steer completely clear of anything suggestive! We take a lot of care with lyrics because we don't want to offend anybody. The music is the main thing, and it's just as easy to write acceptable words.[7]

For a time, ASCAP was effective in encouraging radio stations to play their songs (invariably recorded by major companies) rather than BMI songs. But, particularly after Alan Freed moved from Cleveland to New York, in 1954, an increasing number of disc jockeys on stations oriented to white audiences began to feature independently recorded BMI songs. And as this opened up a previously inaccessible market to independent companies and their singers, some of the companies began to orient their records deliberately to the white audience.

Although Alan Freed did not, as he sometimes claimed, coin the expression "rock 'n' roll" or create a new music single-handed, he did play an incalculable role in developing the concept of an exciting music that could express the feelings of adolescence. When he first used the term "rock 'n' roll," he was applying it to music that already existed under another name, "rhythm and blues." But the change in name induced a change in the music itself. "Rhythm and blues" had meant music by black people for black people. "Rock 'n' roll" meant at first only that this music was being directed at white listeners, but then, as the people producing the music became conscious of their new audience, they changed the character of the music, so that "rock 'n' roll" came to describe—and be—something different from "rhythm and blues."

♪ The Electric Guitar

How We Got from Andrés Segovia to Kurt Cobain

By Monica M. Smith

Some things were invented for obvious reasons. With others, the motivation is less clear. Consider, for example, the electric guitar. When guitarists first crudely electrified their instruments in the 1920s, what were they trying to do? Why change something that had been successful for hundreds of years? Could they have envisioned that the instrument that inspired some of Vivaldi's and Boccherini's most beautiful compositions would one day be used by Motörhead and blink-182?

In fact, the driving force behind the invention of the electric guitar was simply the search for a louder sound, a desire that had existed long before the development of electronic amplifiers and speakers in the 1920s. As musical performances moved to increasingly large public spaces over the course of the nineteenth century, the sizes of ensembles grew correspondingly, and musicians needed more volume. For this and other reasons, Americans had been making innovations in guitar design since before the Civil War.

Christian Frederick Martin, Sr., founder of the C. F. Martin Company, was probably the most influential American guitar maker in the nineteenth century. He was born in Germany in 1796 and immigrated to the United States in 1833. During the 1850s Martin developed X-bracing, the use of crossed wooden strips in the guitar's top for structural reinforcement. He also developed other design features, such as a body shape that was smaller above the sound hole than below.

In the late 1890s Orville Gibson, founder of the Gibson Mandolin-Guitar Manufacturing Company, designed a guitar with an arched (or curved) top, as is found on a violin. It was both stronger and louder than the earlier flat-top design. (The top of a guitar is the side with the strings.) It helped, but guitars were often still hard to hear.

The quest for volume intensified during the 1920s with the advent of big-band music and commercial radio and the rise of the recording industry. By the end of the decade the big-band era was in full swing, but the guitar was stuck in the rhythm section and couldn't be heard in crowded, noisy clubs, bars, and dancehalls. Since recordings were made directly to phonograph disks, using either an acoustical recording horn or a single electric microphone for the whole band, there was no way to boost the guitar's sound in the studio either.

Around 1925 the banjo and guitar maker John Dopyera came up with a nonelectric remedy. Borrowing an idea from the banjo, he designed a metal-body guitar with metal resonating cones built into the top. Unlike earlier acoustic guitars, this one's sound was created by the vibrations of the resonator cones, not those of the body itself. Resonator guitars produced a loud, brash tone that was popular with some Hawaiian and blues guitarists but was unsuitable for many other types of music.

Another solution was to use steel strings instead of gut. The guitar had to be altered structurally to withstand the increased tension of the heavier strings, and in many cases this meant ever-larger bodies with more internal bracing and stronger necks. The C. F. Martin Company became known in the 1930s for its Dreadnought, a large steel-string flat-top acoustic guitar that was widely imitated by other makers, including Gibson.

These mechanical fixes helped, but only up to a point. So guitarists began to look at the possibilities offered by the new field of electronic amplification, which had been made possible by recent advances in vacuum tubes. Simply putting a microphone in front of the guitar would work in a solo setting or a small group, and this method is still common among folk singers. But in a big band, the microphone would amplify the rest of the band nearly as much as the guitar. What guitar players needed was a way to separate the guitar's sound and boost it in isolation.

Guitar makers and players began experimenting with electrical pickups. On today's electric guitars, a typical pickup consists of a permanent bar magnet that is wrapped tightly with a coil of wire. The ends of the coil are connected to an amplifier. When a metal string vibrates next to the pickup, the bar magnet's field induces an electric current in the string. The current varies rapidly as the string vibrates back and forth. This varying current, in turn, creates a varying magnetic field of its own, which induces a current in the wire coil. That current, called a signal, is boosted by the amplifier and then used to create sound waves by making a speaker cone vibrate. Instead of a single large magnet, a pickup may contain a series of magnets, sometimes one for each string, but they will usually all be wrapped with the same coil.

The first guitar pickups were much less refined. A Gibson engineer named Lloyd Loar, a musician himself, developed a functional coil-wound pickup as early as 1923, but Gibson was not yet interested in producing electric instruments, so it never introduced Loar's invention onto the market. Even if it had, the technology needed to amplify the signal and reproduce it through loudspeakers was still a few years away from being commercial.

Loar's pickup was not electromagnetic in the modern sense. Instead, it used the instrument's physical vibrations, as transmitted through the bridge, to vibrate a diaphragm stretched over the pickup and create an electrical signal. The first commercially advertised electric guitar, offered by the Stromberg-Voisinet company of Chicago in 1929, used a similar pickup connected to the soundboard. Both systems had trouble creating a strong enough signal. In 1933 Loar began marketing electric guitars, mandolins, and keyboards under the Vivi-Tone label, but he found few buyers.

The guitarist Les Paul also started experimenting with electrical amplification in 1929. Still in his early teens, he jammed a phonograph pickup into his acoustic guitar, slid a telephone mouthpiece under the strings, and wired them to his parents' radio, which he used as an amplifier. The experiment was not immediately successful. Among other things, a conventional guitar's sound is meant to resonate through its body and be heard from the outside, so amplifying the vibrations directly under the strings gets the acoustics all wrong. Still, it inspired Paul to embark on a lifelong dual career of performing and engineering. He went on to pioneer multitrack recording and sound-on-sound techniques and develop many devices and methods to expand the electric guitar's capabilities and revolutionize the recording industry.

Trying to name a single inventor as the first to build a modern electric guitar would be fruitless, but the credit for making the technology commercially viable goes to the Rickenbacker International Corporation (originally the Ro-Pat-In Corporation and then the Electro String Instrument Corporation). The company was founded by George Beauchamp (pronounced "Beechum") and Adolph Rickenbacker, a distant cousin of the World War I flying ace Eddie Rickenbacker. Adolph's name was originally rendered Swiss-style as Rickenbacher, and this spelling was used on the company's earliest guitars.

In late 1931 Beauchamp built an electromagnetic pickup by placing a pair of horseshoe magnets end-to-end to create an oval, which wrapped around the strings. The coil was placed inside the oval as well, underneath the strings. Since it did not depend on physical contact with the vibrations of the guitar body, this pickup had a much cleaner sound and a stronger signal than earlier models. The horseshoe pickup was introduced on the market in a hollow cast-aluminum lap-steel guitar nicknamed the Frying Pan because the playing area consisted of a small round disk. The Frying Pan (officially called the Electro Hawaiian) was the first commercially successful electric guitar.

Most early commercial electric guitars were Hawaiian, or steel, versions. The Hawaiian lap guitar, introduced to the mainland around 1900, differs from the standard Spanish-style guitar in that it is played horizontally, on a stand or in the player's lap, and has a sliding steel bar that can be moved along the frets for a glissando effect. The ease of learning and playing the Hawaiian guitar made it popular with users and teachers. Its alluring effect of sliding between notes particularly endeared it to Hawaiian, country, and blues musicians. The Hawaiian guitar was especially prominent in American music in the 1920s and 1930s.

Beauchamp filed his first patent application for the Frying Pan in 1932, shortly before it went into commercial production. A second, greatly revised application was submitted in 1934, but it ran into problems. Although the Frying Pan was already on the market, two successive patent examiners questioned whether the instrument was "operative." To prove that it was, Rickenbacker sent several guitarists, including the well-known Hawaiian musician Sol Hoopii, to perform for the examiners at the Patent Office in Washington, D.C. The patent was finally granted in 1937. By that time other inventors had developed and marketed electric guitars of their own.

The Gibson ES-150 (E for Electric and S for Spanish), introduced in 1936, was the first Spanish-style electric guitar to achieve commercial success, with most of its sales going to professional musicians. Its pickup was much more elegant looking than Rickenbacker's bulky horseshoe version. Instead of wrapping around the strings, this bar pickup had two long magnets mounted below the guitar's face, leaving only a small coil-wrapped metal rod visible beneath the strings.

By the end of the 1930s electronic amplification was firmly established as the best way to make a guitar louder, despite some misgivings among traditionalists. Detractors complained that it did not produce a pure, "authentic" tone, and in a sense they were right: Bypassing the resonance created by the hollow body meant altering the instrument's traditional timbre. But musicians were championing the electric's louder sound, which enabled the guitar to compete with other instruments in ensemble performances. Instead of trying to duplicate the warmth and lushness of an acoustic guitar, musicians and engineers tinkered with their equipment and ended up creating an entirely new kind of sound.

The jazz musician Charlie Christian is generally credited with introducing the electric guitar solo. In 1939 he joined Benny Goodman's band and began stepping to the front of the band and performing long, complicated passages that imitated the style of horn playing. He explained, "Guitar players have long needed a champion, someone to explain to the world that a guitarist is something more than a robot pluckin' on a gadget to keep the rhythm going." Christian's role in popularizing the electric guitar among musicians and the public, and his association with the Gibson ES-150, led to its pickup's being nicknamed the "Charlie Christian pickup."

Yet along with its benefits, the new technology brought problems. Reverberation of the sound through the instrument's hollow body, which was responsible for the guitar's lovely timbre when played acoustically, caused distortion, overtones, and feedback when combined with electromagnetic pickups. But as the electric guitar developed its own sonic qualities and style of play, musicians and manufacturers realized that it should be designed from scratch with amplification in mind. This led a few innovators to think about replacing the hollow body with a solid one.

Some experts argue that the Rickenbacker Electro Spanish, introduced in 1935, was the first Spanish-style solid-body electric guitar, even though it did not actually have a solid body. Parts of it were hollow, but solely in the interest of reducing weight. In design and performance, it functioned as a solidbody guitar, virtually eliminating the acoustic feedback that plagued early hollow-body electrics. It was made of Bakelite, the first synthetic plastic, which, because of its weight, resonates less readily than wood. The Electro Spanish had stainless-steel cavity covers to hide the hollow parts of the guitar, a detachable neck, and horseshoe pickups. Because Bakelite is very heavy, it was smaller than other guitars of the period, and it must have been awkward to play.

However, since the Rickenbacker Electro Spanish was not intentionally conceived of as a solid-body guitar, the credit for inventing the solid-body goes to others, including Les Paul. In 1941 he made a solid-body guitar that he dubbed "The Log" by attaching a Gibson guitar neck to a four-by-four-inch pine board about a foot and a half long and fitting it with strings and two homemade pickups. Later he cut up and glued the body of a traditional acoustic guitar to the board to make it look slightly more conventional.

Then around 1947 Paul Bigsby, a Los Angeles machinist, teamed up with the country singer and guitarist Merle Travis to design a solid-body electric guitar that more closely resembled the ones we know today. Bigsby also developed a tremolo arm, sometimes known as a vibrato arm or whammy bar, that altered the pitch of notes by changing the tension on the strings when it was moved up and down.

But it was Leo Fender who first successfully mass-produced and sold a solid-body Spanish-style electric guitar. His simply constructed Fender Broadcaster of 1950 (renamed Telecaster in 1952 as the result of a trademark dispute), with its bolt-on neck, was initially derided by competitors as too simple and lacking in craftsmanship. Gibson's president, Ted McCarty, dismissed it as a "plank guitar." Yet everything about its patented, practical design was optimal for production in large quantities. The Broadcaster/Telecaster was immediately successful, spurring other guitar companies to follow Fender's lead.

Some dispute remains about whether the Broadcaster's design was adapted (or stolen, depending on one's viewpoint) from the Bigsby/Travis guitar. We do know that Leo Fender was already familiar with the concept of solid-body construction, since he had made lap-steel guitars out of solid planks of wood in the 1930s and 1940s. In any event, Fender was the one who made the solid-body electric guitar cheap enough for the masses; people called him the Henry Ford of the Electric Guitar.

Fender revolutionized the music world again with his 1951 electric Precision Bass. Although there had already been electric standup basses, the "P Bass" was the first commercially successful model to be played like a guitar. (Paul Tutmarc, of Seattle, had built electric guitars, including basses, starting in the mid-1930s and sold them through his company, Audiovox Manufacturing, but they were never widely used.) The Fender Precision had frets like a guitar, making it easier for players to hit an exact note, hence the name Precision. Monk Montgomery, the bassist with Lionel Hampton's band, is credited with making the instrument a musical sensation, and even today *P Bass* is often used generically for any electric bass guitar.

Not only was the Precision cheaper to buy and easier to learn than a standup bass, but by being much more portable, it helped the bass guitar develop into part of the standard lineup of a rock band. Some historians suggest that entire genres of music, such as reggae and funk, could not exist without the electric bass.

In 1952 Gibson became Fender's first major competitor in the solid-body market. The Gibson Les Paul was created in direct response to the success of Fender's Broadcaster/

Telecaster model. It was primarily designed by Gibson's Ted McCarty, but it was endorsed by Les Paul, who had been a popular guitarist since the mid-1930s. Paul's design input to the Gibson apparently included the original trapeze-style combination bridge-tailpiece, which allowed him to damp the strings with his hand, and the gold finish, which inspired the instrument's nickname, the Goldtop. The gold color was intended in part to disguise from competitors that the guitar had a maple cap on a solid mahogany body. According to a company history, the idea of using two kinds of wood was to "balance the bright attack of maple with the warmth and richness of mahogany."

After its introduction, the Gibson Les Paul went through a variety of modifications that culminated in 1958 in the still beloved Standard, with its sunburst finish and newly perfected double-coil, or humbucking, pickups. The humbucking pickup transmits less background interference, or hum, from electrical equipment, which can be a particularly annoying problem during recording sessions. It also cuts out some high frequencies, yielding a "warmer" sound that may be desirable or undesirable, depending on the music and the performer.

Fender responded to the success of the Goldtop by introducing the Stratocaster in 1954. This model may be the most influential electric guitar ever produced. It is easily identified by its double cutaway design and three pickups; previous guitars had two at most. (Since the strings vibrate differently at different points along their length, each pickup has its own character, and they can be combined in various ways, in or out of phase, to create numerous effects.) It also features Leo Fender's patented tremolo system, a combination vibrato unit, bridge, and tailpiece.

In the hands of Buddy Holly and others, the Fender Stratocaster became an American icon, like the Harley-Davidson motorcycle. This is only fair, for most innovations of any importance involving the electric guitar have taken place in America (which may explain, at least in part, why rock 'n' roll was invented and flourished here). One celebration of the Strat's role in American vernacular culture can be found in Jonathan Richman's 1989 song "Fender Stratocaster": "Like the Dunkin' Donuts in Mattapan / Like the Thrifty Drugs in Santa An' Fender Stratocaster, well there's something about that sound." A few years later Die Goldenen Zitronen (The Golden Lemons), a German punk band, paid homage to Richman's composition with a song of their own, also called "Fender Stratocaster." Such cross-cultural borrowing, which is virtually as old as rock itself, shows how the electric guitar has permeated the international music scene, making it one of America's most successful cultural exports.

Fender and Gibson weren't the only companies making solid-body electric guitars, but they were the pioneers, and their instruments are among the most sought after on the vintage market. Major competitors included Rickenbacker and Gretsch, although the latter is better known for its hollow-body electrics, which came to be appreciated for their tonal qualities after engineers learned to control the feedback problems. In 1964 Rickenbacker introduced its 360-12 model, the first commercially significant 12-string electric guitar, which was popularized by George Harrison in the Beatles' 1964 movie *A Hard Day's Night*. When Jim (later Roger) McGuinn saw the movie, he went right out and bought himself a

12-string Rickenbacker, which would soon give McGuinn's group, the Byrds, its instantly recognizable jangling sound.

Because the sonic character of a solid-body electric does not depend on its shape, makers could experiment with a wide range of imaginative designs. The Stratocaster, modernistic and space-age yet still recognizably guitar-shaped, remains a classic of 1950s design. The Gibson Flying V was the firm's first boldly shaped electric guitar. It was introduced in 1958 as part of a modernistic line of guitars, along with the angular, asymmetrical Explorer. These designs proved too extreme for the market and were soon discontinued. In the late 1960s, however, musicians like Albert King and Jimi Hendrix (who was recently named the greatest guitarist of all time by *Rolling Stone*) helped revive the Flying Vs popularity, encouraging guitar makers to develop other adventurous shapes.

While the electric guitar was feeding rock 'n' roll's explosive growth, what about the genre of music that had started it all? In jazz the guitar lost its role as a rhythm instrument with the demise of the big bands in the 1950s. As a solo instrument, the electric guitar is still struggling to free itself from its associations with fusion (jazz for rock fans) and smooth jazz (jazz for office workers). Those genres do have their adherents, of course. And with such virtuosos as George Benson and Pat Metheny, jazz guitar is still alive and doing about as well as anything else in jazz. Yet if there had been no electric guitar, jazz today would sound pretty much the same, whereas rock 'n' roll would not exist at all.

As for blues, the electric guitar revitalized the genre, as its versatility gave musicians fresh ways to express emotion. Beginning in the 1940s, a new, urban-edged style of blues, born in Chicago, was built entirely on amplified sound. Bluesmen like Muddy Waters and the Texan great T-Bone Walker (who has been called the Father of Electric Blues) also took up the amplified guitar and, along with Charlie Christian, inspired a new generation of performers, led by the likes of B. B. King.

During the 1950s blues-based music that had strayed too far from its roots became known as "rhythm and blues," a term that was as nebulous then as it remains today. Eventually, of course, in the words of Muddy Waters, "The blues had a baby, and they named the baby rock and roll." Early rockers clung to the notion that the baby was destined to take after its father, so they idolized and often imitated the great bluesmen. The blues remained an obsession for most rockers into the 1970s, and when the talent scout Danny Fields first heard the Ramones at CBGB's in 1974, he was ecstatic at finally finding music that was "all rock and no blues"—chiefly because, like most punk bands, the Ramones were nowhere near good enough to play blues convincingly.

The most powerful demonstration of the electric guitar's role as a sociopolitical symbol came at the 1965 Newport Folk Festival, when Bob Dylan, a tireless innovator in folk and blues idioms and a protest singer of solidly liberal values, plugged in an electric guitar amid boos and catcalls from the audience. On one level, it was a betrayal; the young genius who could have led a new generation of fans to the timeless joys of American folk music was instead (as the folkies saw it) pandering to the tastes of teenyboppers. More than that, however, Dylan's act of plugging in symbolized the merger of the political left with the counterculture. The divergent paths Dylan's music was taking were not what alienated fans; it was the electric guitar. Dylan could get as experimental as he wanted, and everything would have been fine as long as he didn't plug in.

What gives the electric guitar such potency? For all the basic and straightforward nature of much rock music, the electric guitar's most important quality may be its versatility. Once guitarists got accustomed to changing the sound by using tone and volume knobs and the tremolo bar, they began to look further. In the early 1960s artificial reverberation created the distinctive "surf-style" instrumental sound of the Ventures and, in Britain, the Shadows. Producers learned that feedback and interference could be their friends, developing circuits and devices that allowed fuzz, delay, wah-wah, compression, and a host of other embellishments to be invoked on demand.

The most influential master of manipulated sound in the 1960s was Jimi Hendrix, whose influence remains strong after nearly four decades. With techniques such as maneuvering the guitar's tremolo arm and playing close to the amplifier, not to mention setting the guitar on fire, Hendrix achieved spectacular effects: "Sometimes I jump on the guitar. Sometimes I grind the strings against the frets. The more it grinds, the more it whines. Sometimes I rub up against the amplifier. Sometimes I play the guitar with my teeth, or with my elbow. I can't remember all the things I do."

Through the 1970s and 1980s rock guitarists continued experimenting. One genre emphasized raucous power chords, flashy solos, and overall loud volume. It came to be known as "heavy metal." Eddie Van Halen, of the band Van Halen, experimented with stunts like dive-bombing, using the tremolo arm to drive the guitar's lowest note even lower. Hendrix had done this, but he usually forced the guitar out of tune as a result. However, by the mid-1980s the inventor Floyd Rose had improved solid-body guitar tremolo systems, making it possible to dive-bomb repeatedly.

Guitarists increasingly regarded their instruments as identifying signatures and had makers customize them. Eddie Van Halen decorated his with colored sticky tape, while Prince had guitars of all shapes and sizes created for his stage performances. The country musician Junior Brown took the customization of his guitar a step further. To solve the problem of switching back and forth between a Spanish-style electric and a lap-steel electric, Brown put the two together to form a hybrid "guit-steel."

In keeping with its status as a symbol of America, the electric guitar is the most democratic of instruments. It is extremely accessible in terms of both cost and learning curves. A beginner can manage a few chords after a lesson or two, and sometimes that's all you need. And while electric-guitar players are still overwhelmingly male, women are increasingly making their mark. Once the very act of playing an electric guitar seemed inherently aggressive and masculine, but since the 1970s female guitarists like Bonnie Raitt and Joan Jett have become prominent. Raitt got her start playing blues, and her musical style continues to evolve, combining elements of blues, pop, and rock. Jett and her band the Blackhearts made a splash in the 1980s with their harder edge. Jett's influence on the music scene earned her a place on *Rolling Stone*'s top 100 list, one of only two women included (the other was Joni Mitchell).

The electric guitar is a prime example of the law of unintended consequences. At first it just wanted to be heard, but it ended up taking over popular music and revolutionizing society along the way. Amplified musical technology is now at the forefront, and since most of the music we hear is electrified and synthesized, performing "unplugged" has become the exception rather than the rule. Today, more than seven decades after bursting onto the scene, the electric guitar is played and enjoyed worldwide and has achieved iconic status as a symbol of American culture.

MONICA M. SMITH is a historian and exhibit specialist at the Smithsonian Institution's Lemelson Center for the Study of Invention and Innovation.

♪ Part II

Rock Rises from American Song Traditions:
The Blues, Folk/Country and Popular Song

It is tempting to view rock 'n' roll as a stylistic hybrid that came out of nowhere—a mixture that rose phoenix-like from the blues, country, and the first folk revival. That temptation leads to a dead end, and rock 'n' roll has proven that it is not a dead end. The rock music that materialized from American song traditions was a mix of everything that artists heard throughout their collective careers, including minstrel shows from the South, the music of Tin Pan Alley, cowboy ballads from the Southwest, and mountain music from Appalachia.

Artists and songwriters from different American song traditions often had diverse priorities, which helped shape their musical focus. Bluesmen, for example, were likely influenced by the use of language, specifically lyrics; and black blues artists often incorporated white style and covers into their traveling shows (Robert Johnson rarely performed his own works in the juke joints). Popular song, in contrast, was often preoccupied with form and chord progression, which were frequently expressed in cover versions of songs from other genres. The folk revival appropriated old and traditional songs and transformed them into something new and different.

Rhythm and blues, folk, the blues, country, and pop—the music that immediately preceded rock 'n' roll—are responsible for the first creative explosion by rock's early artists Fats Domino, Little Richard, Elvis Presley, Bill Haley, and Carl Perkins. As many rock artists of the 1960s and 1970s noted, this "new" music didn't come out of nowhere; often it came from local entertainment venues.

William Barlow, a researcher at the Media Research Hub and affiliate of the School of Communications at Howard University in Washington D.C., discusses the emergence of the blues in the late nineteenth-century rural South and traces its journey to urban centers in Chicago, Cincinnati, and Kansas City. The blues, which was initially a unique musical style among rural agricultural workers, moved to juke joints and red-light districts during the first decades of the twentieth century. Recordings of all types of music became more widespread, and the recording industry became a powerful vehicle as this music moved from rural venues into the mainstream of American popular music. As the popularity of the blues waned, primarily among black audiences following World War II, it gained

young, white listeners and began to morph into rhythm and blues (R&B), an early dominant influence on the development of rock 'n' roll.

For many contemporary listeners, what was first called country-and-western and now
just country is a fusion of the traditions of the cowboy ballad from the West and the
Appalachian country/folk ballad. Although many contemporary bar bands joke that they
play both "country" and "western," in truth these are actually separate and distinct styles.
The unique character of the cowboy ballad is beautifully detailed in James Miller's essay,
"El Paso," from *The Rose and the Briar: Death, Love and Liberty in the American Ballad*.
He uses "El Paso," a more recently composed and performed "cowboy" ballad by Marty
Robbins, to explore how these ballads portrayed the romance of the American cowboy.
Marty Robbins describes "El Paso" as "the type of song you would have heard eighty years
ago. That's not country-and-western." Robbins, who was a cast member of Nashville's
Grand Ole Opry for many years, wrote and recorded country-styled love songs with a
crooner voice, but he also scored a pop-rock hit with *A White Sport Coat and a Pink
Carnation* in 1957. His epic cowboy ballad, "El Paso," though newly composed, sounds
like an old, authentic cowboy song passed down from generation to generation through
the oral tradition. As we will see, beginning in the early 1960s, many of Bob Dylan's newly
composed ballads in the folk tradition have the same, authentic feel.

A sea change for American popular music began in the late1950s at the Brill Building
in New York City. New York was the home of Tin Pan Alley, the source of the American
songbook from the middle of the nineteenth through the middle of the twentieth centuries,
where teams of lyricists and composers pounded out hits on out-of-tune upright pianos
in tiny rooms so close together that it was possible to eavesdrop on the creative process.

With the rise of the baby-boom generation in the 1950s, a new record-buying demographic emerged. Teenagers had money and a taste for music that was different from what
their parents listened to. Tin Pan Alley songwriting teams since the Great Depression and
before had been churning out songs for crooners such as Bing Crosby, Dinah Shore, and
Frank Sinatra. Disinterested in buying this kind of music, baby boomer teens themselves
donned the mantle of songwriter. By 1959, young songwriters/producers Leiber and
Stoller had produced hit after hit with the Drifters and the girl-group sound. Another
production team, Al Nevins and Don Kirshner, created Aldon music and hired several
teams of young songwriters including Neil Sedaka and Howard Greenfield, Barry Mann
and Cynthia Weil and Carole King and Gerry Goffin. The new, young songsmiths in the
Brill Building produced songs for teens by teens and the American songbook was forever
changed. Paul Zolo interviewed more than sixty songwriters in *Songwriters on Songwriting*.
He interviewed Carole King and Gerry Goffin in 1989.

♪ The Music of the Dispossessed

The Rise of the Blues

By William Barlow

The blues have a century-long history in the development of American popular music. They emerged as a unique musical style among black agricultural workers in the rural South during the 1890s. Over the next three decades, this new music and its makers spread to urban centers in the South and the North with the rising tide of African-American migrants. Once in the cities, the rural blues were transformed, stylistically and in content, to express better the grim realities of urban living. By the 1920s, blues were the music of choice among the growing black work force migrating to the cities in search of jobs and a better life. The popularity of the blues finally attracted the attention of the music industry, particularly the record companies, which began manufacturing blues recordings for sale, primarily to black consumers. The blues continued to be the favorite music of the African-American working class throughout the Great Depression and World War II. During this period, their popularity reached its zenith in urban black communities. But by the onset of the 1950s, urban blues were being eclipsed by a more diverse mixture of black musical styles, which came to be known as rhythm and blues. This was especially the case among the younger generation of African Americans growing up in the cities. The blues were still alive in certain black musical enclaves around the country, and they continued to influence other styles of American popular music; however, they were no longer as culturally and commercially dominant as they had been in the pre–World War II era.

Ironically, the demise of urban blues as a popular black musical style coincided with their sudden popularity among young white middle-class listeners, who began discovering the blues, and then learning to play them, in the 1950s. During the 1960s, these white blues enthusiasts spearheaded the so-called blues revival, which "rediscovered" a number of the older blues veterans while broadening their appeal to a white audience. Within the music industry, however, the blues have been segregated from the pop mainstream and relegated to the bottom of the economic pecking order since the 1920s. Blues records and albums have historically been under-promoted by the industry; hence, they seldom get airplay on commercial radio or make it to the pop charts. Even the most popular blues musicians do not fill large concert halls, much less football stadiums; for the most part, they are treated like minor league properties. In a nutshell, the blues get little respect or support from the music industry, despite their many contributions to its prosperity over the years. Nevertheless, the blues have shown a remarkable resiliency; they have managed to survive as both a musical style and a subculture. Accordingly, they continue to inspire and influence current trends in popular music, if only beneath the surface as an insurgent roots music. Moreover, since the end of World War II, the blues have been discovered and acclaimed by people from various cultures all over the world. Today they are universally perceived as a music capable of articulating the sorrows, grievances, hopes, and aspirations of downtrodden people everywhere.

From the beginning, the blues have been characterized by a twelve-bar, three-line (AAB) stanza structure within which the second line is almost a repetition of the first line, and the third line is a response to the first two. Complementing the vocal line of the stanza is at least one instrumental accompaniment, usually a guitar, which establishes the groundbeat and the chord progressions, while also responding to the vocal lines in a call and response pattern. Although the twelve-bar blues became standard fare, the length of the blues stanza could, and often did, vary, especially in the early years.

The musical roots of the blues can be found in African-American field hollers, work songs, and ballads, all popular in the rural South during the post-Reconstruction era. The field hollers, also known as "arhoolies," can best be described as African yodels—a kind of tonal language used by slaves working on plantations in the South. As such, they were used not only as audio calling cards but also as a means of disguising messages between the captives. Arhoolies always employed "blue notes" in their descending vocal lines. Blue notes are "bent" or "flattened" notes sung in between certain major and minor keys of the European diatonic scale but more musically attuned to the African pendantic scale. They were the major musical breakthroughs, along with the use of cross rhythms, in early blues music.

The collective voice and labor-intensive work songs were also sung during slavery and then remained in circulation on prison farms in the South with large black convict populations. They were call-and-response vocal chants sung by a lead singer and chorus, to the rhythms of forced penal labor. The subject matter of the work songs often drew on local prison folklore; it was ready-made for early blues repertoires. The black ballads were first sung by African-American songsters in the post-bellum era. These songsters were in many ways the precursors of the early blues musicians, their ballads based on traditional Anglo-American ballads from the rural South. They were, however, much more rhythmic compositions, and they featured African-American folk heroes, including renegade outlaws, in their storylines. The fusion of these three musical entities led to the formation of blues styles and repertoires in the rural South before the turn of the century. These rural-based musical formations took place in at least three discernible regions, thus generating three separate blues traditions: the Mississippi Delta, East Texas, and the Piedmont.

The Mississippi Delta is located in the heart of the soil-rich farmlands spreading out on both sides of the Mississippi River, between Natchez, Mississippi, and Memphis, Tennessee. The farmlands in this area were initially wild, lush swamplands. After the indigenous Indians were driven from the area, the swamps were drained, the vegetation burned off, and the land prepared for cotton cultivation. With the help of a federally funded levee system to hold the river's seasonal floods at bay, large cotton plantations were eventually carved out of the Delta wilderness, using slave labor in the antebellum era, and then hired as convict labor, in the postbellum era. With the passing of slavery, the Delta plantation owners turned to share-cropping and tenant farming, which enabled white planters to reap huge profits from their cotton crops while keeping their black fieldhands in economic servitude. By the 1890s, the Delta had the most concentrated black population in the nation, with blacks outnumbering whites by close to a four-to-one ratio. The economic peonage inherent in the sharecropping and tenant farming system, the rigid jim crow legal system, and the lynch rope were all used to keep the region's large black work force segregated from the white populace, dependent on their white landlords, and resigned to their second-class status in the social order. This was the historical situation out of which the earliest Delta blues emerged; in many respects, they were a defiant response to the oppressive social conditions engulfing their inventors.

Blues in the Delta may have originated in the cotton fields, but they soon became the centerpiece of black plantation workers' recreational life. At house parties on weekends, they supplemented the traditional country dance music; guitars and harmonicas took the place of banjos and fiddles. In the barrelhouses and the juke joints, the blues replaced ragtime as the music of choice. Delta blues pioneers like Charley Patton, Tommy Johnson, Son House, and Skip James made their reputations playing for crowds at these places and occasions. They were followed by a second wave of Delta blues legends: Robert Johnson, Rice Miller, Muddy Waters, and Howlin' Wolf, who not only made a name for themselves among Delta blues fans but also played a major role in transforming the blues from a regional to a national phenomenon. The Delta blues were dominated by two contrasting vocal styles: the rough, guttural declamatory shouting of Charley Patton and Howlin' Wolf, and the tormented and introspective falsettos of Skip James and Robert Johnson. The most prominent guitar techniques associated with the Delta blues were the use of intense chord repetitions building toward a droning crescendo and the use of a slider, such as a bottleneck on a finger, to create a poignant voice like a crying effect. The latter was derived in part from the widespread use of homemade one-string guitars by the black youth in the Delta.

East Texas was also a cotton-producing region tied to the South's plantation economy. As slavery's last refuge in the waning days of the Confederacy, the Lone Star state took in a sizable black slave population in order to keep them in bondage as long as possible. After being released, most of the former slaves had no choice but to continue to work in the East Texas cotton fields as sharecroppers and tenant farmers. However, they were not as concentrated there as their Delta counterparts, due to the paucity of the soil and the availability of land to the west. The exception was along the Trinity and Brazos rivers, where the topsoil was rich and thick. These riverlands were not only the site of the state's most prosperous cotton plantations but also a chain of the South's most notorious prison farms. The work songs shared among the black prisoners on these penal farms proved to be a motherlode for the East Texas blues tradition. A number of these work songs, or portions of their verse, were integrated into the repertoires of the major East Texas blues pioneers: "Ragtime Texas" Henry Thomas, the father of the railroad blues; Blind Lemon Jefferson, the blind blues bard who went on to become the nation's most recorded rural blues-man; and Alger "Texas" Alexander and Huddie Leadbetter ("Leadbelly"), both of whom served time on the infamous Texas prison farms. Leadbelly later recorded his entire repertoire of Texas prison work songs for the Library of Congress. The next generation of East Texas blues innovators—guitarists Sam "Lightnin'" Hopkins, Clarence "Gatemouth" Brown, and Arron "T-Bone" Walker; pianists "Ivory" Joe Hunter, Joe Liggins, and Charles Brown; and saxophonists Buster Smith and Arnett Cobb—all helped to shape the region's blues into a taut, dance-oriented ensemble music highlighted by rolling piano accompaniments, riffing horns, and imaginative single-string-guitar solos. T-Bone Walker is credited with being the first blues musician to experiment with this style on an electric guitar, which changed the sound of the blues irrevocably. Along with peers like Hopkins, Liggins, Hunter, and Brown, Walker helped to position East Texas blues at the center of West Coast rhythm and blues during and after World War II.

The Piedmont is the largest of the three rural blues homelands, stretching from Richmond, Virginia, south to Atlanta, Georgia. It is bounded by the Atlantic coastal plain to the east and the Appalachian Mountains to the west. The area from Richmond down to Durham, North Carolina, and then west to the mountains has historically been tobacco country; farther south cotton was king. Black workers in the cotton and tobacco fields were the source and inspiration of the Piedmont blues, which seem to have emerged almost a decade after their initial appearance in the Mississippi Delta and East Texas. The first documented folk blues in the region were reported in rural southeast Georgia in 1908. In the 1910s, Greenville and Spartenburg, South Carolina, were the centers of gravity for a loose network of blind blues oracles, including Simmie Dooley, Willie Walker, and Gary Davis. In the 1920s, Atlanta was the hub for Piedmont blues giants like Blind Willie McTell, Peg Leg Howell, Eddie Anthony, and the Hicks Brothers, Charlie and "Barbecue" Bob. By the depression era, Durham was the region's blues hotspot, with musicians like Blind Boy Fuller, the Reverend Gary Davis, Sonny Terry, and Bull City Red based there. The Piedmont blues sound was sweet, light, and flowing—a dramatic departure from the deeper and darker Delta blues and the more jazz- and dance-oriented ensemble sound that came to the forefront in East Texas blues. Piedmont blues pioneers favored lilting melodies for their solo blues numbers, which they sang in high, plaintive voices. They drew their material from the folk songs, ballads, and show tunes performed by songsters working in black minstrelsy, which had a large following in the region from its origins in the Reconstruction era to its demise in the wake of World War I. In addition, the early Piedmont blues innovators, like Blind Arthur Blake, incorporated ragtime playing techniques into their guitar styles; they did so by "ragging" their blues melodies in order to create the desired cross-rhythms between voice and guitar, which gave the songs their tension and drive. Blake's ragtime-influenced blues guitar style stressed finger-picking dexterity; his fast-paced runs with a deft touch on the strings became the dominant blues guitar style in the Piedmont. Another musical trait of the region was the guitar and harmonica duos, which flourished in the northern Piedmont in the pre–World War II era. They featured intricate call-and-response patterns that were interchangeable and often overlapped. Unlike the Delta and East Texas traditions, however, the Piedmont blues were unable to adapt to an urban environment. They never found an equivalent urban sound and hence never caught on in eastern seaboard cities with large black migrant populations, like Washington, D.C., Baltimore, Philadelphia, and New York. The popularity of the Piedmont blues peaked in the region in the 1930s and were a musical relic of the past by the late 1940s.

When the blues reached the cities in the South and then the North, they came under the influence of two disparate cultural forces; the music industry and the ghetto tenderloins, also known as red-light districts. Both of these urban phenomena had contradictory effects on the blues—effects that dramatically transformed their soundscape and their lyrical content. The music industry introduced blues recordings to a nationwide black audience, as well as to a more select white audience; in the process, it documented some of this new folk music for posterity. However, the music industry also attempted to standardize the blues form, trivialize their contents, and financially exploit blues artists. The red-light districts also had a paradoxical influence on the music. The underworld economies at the heart of these tenderloins provided blues musicians with jobs playing their own music, which in turn gave them the social and physical space to experiment with their art form among peers. In addition, the red-light districts infused the blues with the restless and rebellious ethos of the resident black underclass. But the decadence, violence, crime, vice, alcohol and drug addiction, disease, and poverty endemic to the ghetto tenderloins eventually took their toll on blues musicians, like everyone else living there. As a consequence, many of the most talented urban blues artists of the twentieth century never got a chance to record their own music or to reach their full potential due to their premature deterioration or death. Ultimately all of these contradictory factors came into play in the sudden rise, and then the slow decline, of urban blues in the twentieth century.

Show business proved to be the high road for the blues migrations into the cities. In the wake of the Civil War, black entertainers began to replace their white counterparts in the blackface minstrel shows, popular since the 1830s. By the end of the century, black minstrelsy was well established as a favorite leisure-time activity among African Americans living in the South, especially in the Piedmont region. The traveling tent shows featured a wide variety of entertainers: dancers, comics, songsters, and an all-purpose band. In the postbellum era, male comedians like Billy Kersands became black minstrelsy's major attractions, but by World War I, the up-and-coming new blues divas began to rival the male comics for top billing. Foremost among these women were Gertrude "Ma" Rainey and Ida Cox, both of whom ran their own tent shows during this period. Concurrently the launching in 1909 of an urban vaudeville circuit for African Americans, the Theatre Owners Booking Agency (TOBA), gave black minstrelsy a new lease on life. Staging the shows at theaters in the cities was more lucrative, and they soon attracted the attention of the urban-based music industry. By the 1920s, blues divas like Bessie Smith, Ethel Waters, and Mamie Smith were the major stars of the TOBA; moreover, they were the first African Americans to record the blues. By that time, the music industry's Tin Pan Alley tunesmiths, following the lead of W. C. Handy, had already popularized their own watered-down versions of the blues. The bulk of these early 1910s recordings, however, were made for a white middle-class audience and featured white singers like Sophie Tucker. Only inadvertently, the music industry discovered that there was a more profitable blues market among African Americans, especially if the music was recorded by black artists. At first, only the smaller record labels ventured into the black blues market; this enabled some of the new record companies, like W. C. Handy and Harry Pace's Black Swan label, to gain a foothold in the industry. But eventually the larger companies, like RCA Victor and Columbia, bought out the smaller labels and took over the race record market, as it came to be known. Black women, later referred to as the "classic blues singers," first recorded the blues in the early 1920s. Later in the decade, the major race record operations sponsored field trips to the South to make recordings of rural and urban bluesmen. They were not especially interested in giving these indigenous blues artists national exposure or in documenting their folk blues; they were seeking new songs to use for financial gain. This was done by copyrighting the blues compositions they recorded under the auspices of their own music publishing firms, which then collected all the royalty monies generated by the songs; the original composers were left out of the financial equation, save for the few dollars they were paid to record their blues composition. This exploitation of black musicians by the record companies and their agents was business as usual in the music industry, especially where the blues were concerned.

The ghetto tenderloins proved to be the low road for blues migrations into the cities. The emergence of these red-light districts coincided with the accelerated growth of industrialism in the nation's burgeoning urban centers in the late 1800s and early 1900s. The rapid influx of immigrant and migrant laborers seeking work in the new industries changed the landscape of the cities. Overcrowded ethnic ghettos gave birth to local ward political organizations; they delivered the ethnic vote to city hall in exchange for patronage. These organizations became the backbone of a number of urban political machines, which gained control over the political and economic life of key industrial cities with large working-class populations. The machines not only doled out patronage to their ethnic constituencies (Irish, Polish, Italians, African Americans, and others); they also sanctioned the underworld vice operations—gambling, prostitution, illegal drugs and alcohol—that flourished in the ghetto tenderloins; this was done for a share of the profits from these operations.

New Orleans has a long history as the nation's foremost city of pleasure, dating back to the pre–Revolutionary War era. The legendary French Quarter is world renowned as both a red-light district and an incubator of innovative black music. Although recognized as the birthplace of jazz, New Orleans also played an important role in the origins of urban blues. In fact, it was the inclusion of blues in the repertoires of local black musicians, like cornet legend Buddy Bolden, that led to the birth of jazz in New Orleans around the turn of the century. The pioneering blues pianist, Ferdinand "Jellyroll" Morton, recalled first hearing the blues in New Orleans in 1902. The performer who introduced him to this new music was Mamie Desdoumes, one of the many local pianists who made a living playing in French Quarter bordellos. In addition to being adopted by tenderloin pianists, the blues were being featured in the music of local black bands. Bolden's jazz band was the most famous example; "Funky Butt Blues" was its signature piece. But a number of local bands played the blues during this period; the Johnson Family string band, for example, performed in the streets of the French Quarter. The youngest member of this band was Lonnie Johnson, who blossomed into the 1920s premiere urban blues guitarist. Unfortunately, Johnson, like many other talented black musicians from New Orleans, had to move on to make his mark in music. The French Quarter went into a decline with the advent of World War I and was even shut down for awhile at the behest of the U.S. Navy. As a result, many black musicians left New Orleans to seek work in the red-light districts that continued to flourish in urban centers throughout the war years and well into the 1920s.

A number of cities in the South featured their own unique brand of early urban blues, the most prominent being Atlanta, Birmingham, Dallas, and Houston. The southern city that had perhaps the most profound influence on the development of urban blues in their formative years was Memphis, Tennessee. Like New Orleans, it was a bustling riverport trade, transportation, and manufacturing center, with a tenderloin haven for pleasure seekers and for talented black musicians. The city's political machine was lorded over by "Boss" Crump, a wily segregationist politician who garnered the local black vote in exchange for patronage and the sanctioning of a wide-open tenderloin nightlife on Beale Street. Cocaine use was rampant in this red-light district, as was murder. Due to the skyrocketing homicide rate, Memphis was christened the "murder capital" of the nation in 1923 by the local press. As for music, Beale Street became a magnet for Delta blues performers, as well as for rural blues musicians from the surrounding Tennessee and Arkansas countryside. In the 1920s, the city was base for a number of influential jugbands that played a rudimentary but lively brand of urban blues. These bands used guitars, banjos, harmonicas, kazoos, and whiskey jugs. The most prominent were Gus Cannon's Jug Stompers, which featured the legendary Noah Lewis on harmonica, and the Memphis Jug Band, featuring Will Shade on harmonica and "Laughing" Charley Burse on guitar and vocals. Burse's suggestive hip-shaking routine and his use of his guitar as a phallic symbol would be imitated much later in his career by an impressionable young white guitarist and singer named Elvis Presley. These borrowed stage antics helped to launch Presley's career as a rock and roll star. Other important Memphis-based blues musicians active in its pre–World War II heyday were guitarists Furry Lewis, Frank Stokes, and Memphis Minnie Douglas; pianists Jab Jones and Memphis Slim; harp players Hamie Nixon and John Lee "Sonny Boy" Williamson; and Sleepy John Estes, the groups' most talented blues composer. In the postwar era, Memphis continued to be a hub of blues activity, although Boss Crump's political machine was finally dismantled and Beale Street fell into disrepair. Urban blues artists like Howlin' Wolf, B. B. King, Bobby Blue Bland, Junior Parker, and James Cotton all cut their teeth on the postwar Memphis blues scene before moving on. In the case of B. B. King, this involved becoming the nation's premiere electric blues guitarist and ultimately an international symbol of the music.

Chicago proved to be the mecca of urban blues in America. The city was not only the site of a large ghetto tenderloin, overflowing with black migrants, mostly from the Mississippi Delta; it was also the site of a large race record operation, which was second only to New York's size and influence. The massive influx of rural African Americans began in earnest during World War II, when the *Chicago Defender* launched its "Great Northern Drive" to bring southern black migrants to the city. By the 1920s, Chicago's Southside ghetto had more African Americans living there than anywhere else in the country, with the exception of Harlem in New York City. The major blues musicians active in the city during this early period included guitarists Big Bill Broonzy, Tampa Red, Lonnie Johnson, and Kokomo Arnold; pianists Cow Cow Davenport, Cripple Clarence Lofton, Her-sial Thomas, Clarence "Pinetop" Smith, Thomas Dorsey, and Jimmy Yancy; and vocalists Washboard Sam, Sippie Wallace, and Alberta Hunter. During the depression years, boogie-woogie pianists like Albert Ammons and Mead Lux Lewis came to the forefront of the Southside blues scene. In addition, the early urban blues bands, like those organized by Sonny Boy Williamson and Memphis Slim, began to transform the traditional Delta blues into the forceful ensemble dance music that would characterize Chicago blues. Sonny Boy's band featured his harmonica playing, an electric guitar, a rhythm guitar, then a bass, and eventually drums and piano. It was a prototype of what would follow in the postwar era, which proved to be the golden age of Chicago blues. The bands of Muddy Waters and Howlin' Wolf, along with their recordings on Chess Records, not only pioneered the soundscape of postwar Chicago blues but influenced the future course of popular music in America for years to come.

There were other urban blues hotbeds in the Midwest, in particular, Louisville, Indianapolis, Cincinnati, and Kansas City. Yet none was as bountiful as Chicago's during its heyday. After the ascendancy of urban blues in the 1920s and their impressive resiliency over the next three decades, they were finally overtaken in the late 1940s and early 1950s by fresher black musical styles favored by African-American youth. This decline in popularity coincided with a diffusion of the blues into the more current musical trends, both black and white—a process that accelerated in the 1950s. Hence, blues diffusions can be traced to African-American rhythm and blues, soul, and even rap musical styles. Moreover, they can be traced to the flowering of rock and roll, and then rock music, among white youth. As for country music, it has been diffused with the blues since its commercial origins in the 1920s.

In addition to the diffusion of the blues into much of American popular music, they have played a vital role in African-American cultural resistance to white domination. The blues texts were black working-class discourses on American society, as seen and experienced from the bottom up. The blues sounds were "off key" and "dirty" by Eurocentric musical standards, while being true to their African musical roots. Blues performances were collective healing rituals involving audience and artist in a self-affirming catharsis that purges the despair and pain of the past. And blues artists historically have been cultural rebels; their music and their life-styles were implicit critiques of their second-class status in the white-controlled social order. These four aspects of the blues tradition have helped to infuse African-American culture, from the bottom up, with a resilient outlook that has resisted domination, from both outside and top down. For example, the rural blues were a grass-roots cultural response to the domination of older styles of fiddle and banjo music in the South. In a similar fashion, urban blues were a grass-roots cultural response, this time to the domination of Tin Pan Alley musical styles. Even today, after having changed the landscape of American popular music, the blues remain a working-class-roots music constantly at odds with the commercially dominated pop mainstream.

Bibliography

Albertson, Chris. *Bessie.* New York: Stein & Day, 1974.

Bastin, Bruce. *Red River Blues: The Blues Tradition in the Southeast;* Baton Rouge: Louisiana State University Press, 1986.

Bruyuoghe, Yannick. *Big Bill Blues.* New York: Oak Publications, 1969.

Charters, Samuel. *Sweet as Showers of Rain.* New York: Oak Publications, 1977.

Dance, Helen Oakley. *Stormy Monday: The T-Bone Walker Story.* Baton Rouge: Louisiana State University Press, 1987.

Handy, W. C. *The Father of the Blues: An Autobiography.* New York: Macmillan, 1942.

Harrison, Daphine Duval. *Black Pearls: Blues Queens of the 1920s.* New Brunswick, N.J.: Rutgers University Press, 1988.

Levine, Lawrence. *Black Culture and Black Consciousness: Afro-American Folk Thought from Slavery to Freedom.* New York: Oxford University Press, 1977.

Lieb, Sandra. *Mother of the Blues: A Study of Ma Rainey.* Amherst: University of Massachusetts Press, 1981.

Oakley, Giles. *The Devil's Music: A History of the Blues.* New York: Harcourt Brace, Jovanovich, 1976.

Oliver, Paul, *The Story of the Blues.* New York: Chilton Books, 1966.

Palmer, Robert. *Deep Blues.* New York: Viking, 1981.

Rowe, Mike. *Chicago Breakdown*. London: Eddison Press, 1973.

Sawyer, Charles. *The Arrival of B. B. King*. Garden City, N.Y.: Doubleday, 1980.

Shaw, Arnold. *Honkers and Shouters: The Golden Age of Rhythm and Blues*. New York: Macmillan, 1978.

 El Paso

By James Miller

> I don't consider "El Paso" a country-and-western song. It's a cowboy song, early American folk music from the western United States. It's not an old song—I wrote the song—but it's the type of song that you would have heard eighty years ago. That's not country-and-western.[1]
>
> —MARTY ROBBINS (1925–82)

As a multimedia child of the early fifties, weaned on the cross-merchandising of six-shooters and lunch pails blazoned with pictures of Hopalong Cassidy and Davy Crockett, I naturally assumed that cowboys and the songs of the West were a key part of my patrimony. I was encouraged in this assumption by my parents, who had a copy of the famous John and Alan Lomax anthology, *Best Loved American Folk Songs*. My mother would sometimes play songs from the book—"Home on the Range," "The Old Chisholm Trail"—on our upright piano.

For John Lomax, this music shed light on "that unique and romantic figure in modern civilization, the American cowboy"—a figure that Lomax dramatically placed "on the skirmish line of civilization. Restless, fearless, chivalric, elemental, he lived hard, shot quick and true, and died with his face to his feet."[2]

For my mother, cowboy songs had no special significance; they were simply part of an American boy's common culture, like baseball and apple pie. But for my father, the ballads cut closer to the bone in ways that I didn't understand until I was much older.

---

[1] Quoted in Alanna Nash, *Behind Closed Doors*, p. 446. For full citations, see Notes, Books and Recordings.

[2] John A. Lomax, *Cowboy Songs* (1925), "collectors note."

He was born in 1920, on Cactus Hill outside Bartlesville, Oklahoma, where cowboys still tended cattle. The son of an oil worker active in the local union, he had grown up watching the films of Gene Autry, listening to the Western swing of Bob Wills and his Texas Playboys—and helping his dad recruit new members for the union. The first in his family to receive a Ph.D., he had a scholarly interest in Western music as well. Besides the Lomax book, he had acquired a number of the albums of union songs and folk music, including cowboy ballads, recorded by Woody Guthrie, Burl Ives, and Pete Seeger for Moses Asch and his Asch label in the 1940s.

As I grew older, I put away my toy spurs and coonskin cap. But I never quite outgrew the Western music I was raised on—which helps explain my continuing affection for one of the greatest cowboy ballads of the twentieth century, Marty Robbins's "El Paso."

Marty Robbins was of my father's generation and came of age at the height of the Great Depression. But whereas my father grew up in the Dust Bowl, Robbins was from the outback of Arizona.

Born in 1925 in a high-desert homestead outside of Glendale, northwest of Phoenix, Robbins was one of nine children. His father, an immigrant from Poland, was only intermittently employed—the family was sometimes forced to live in a tent.[3]

One of his earliest memories was of listening to the tales of the Wild West told by his maternal grandfather, Bob Heckle, a former cowpuncher and Texas Ranger who had also traveled with medicine shows, hawking books of his own cowboy poetry. "The stories that, he would tell me were cowboy stories that he heard around the campfire," Robbins later recalled. "My grandfather inspired me to be a cowboy, I guess. That's what I wanted to be. Because I thought a lot of him, and he was a cowboy, you know."

Grandpa Heckle died when Robbins was six, but the boy was hooked: he became an avid reader of Western fiction (and would later in life publish a Western novel of his own). He picked cotton so that he could see the latest Westerns at the local picture show.

"I first started praying to be a cowboy singer," Robbins once explained. "I wanted to be Gene Autry. I wanted to ride off into the sunset."[4]

And so the young Robbins became a singer of cowboy songs, coming to master the "western" part of country-western—a mishmash of tall tales, old Irish music, and minstrel hokum. He doubtless knew the first popular recording of a cowboy ballad, "When the Work's All Done This Fall," a song based on a poem written by Montana cowboy D. X O'Malley in 1895, reprinted in John Lomax's first book, *Cowboy Songs and Other Frontier Ballads,* in 1910, and sung by 'Carl T. Sprague, once a real cowboy too' in the 1925 recording that turned it into a Western standard. (It would be recorded by Robbins himself thirty-six years later.)

In 1929, the Arizona Wranglers, from Phoenix, recorded "Strawberry Roan," the saga of a bucking bronco that couldn't be broken; it became the basis of a 1933 movie,

---

[3] Colin Escott, notes to *Marty Robbins at Town Hall Party.* Bear Family DVD 20007 AT (2003).

[4] Quoted in Nash, *Behind Closed Doors,* p. 442.

The Strawberry Roan, featuring Ken Maynard, Hollywood's first "Singing Cowboy," who delivered the song in an abrasive nasal monotone. (Robbins would record "The Strawberry Roan," too, in 1959.)

As a result of the growing popularity of musical Western films, demand started to outstrip the supply of more or less genuine cowboy songs. This created an opportunity for new singers and new songwriters, like the Sons of the Pioneers, a Hollywood-based harmony group with no firsthand experience of the frontier but a knack for imagining what it was like and writing tunes that evoked its wild beauty. Their 1934 recording of "Tumbling Tumbleweeds" was a national hit, and a year later the song became the centerpiece of the film that turned Gene Autry into a Hollywood star—*Tumbling Tumbleweeds.*

A veteran of medicine shows, Gene Autry had first achieved fame as "Oklahoma's Yodelin' Cowboy" performing on radio station KVOO in Tulsa, Oklahoma, before moving on to WLS and joining the cast of its *National Barn Dance* in Chicago. Autry had style; he sang with a bluesy twang, like the Singing Brakeman, Jimmie Rodgers, but his delivery was relaxed and his diction clear, like Bing Crosby, the Old Groaner.

In- *Tumbling Tumbleweeds,* as in the many films that followed, Autry wasn't only a cowboy who happened to sing; he was *Gene Autry,* frontier good guy invariably playing himself, he was miraculously able to defeat crooks and killers with a song and a sunny disposition—or, if that failed, some sharp shooting. Even in the depths of the Great Depression, a Gene Autry film seemed to promise, there was one place in America where justice would prevail that was back home on the range—"where you sleep out every night, and the only law is right," as Autry sang in "Back in the Saddle Again," his radio theme song.

In December of 1959, my radio theme song became "El Paso."

At a time when the radio was full of watered-down rock 'n' roll sung by pretty boys bereft of talent, Marty Robbins and "El Paso" had the narrative arc of an epic film. The music was lilting, the singing gorgeous. The recording lasted for nearly five minutes, an eternity by the standards of the time. The lyrics told the story of a cowboy who kills, and in turn is killed, all for love of Felina, a Mexican girl. Even more memorably, the outlaw narrates his own death. He sings of the bullet going deep in his chest, the girl kissing his cheek, and his very last words: "Felina, goodbye!"

At the time, I was twelve years old. Though the killing spree of Charles Starkweather and Caril Fugate had terrorized my hometown of Lincoln, Nebraska, the year before—and though my grade-school teachers had taught me to duck and cover in the event of nuclear' war—I knew little about life and less about death. An introvert by temperament, I spent much of my youth daydreaming. Thanks to *Gunsmoke* and *Have Gun Will Travel,* two favorite TV shows, the image of a lawless frontier was vivid in my mind. But most of the time, it bore no resemblance to the world I thought I knew.

That winter, my family drove across Iowa to Moline, Illinois, to celebrate Christmas with my mother's extended family, the Anderson clan. There, were six brothers and sisters still living on the banks of the Mississippi in 1959, all of them descended from Swedish stock, all of them still churchgoing Lutherans like my mother, and they were one image of a good community—loving, cozy, civilized.

Grandpa Anderson worked at the local Chevrolet dealership, which one of his older brothers owned. On this visit, I was to earn some money and learn some discipline by helping him take inventory in the parts department. It was a dirty job. The weather was bleak. Driving to the dealership every morning under sleet-gray skies, I would warm up by listening to the radio—and what warmed me the most was hearing "El Paso."

I tried to interest my grandfather in the saga of the amorous outlaw and his inevitable death. But "El Paso" left him cold. Like most of the other members of his clan, grandpa Anderson was a loyal company man and a lifelong Republican, with little interest in the wilder side of life. He didn't much like Westerns, he explained, and he would rather listen to Dinah Shore—Chevrolet sponsored her TV show, after all.

Marty Robbins recorded "El Paso" in the course of an all-day session held in Nashville, Tennessee, on April 7, 1959. The session produced twelve songs that would appear later that year as a long-playing album entitled *Gunfighter Ballads and Trail Songs.*

A cast member of Nashville's "Grand Ole Opry" since the early 1950s, Robbins first achieved fame in the country field by writing and singing love songs in a smooth, sweet tenor, like Eddy Arnold in the 1940s. When sales of his love songs began to sag, Robbins tried his hand at rock 'n' roll. In 1954, he cut a version of Elvis Presley's first ' record, "That's All Right," and had a country hit with it, unlike Presley. He cut a version of Chuck Berry's "Maybellene" and had a modest hit with that, too. Then, in 1956, his version of "Singing the Blues" became a number-one country hit, edging out Elvis Presley's "Hound Dog."

The following year, Robbins traveled to New York to work with veteran pop producers Mitch Miller and Ray Conniff. Targeting Presley's teen audience, Robbins recorded a new composition of his own, and in the spring of 1957 "A White Sport Coat and a Pink Carnation" rivaled the mainstream popularity of Presley's "All Shook Up." More pop hits followed—"The Story of My Life" in 1957, and "Just Married" in 1958—all of them featuring the kind of close-blended vocal accompaniment that Presley had made a fixture of his hit recordings with the Jordanaires.

To reproduce the sound of his pop records on the road, Robbins hired a group of vocalists, the Glaser Brothers, a trio of Jewish farm boys from Nebraska. "We grew up in Spaulding," recalled Jim Glaser many years later, "and the nearest town was sixty miles away. The town wasn't on our side. A lot of people thought you had to be illiterate to like country music." Ironically rescued from a life of rural idiocy by their mastery of song forms symbolically associated with rural idiocy, the brothers joined Robbins and his touring show.

"In those days, Marty traveled in two cars, or sometimes station wagons," Jim Glaser says. "Marty carried a little ukulele, made by the Martin Guitar company, and would often pass the hours and miles by singing every song he could think of, with Bobby and me adding harmony. Many of the songs were Western songs, and it was during this time that Marty decided to do an album of these songs."

Robbins also began to make up new Western songs of his own. One of the first was "El Paso"—inspired, he would later say, by driving through the West Texas town on a family car trip from Tennessee to Arizona.

"The song took him several months to write," recalls Jim Glaser: "Each time we went out on tour, Marty would sing the latest verses. … By the time we accompanied Marty into the studio to record the song, we had it down so well that it only took four takes to get the final version, and two of those were false starts."[5]

"El Paso" shares some of its ingredients with the Western music that enchanted Marty Robbins as a boy. The song as a whole projects an aura of authenticity, like the ballads of Carl T. Sprague; it is sung with the sort of open-hearted sincerity that Gene Autry made a trademark; and the vocal blend of Robbins with Jim Glaser and Bobby Sykes evokes the freedom of the open range as surely as do the soaring. harmonies of "Tumbling Tumbleweed."

But the *music* itself bears no resemblance at all to the sorts of songs sung by Sprague, Autry, and the Sons of the Pioneers—and neither do the lyrics, which invert the exaggerated optimism of the singing cowboys of the 1930s.

Robbins's West is a dangerous place of large passions and empty violence, where death and eros are intertwined. Though *Gunfighter Ballads and Trail Songs* included such traditional numbers as "Billy the Kid" and "Utah Carol" its keynote songs were "El Paso" and "Big Iron." Here he evokes a specifically American fear of falling on the wrong side of the skirmish line of civilization, a fear that also informs the noir Westerns, that Hollywood had begun to make after World War II: from *Red River* and *Winchester '73* to *High Noon* and the TV series *Have Gun Will Travel*.

There are decent men in this West—but they are loners and outriders, and there is always a chance that a good man's blood brother will turn out to be evil incarnate (as happens in *Winchester '73*). The Paladin character in *Have Gun Will Travel* is a bounty hunter with a brain and what seems like a good heart—though where he found his moral compass is obscure, not least to some of the 'outlaws he brings to heel. (For the album cover of *Gunfighter Ballads,* Robbins wore *vaquero* black, just like Paladin.)

The unrequited lover who narrates "El Paso" is not quite beyond good and evil. He expresses shock at his ability to kill a stranger in a jealous rage. But he is irresistibly drawn by his love for Felina, who is "wicked" and "evil" and "casting a spell." His violent end is as sublimely preordained as that suffered by any hero in Greek tragedy.

The song is cast in the form of a *ranchera,* the Mexican brand of "ranch" music associated in the 1940s with Jorge Negrete and Pedro Infante, impassioned singers who were also Mexican movie stars, personifying on screen "El Charro Cantor" Mexico's version of the Singing Cowboy. The outlaw who sings "El Paso" tells his story in an operatic idiom

5 Memo from Jim Glaser to Norma J. posted on her Web site devoted to Jim Glaser: http://normal00.com/glsrobbnsl.html.

that his Mexican maiden will surely understand. The song is taken at a brisk waltz tempo characteristic of *ranchera*—mariachi horns would be a natural addition. (In 1960, when Robbins tried to recapture the epic spirit of "El Paso" by recording a new gunfighter *ranchera*, "San Angelo," he in fact added mariachi trumpets.)

The music itself proves how porous cultural borders can be. Robbins's cowboy is trapped by a passion that bursts forth in a song-form that belongs to another world. Virtue and vice blur along this borderline. In the badlands the song evokes, power grows out of the barrel of a gun—and death seems almost a form of deliverance.

A similarly ambiguous moral universe was dramatized in the most popular Hollywood Western of 1959, *Rio Bravo,* a movie set in an anarchic border town much like the "El Paso" of Robbins's song. As in "El Paso," much of the action takes place in a cantina. "Every man should have a little taste of power before he's through," declares an outlaw who has just been forced to lay down his guns by the town's often unreliable deputy sheriff, an alcoholic gunslinger played by Dean Martin. As the film's director, Howard Hawks, famously quipped, he had made the movie, in part, as a rejoinder to *High Noon* with its picture of a high-minded lawman who must beg for help. "I didn't think a good sheriff was going to be running around town like a chicken with his head off asking for help."

The taciturn sheriff in *Rio Bravo,* played by John Wayne, gets help without asking for it. The sharp-shooting rifleman takes his name from the hostile power that he has mastered: "Chance" is fearless, independent, and a natural-born Stoic whose virtue is tested not just by killers but by a lady of low repute, like Felina from "El Paso."

When outlaws roll into the border town to spring a comrade from jail, the gang's leader tells the cantina's band to play "The Cutthroat Song"—a sinister mariachi that the Mexican Army used to break the will of the men defending the Alamo. Waxing philosophical, Chance explains the meaning of the music: "No mercy for the losers."

The *ranchera* in "El Paso" is similarly evocative. From the moment the music starts, it rushes forward to embrace death—like the cowboy who sings the song.

The Nashville recording session for "El Paso" involved four musicians in addition to Robbins and the Glaser Brothers. The players—Louis Dunn on drums, Bob Moore on bass, Jack H. Pruett on rhythm guitar, and Grady Martin on lead guitar—included several members of Nashville's A-Team, as the city's best pickers were called. The most important of these was Grady Martin, whose calling card was an uncanny ability to alter his sound to fit the needs of virtually any song—from the fleet boogie-woogie he plays on Red Foley's 1949 recording of "Chattanooga Shoe Shine Boy," to the thundering 12-string guitar riff that he uses to open Roy Orbison's 1964 recording of "Oh, Pretty Woman."

But all of Martin's other achievements pale beside the gut-string solo he improvised for the recording of "El Paso." For chorus after chorus, the guitarist accompanies Robbins's narrative with a nonstop sequence of runs, flourishes, and fills that are more redolent of

Gypsy flamenco, or of Les Paul's playing on "Vaya con-Dios," than of anything commonly heard in a *ranchera* or an ordinary Nashville session.

Martin's guitar becomes a second solo voice. It dances and gallops, and it makes the song seem to lift off the ground.

As a result of the popularity of "El Paso," Marty Robbins was able to fulfill a childhood dream. He starred in a Hollywood Western, *Ballad of a Gunfighter (1964)*.

Like Gene Autry in all of his films, Marty Robbins appears as himself in *Ballad of a Gunfighter*. He is a frontier Robin Hood who steals gold that he gives to the local padre and the poor of San Angelo, a Texas border town. The town's cantina is home to a bordello full of Mexican maidens, including Felina from "El Paso" and Secora, the heroine of that song's sequel, "San Angelo."

In the film, "Señor Marty" falls in love with Secora. With the help of the padre, he tries to convince Secora that there is good in everyone, even a whore like her and a thief like himself—to become good, all you need is love.

The soundtrack opens with symphonic variations on "El Paso" and climaxes with Robbins's recording of "San Angelo." A corrupt sheriff traps Robin Hood by kidnapping Secora and forcing her lover to ride into an ambush. As in the song, Secora dies—and so does Marty Robbins.

The religious imagery could not be more explicit. In the film, the padre smiles beatifically as Secora and Robbins die. The cowboy is a kind of saint—a martyr, redeemed by his transcendent love, a love stronger than death.

Years after "El Paso" first captured my fancy, I asked my paternal grandfather to tell me about his life. We talked in the living room of a refrigerated bungalow in suburban Houston, where grandpa Miller had moved after he retired from the Phillips 66 petroleum company. He had worked as a roustabout for Phillips for almost his entire adult life. . Since I had developed an interest in the history of the American left, I pressed him about his political beliefs as a young man. Almost offhandedly, he revealed a fact that even my father didn't know: Phillips had banished him from Tulsa to remote Shidler, Oklahoma, to punish him for his union activism. A onetime socialist, he became a lifelong Democrat with a sharp sense that there is no justice in this world.

The ice broken, we kept talking—he was normally a man of few words. Before settling down to raise his family in Oklahoma, he explained, he had gone north to find work in the coal mines of Kansas. His earliest memories were of Texas at the turn of the twentieth century. As a teenager, he had hawked newspapers on the streets of Fort Worth. He recalled traveling in a covered wagon, and he recounted how, as a child, he and his parents had had a frightening encounter with Indians on the open range (nobody got hurt).

The West that Marty Robbins conjured up in "El Paso" never existed, of course, any more than the West depicted in "Home on the Range" or in John Wayne's *Rio Bravo* did.

But as I came to understand while talking to my grandpa Miller shortly before his death, the West was a bigger part of my real patrimony than I had previously understood.

Though not a cowboy, my grandfather had certainly lived on the skirmish line of civilization—and he had certainly fought the good fight in a morally uncertain universe.

And that is another reason why I still warm to hearing Marty Robbins exalt a lost world of rough passion and stoic courage—in what may be the last great cowboy ballad.

Gerry Goffin/Carole King Interviews

Songwriters on Songwriting

By Paul Zollo

Though it was a cold day for Los Angeles, only five days before Christmas, meeting with Gerry Goffin at his home was a warm experience. With his four-year-old daughter dressed as a fairy princess with cat ears and a magic wand, playing with the kittens scampering about in the sparkling light of an enormous Christmas tree, Gerry tuned out all of these homey distractions and spoke at length about the early days of rock and roll and about writing with his former wife and collaborator Carole King.

It was the last days of Tin Pan Alley, when writers would go to their offices in the Brill Building (and nearby) in New York every day and churn out new songs like factory workers turning out cars. These were the days when a song could be written, recorded and released all within a month, as was Goffin and King's first hit, "Will You Love Me Tomorrow?" which was recorded by the Shirelles.

Then came the age of the singer-songwriter and Carole began performing her own songs, rather than writing them for others. And though many of the songs on her landmark *Tapestry* album were Goffin/King collaborations, Gerry didn't feel right "putting words in her mouth," and the two stopped writing together for years.

He was born in New York in 1941 and met Carole King at Queens College in 1958, where they found few things more engaging than writing songs. Though Gerry insists that they wrote an abundance of bad songs for years, they soon started writing hits, and generated many that have since become standards, including "The Loco-Motion," "Up on the Roof," "One Fine Day," "Chains," "Natural Woman" and many more.

Gerry has since written words to the tunes of other composers, most notably Michael Masser, with whom he wrote "Saving All My Love for You" for Whitney Houston and "Theme from Mahogany" for Diana Ross.

After our interview was over, I was happily surprised when he asked me to join him for a game of chess. Though the last time I played was around the time *Tapestry* was first released, I agreed, and Gerry brought out his ornate set. Using the same thrifty acumen he brings to lyric writing, he beat me quickly and easily with a minimum of moves, checkmating my king without even capturing many of my pieces. "I never win," he said afterward with a smile. "You can play me anytime."

One thing that you and Carole did was to bring traditional songwriting structures, such as the use of inner rhymes, to rock and roll.

Yeah, it was sort of a synthesis. We didn't really write what you would call a rock and roll song like Chuck Berry or Little Richard wrote a rock and roll song.

How, in your mind, were they different than those kind of songs?

Well, Carole had a great capacity to write great melodies. She was aware of chordal structures. She didn't use the typical I-IV-V chord progressions. It was a great experience for me. She was studying to be a schoolteacher and I was studying to be a chemist, and I think we made out pretty good [laughs] as far as an easier life.

Did you and Carole enjoy the same kind of songs back then?

Carole liked some music that rubbed me the wrong way. I'd rather not name the music, but it was the kind of music that just went so far lyrically. And the songs didn't seem to have the soul that I wanted to put into a song. And we ended up writing in an entirely different way than all of them.

We liked all the music that was out. It was a great time. It was like music coming from the streets. I know when I was growing up, most songs sounded great. We loved everybody's music just as much as our own. And now it seems like there's maybe fifteen to twenty good songs a year that really stick with you. The rest sort of get in this collage of the same electronic sounds. …

Do you remember when you knew you could make your living as songwriters?

Well, Carole's parents were very much against the idea of songwriting. My father encouraged me but my mother said I was crazy. My marks in school fell down a whole lot.

I remember telling my mother I could still do both. Carole ended up coaching me on all my subjects one day and failed all of hers. [Laughs]

The big change happened when we met Don Kirshner. He was a great publisher and he gave us confidence. He gave us money to live on—not too much [laughs] but he gave us money to live on.

I was working as an assistant chemist, I was in the Marine Corps Reserve, I was going to night school. I wasn't putting my eggs in one basket. I came from a middle-class background, you know, where there are not too many successful songwriters.

Did you wait until you had your first hit before making a commitment to being a songwriter?

I had trouble making a commitment until I was thirty-two, even after I had maybe fifteen or twenty BMI awards. I still had doubts as to whether this was a fit occupation for somebody. I went back to school and got a job as a chemist for eleven thousand dollars a year. Then I said, "The hell with this," and went back to writing songs. I realized then that I didn't want to play with test tubes anymore.

You said that you and Carole wrote about 150 songs that weren't any good before you wrote "Will You Love Me Tomorrow?"

Oh yeah, they were terrible. The way "Will You Love Me Tomorrow?" was written was that I was out bowling. She went to play mah-jongg [laughs] with her mother. I came home and I found this melody on tape and I wrote it all down, except for the bridge.

We had this huge Norelco tape machine. The words just got written in about fifteen minutes. She came home from playing mah-jongg and we wrote the bridge together. About two days later the Shirelles recorded it. Carole did a great string arrangement on it.

It almost happened overnight. All of a sudden we were writing bad songs and then we keyed into what was happening and what was necessary for the market. We still wrote our share of bad songs, but the majority of them were good. We had, from about 1960 to 1965, almost eighty Top Thirty records.

So that's primarily how you learned to write songs, from doing it?

Yeah. It's something I can't do today because I don't get the opportunity to write as much. But we always kept the flow going. We always had this work ethic going where we learned by working. And we tried to write every day. You can't write a great song every day, but we kept the flow and our minds were in tune. Now I throw out the ideas that are bad. In those days, I didn't.

As for advice for young songwriters: Don't be afraid to write a bad song because the next one may be great. It's just like anything else; you've got to keep the synapses in your brain going. And you have to think about it every day. The main thing is keeping your head free just to think about songs, which is a hard thing to do when you're raising kids or you've got a job and you're hustling for money. It's a hard thing.

Is being married to your collaborator a good way to keep the creative flow going? Or does that closeness get in the way?

Being married … our daughters sort of suffered because as soon as we made some money, we got someone to take care of the kids so that we were free to write.

It's all part of the hunger of being young. The energy you have. I wish I had that energy right now.

Did you and Carole have any routine way of working together? Would you bring in a finished lyric or write a lyric to a finished melody?

Both ways. I'd write a lyric first, or else she'd play a chord progression on the piano and I'd write a melody over it. I can't do that now because melodies are more sophisticated and not as symmetrical. And I don't sing on key that well, but Carole was always able to change a melody enough to make it interesting.

She mentioned to us that you would often come up with melodic ideas.

On the better songs she wrote most of the music. Songs like "Take Good Care of My Baby"—I wrote most of the music to that. Very obvious melodies. Melodies that wouldn't hold water today, but for those days they were good enough.

Carole had this great songwriting piano feel that everybody loves. If I was doing a session, I don't know if I would hire her to play piano. But she had a way of playing where you could hear the record just by her piano feel.

Also, she would put arrangement ideas on demos. We would go to make demos, and Donny Kirshner was always trying to get us to save money on demos, so Carole would put down a basic piano feel; if we were lucky, we would have a drummer or a bass. We had no synthesizers, so Carole would just put string lines on the piano. So it was piano over piano over piano over piano.

Some people say that there's a new generation of music every three years. And I've been writing songs for thirty years, so I must have lived through ten generations of popular music. I've learned there's no one way to write a song.

You've written a number of songs that have been huge hits in today's market. "Saving All My Love for You," for example, which you wrote with Michael Masser, was a big hit for Whitney Houston. Do you consider that an old-fashioned song to have been a hit nowadays?

"Saving All My Love" could have been written in the thirties. I've got to give a lot of credit to Michael Masser. When he used to play me his melodies, I used to laugh because they sounded like traditional ballads. And I said, "I don't think a traditional ballad is going to make it in today's market." But I'd write to them anyways 'cause I liked his music. And I'm happy he proved me wrong.

Does Masser give you a finished melody to write to?

Oh, it's the most frustrating thing to write with Masser because he finishes a melody completely, and he writes very complicated meters. They don't seem complicated when they come out, but they are.

I'm not used to that because Carole would change a whole melodic line if I had a good line. But Michael won't do that. I have to write exactly to his melody.

So with "Saving All My Love," did you fit that title into his melody?

Well, that was one of the few songs we wrote together. We were both a little drunk *[laughs]* and we just decided to write anything. It's one of the simplest songs and it turned out to be a big hit.

Carole mentioned that one of your strengths was simplicity; saying a lot in a simple way.

Simplicity is necessary to some extent for the mainstream pop market. But if you want to do something artistic, simplicity is in some ways a drawback. I've always been frustrated because I always wanted to write on a higher level. And all of those songs that I would submit never made it. I think that some of my better songs were never recorded.

Do you feel that your ideas for songs come from within you or from beyond you?

Well, Carole always says they come from God. But *[laughs]* I'm not that pretentious to think that God's gonna send me a lyric. *[Laughs]*

You don't feel that there's a source of ideas that you can tap into?

Well, John Lennon used to say that when you've written something good, you know you've been somewhere. Carole says they come from God.

I think it comes from the emotional experience of life's situations. I'm having a tough time writing lyrics now because my life situation's stable now for the first time in my life. We have a young daughter and we make the birthday party circuit on Sundays. Sometimes she lets me sleep through them. It's getting harder. I can't write off experience anymore.

Do you believe an artist needs turmoil in his life?

Yeah. I'm approaching fifty and it's getting kind of hard. But I want to keep going. I don't know, maybe a play or something. When I have a chance to write for a movie, I can write very well because I get into someone else's persona. And I don't have to think about my own life.

Carole said that one way her lyrics differed from yours is that hers were not born out of pain in the way that your lyrics were. It may be pain but it may be intelligent pain.

[Laughs] I always looked at myself as being very lucky to be a lyricist. I remember that before I wrote "Mahogany"—I was living in New York at the time—I was working on a song and it was coming very slow. They were building an apartment house right next to mine. And I said, "Dammit, they're gonna have that apartment house built before I finish this song." [Laughs] So I'm glad I wasn't a construction worker.

But you don't think a songwriter can write good songs while living a happy, settled life?

No. My productivity of late proves it to me. I think living in opulence is a drawback. There has to be a hunger. But a lot of people disagree with me about that.

You wrote many of your great songs in New York. Is it harder for you to tap into that creative energy on this coast?

It's a little harder. For me.

Do you have any method for staying in shape creatively?

When I wrote with Carole, it was an every day, nine-to-five thing. Here in L.A. you can call people and say you want to write today, and they'll say, "I gotta get my car washed today" or "I gotta make this meeting" or "I'm writing with someone else." I wish I just had one partner that I could try to write with every day.

You said that it's important to say old things in new ways. Is it hard to write new love songs after all the love songs that have come before?

Yeah, but I think there are still love songs to be written. It's kind of harder in a high-tech society. People are not as vulnerable to sentiment. It's harder but I still think it's possible.

Do you remember what working with Carole at the Brill Building was like? Was it similar to working a normal, everyday job?

Yeah, it was like going to a normal job. It wasn't really the Brill Building; we worked at 1650 Broadway, around the corner from the Brill Building. The Brill Building had even more of the same madness. Barry [Mann], Cynthia [Weil], Carole and I used to plagiarize each other's songs because we had cubicles directly next to each other. Carole could hear what Barry was playing and I could hear what Cynthia was writing. [Laughs] And we'd end up finishing each other's songs. Some of the ideas sort of drifted through.

Did you have any idea at the time of your contribution to music history?

No, we were just interested in putting food on the table and buying baby diapers.

I know that when Lennon and McCartney started writing songs, they wanted to be the next Goffin and King—

I think they did that twenty times over. In the late sixties, when all these groups came in, I thought it was a more honest thing because you had bands writing their own music and singing what they personally wanted to sing instead of singing what some other song-writer said. I thought it was good, and so did Carole. And that sort of led to our divorce, because she wanted to go out there and make a statement on her own, and I said, "I can't put words in your mouth." And she came up with some pretty good lyrics on her own.

But you did put a lot of great words into her mouth—many of the greatest songs that she did on her own had lyrics that you wrote, such as "Natural Woman."

It's sort of different when you're writing for an artist. My favorite writer is still Bob Dylan; it'll always be Bob Dylan. I always put him on a level way above the average. He sort of blew my mind. When I first started listening to his records, I went nuts. I said, "Nobody ever told me you had to write poetry." *[Laughs]*

Did you like the Beatles' version of your song "Chains"? Oh, yeah. That's a great honor, to have a Beatles record.

Did you have any idea of what a big influence you were on Lennon and McCartney?

I was watching some daytime show that John Lennon was on. He said, "When we were growing up we wanted to be Goffin and King." And that blew me out of my seat. *[Laughs]* That was a great compliment.

After the Beatles came along, we wanted to be the Beatles. [Laughs]

Carole told us that "Natural Woman" was a title that Jerry Wexler suggested to you.

I was in New York and just coming out of the office. A limousine pulled up and it was Jerry Wexler; and he said, "I've got a great title for you: 'Natural Woman.' " I went home and wrote it with Carole, and Jerry produced a great record. It's a classic record.

Do you remember coming up with the title for "Loco-Motion"?

I had that in my head for about two years and it seemed silly. Then Donny Kirshner said, "I got to Didi Sharpe"—this should show you the mentality of the time—"and she wanted a follow-up to 'Mashed Potatoes.'" So I said, "Why not?" We had a girl who took care of the kids called Eva Boyd, who became Little Eva. Donny said, "Hell, if I'm gonna give this to Didi Sharpe," and he put it out as a master. Sold a million-and-a-half copies. …

So it was never the plan for her to be the artist, she just sang the demo?

Yeah. And then she bad-mouthed us in *People* magazine saying Carole and I made all the money out of it. We didn't make all the money. [Laughs] Donny made all the money.

Did Little Eva continue recording after that?

We made three records afterwards. They all went Top Thirty. A terrible song called "Keep Your Hands Off My Baby" was a follow-up. That went Top Ten.

That's a funny song to write for the woman who was taking care of your kids. How did you know she could sing?

I heard her singing around the house. She had a good, pristine voice.

You said that you and Carole didn't write real rock and roll songs. Yet "Loco-Motion" seems like a rock and roll song, even though it does have minor chords in it. Do you think of it as a rock song?

Yeah, but it's still not coming out of Jerry Lee Lewis-type piano. That was what rock and roll was. Carl Perkins. Some of my favorite songs were written by Leiber and Stoller. All the old Coasters' hits, "Yackety Yak," "Poison Ivy." They put a certain intelligence into their writing and producing. All the Drifters' hits I really liked because they used strings but they didn't use them in the conventional ways as sweeteners. They would use cellos as rhythm instruments. They were great producers. That's why I wanted to have Carole do a string arrangement on "Will You Love Me Tomorrow?" I still think that's a great record.

Did you write "Will You Love Me Tomorrow?" to Carole?

No. That was a classic "will you still respect me in the morning" idea from the fifties. You know, "Will you love me tomorrow if I make love to you tonight?" I was a horny young teenager, just like everybody else, and I heard that line a million times.

Is your connection as collaborators as strong as it was when you were married?

Well, now we're like brother and sister. When we were man and wife it was different. She's on her fifth husband, I'm on my third wife. It's time to put all our past grievances behind.

There's less urgency now. And the urgency was what made us write so prolifically. Now she'll come over and if she doesn't have anything and I don't have anything, we'll say, "Let's go out and have some sushi." In the old days, we would just keep pounding away until we got something. We don't push ourselves as hard.

Is there one song that you and she have written together that is your favorite?

I think "Up on the Roof" is my favorite song that I wrote with her.

Do you remember writing it?

I was living in New York, where to get away I wouldn't climb up the stairs but I'd take the elevator [laughs] to the top of the roof and just get a little space away from the electricity of the city.

That was a great melody, a very lasting melody. Carole just came up with it one day when we were driving home in the car. She came up with the melody a capella.

The whole thing?

Well, not the bridge but the verses.

And how would that work then? Would she go home and tape it for you?

No, we had to carry around these big Norelco tape recorders so we didn't mess with tape recorders. [Laughs]

Maybe it's age or maybe it's too many drugs, but I just can't retain a melody like I used to. I have to listen to it over and over again on the tape recorder. Maybe it's just laziness, I don't know.

Would you take her melody and change it at all?

Not on that song. A lot of times when we would work I would bend phrases to fit in the lyrics. Which is sort of cheating according to Masser, *[laughs]* but … it's a lot harder for me nowadays. It's a lot harder, but you make a lot more money on the songs nowadays than you did then.

Nowadays you don't write for singles like you did in the old days. In the old days you could write a single and you'd be working on the follow-up while the single was out. But now you could die before your record comes out. *[Laughs]* It's a long process.

You used to be able to turn them out pretty quickly—

Yeah, there was a momentum you built up.

So you find that being a songwriter is a lot harder these days? It is. It's definitely a lot harder.

Both you and Carole mentioned your use of inner rhymes. Was that something that came to you naturally?

That's where my father's influence came in. He showed me that when I was very young, playing me the songs of Cole Porter or Rodgers and Hart. He'd play "My Funny Valentine" or "I'm in the Mood for Love," and things like that.

I've heard so much great music. Even if I never wrote a song, it would have been rewarding enough to be tuned in to hear so much great music, so many diverse fields. You can go back to "Rock Around the Clock" or "Somewhere Over the Rainbow." Just to be a part of music history is something very important.

* * *

Carole King: New York, New York, 1989

She is one of the most successful female songwriters of all time. Even before her two-sided hit of "It's Too Late" and "I Feel the Earth Move" went to number one in 1971, Carole King had already written eight other number one records. They were co-written with Gerry Goffin, whom she met in 1958 at Queens College in New York. Together, Goffin and King churned out an amazing flow of hit records, inspiring the likes of the Beatles with their success.

Born Carol Klein in Brooklyn on February 9, 1941, she took piano lessons from her mother when she was four and started writing her own music only a few years later. She met a young songwriter at Queens College named Paul Simon, and the two of them teamed up to make demos for others, with Carole covering piano, vocals and drums. She also met Gerry Goffin at Queens, and when they started dating, they found more excitement at the piano than anywhere else, "even the movies," Carole said. So they started to write songs together—Carole generating most of the melodies and Gerry most of the words—and wrote about 150 "bad songs" (according to Gerry) before coming up with their first hit, "Will You Love Me Tomorrow?"

It was when they began working for Don Kirshner's Aldon Music that their success blossomed, writing hit songs for a myriad of artists, including the Drifters, Bobby Vee, the Animals, Herman's Hermits, the Monkees, the Righteous Brothers, and Blood, Sweat and Tears. The Queen of Soul, Aretha Franklin, recorded the classic "Natural Woman," while the Beatles paid a tribute to their idols by recording "Chains" in 1963.

Carole has never been the type of songwriter who pays attention to trends, knowing after all these years that a great song transcends them all. Even at the inception of rock and roll, when most writers were using a variation on a blues progression, she brought a sophisticated harmonic sense to their songs that few other writers were using. And Gerry, brought up on writers like Cole Porter, and Rodgers and Hammerstein, brought traditional lyrical values to the songs, such as the use of inner rhymes. The combined results are deceptively simple songs like "Loco-Motion" (the only song in history to have gone to number one four times) and the eternally jubilant "Up on the Roof."

In 1968, Carole and Gerry ended their collaboration and their marriage, and Carole moved to Los Angeles, where she began to reluctantly perform her own songs. "I never wanted to be the performing artist," she recalled. "I was always the vehicle through which the songs could be communicated to a *real* singer. The switch occurred when I moved to California in 1968. I was encouraged by Danny Kortchmar and Charles Larkey to perform with them as a group, and we made an album called *City*. I didn't have any intention of going out and performing live. It was a way to make a record while hiding behind a group situation. Having done that, the next transition was to do a solo album. I still had no idea about performing live. I was just gonna do the same thing I always did, make demos, only instead of having them go to a real singer, we just figured we would put them out with me singing."

Although the idea of being a recording artist seemed like a natural progression to her from inside the studio, the thought of performing live was horrifying. But thanks to James Taylor, she was eased into it gradually. "Just around the time of *Tapestry* I met James and watched him perform, and he made it look so easy. And he invited me onto the stage to play piano. And then one night he said, 'Why don't we let you play one of your songs?' I think it was 'Up on the Roof,' which he always loved. And I did, and I was pre-loved because they already loved James. And then they knew the songs, so it was really a no-lose situation. I could have been terrible, and they probably would have dug it that I just did it anyway."

In 1971 *Tapestry* emerged an instant classic. Packed with hit after hit, many of them written while still with Gerry, it outsold *Sgt. Pepper*, became one of the best-selling albums of all time, and quickly erased any doubt as to the viability of Carole King as a recording artist.

Do you remember writing your first song?
Not really. Young. Nine?
You were playing piano at that age?

Yeah. I was classically trained but periods of lessons on and no lessons.

Do you remember what it was at the time that made you want to write songs?

I didn't think of them as songs. I thought of them as melodies, I guess. They weren't whole songs. I would just put melodies together and make music.

When I was about fifteen I started writing my own lyrics, and they were so bad that I didn't want to write songs again for a while. Until I met Gerry.

Did you and Gerry have any kind of regular songwriting routine? Would he give you a finished lyric?

It varied. All of the above. It varied then; it varies now.

Was your song "You've Got a Friend" written for anyone in particular?

No. That song was as close to pure inspiration as I've ever experienced. The song wrote itself. It was written by something outside of myself through me.

Is that an unusual feeling for you?

It happens from time to time in part. That song is one of the examples of that process where it was almost completely written by inspiration and very little if any perspiration.

Does that give you the feeling that these songs come from beyond you? Absolutely.

Can you give us any advice about how to get in touch with that source?

Songwriters, both lyricists and melody writers, are often plagued with the thing most often known as writer's block. All writers are, writers of prose as well. I have found that the key to not being blocked is to not worry about it. Ever.

If you are sitting down and you feel that you want to write and nothing is coming, you get up and do something else. Then you come back again and try it again. But you do it in a relaxed manner. Trust that it will be there. If it ever was once and you've ever done it once, it will be back. It always comes back and the only thing that is a problem is when you get in your own way worrying about it.

I'd like to say that I almost never have worried about it. Because when it seemed to be a problem, when I seemed to be … I don't even want to say "blocked" because it seems like too strong a word. But when the channel wasn't open enough to let something through, I always went and did something else and never worried about it and it always opened up again. Whether it was an hour later, which is often the case, or a day later or a week later or sometimes a few *months* later, I just didn't worry about it.

So when you're at the piano and it's not flowing, you don't force it; you just get up and come back to it at a different time?

Right. Another thing that I do is I might play someone else's material that I really like and that sometimes unblocks a channel. The danger in that is that you're gonna write that person's song [*laughs*] for your next song. It's just sit down and, again, if you're a lyric writer, read something that you really like, enjoy something that you really like. Or sometimes I'll play something of my own that I really like, something that is already existing that is *fun*.

Do you find that your hands go to old familiar patterns at the piano? How do you avoid repeating yourself?

I *don't* think about it. If I'm writing something and it sounds too much like something I've already written, I might consciously try to change it but, again, I don't worry about it; I'm not overly concerned with the mechanics of how it's going to work.

Once the inspiration comes, that directs where the perspiration goes, where the work goes. I don't mean to sound like it's some hippie philosophy of *[in a high, fairy-like voice]* you just sit down and it's *all* flowing through you. Because there's a lot of hard work involved in songwriting. The inspiration part is where it comes through you, but once it comes through you, the shaping of it, the *craft* of it, is something that I pride myself in knowing how to do.

I like to be unpredictable. For example, in the songs on my album, *City Streets,* the A&R man looked through them and said, "Each song has a different structure. And not one song has a structure that is recognizable." There isn't one song that's AABA or ABAB. They all turn left somewhere. *[Laughs]* And that's something that I work at.

I do not like to do the predictable thing. That's not to say that it's invalid to do that. Just for me, the challenge and the fun is when you start to write a song that might go AABA, and you might take your B section and go somewhere else before you come back to A. Or you go AA-B-C and then you go back to A. Because one of the things that I try to be conscious about in writing a song and crafting a song is the concept of bringing it home. That is, there's a beginning to a song, and there should be an end of a song, and of course there's a middle. And I like to take the middle any place it wants to go. But whenever I take it to the end, I like to bring it somewhere familiar, someplace that people feel it's resolved, it's settled; it comes back *home* at the end, whatever home means.

Do you ever feel limited by the song form?

No! The song form is limitless. You can do anything you want. Given the fact that a song is generally something that takes between three to five minutes on a record. But if you feel like going seven minutes, you can go seven minutes. If you want to write a really short song, you can do that. I think it's kind of nice because you're given a task to make a statement, musical and lyrical, and you do it and you don't have two hours to do it in. That's kind of nice; but I don't think it's limiting at all. I think it's liberating.

Is there any kind of musical signature you would consider your own, any set of chord changes that defines the Carole King sound?

[Laughs] Well, it's been widely quoted back to me that a four chord with a five bass has been one of my signatures. I guess I still use it. It's one of those things I guess I got known for doing. Musicians have called it the "Carole King chord" although I'm sure I didn't originate it. But I did use it a lot.

I try not to overuse it since it's sort of become a thing you expect. I try to be unpredictable, in my life and in my work. *[Laughs]*

Is there a single song of your own that is your favorite?

I can't say that there is because they're like children. There are some songs that I know are better than others. There are some that I still think about and I still like, and there are others that I've basically forgotten, although sometimes I'll listen to something and say,

"You know, that wasn't bad." But, I don't know, the ones that are standards, the ones that hold up longest I don't want to say I'm proudest of, but they've stood the test of time. You know, "Natural Woman," "You've Got a Friend," "Will You Love Me Tomorrow?" The first and the last I mentioned were written with Gerry but ones I've written myself hold up, too. lb my everlasting surprise.

I want to say something about my writing of lyrics. When you write with Gerry Goffin, you become intimidated, like why bother to write your own lyrics when you have a Gerry Goffin to write with.

But when our marriage ended and our relationship changed a little bit at the time, in terms of ability to work together easily—it was a temporary condition that we weren't able to work together for a little while, and it was only for a little while—that was when I sort of thought about doing it again [writing lyrics] and I really didn't like what I was doing that much, but suddenly it clicked into place for me at that time. It was just before *Tapestry* I guess. By the time we wrote *Tapestry* I was writing with Gerry again but it just didn't click into place, and that's what sort of what motivated me to try doing it myself.

I was always mindful of things that Gerry had taught me about writing lyrics. Above all, try not to be corny. *[Laughs]* Umm, internal rhymes—have fun with internal rhymes. My lyrics are vastly different than his but there's a simplicity about my lyrics that I strive to emulate Gerry in his utter simplicity.

I think that my lyrics are a little more—I want to say childlike—and not born out of so much pain. I think his lyrics reflect either his own pain or the pain of the persona that he's writing for. He has been able to be in touch with a gut level of emotion that I'm only beginning to approach in my lyric writing now. I still look up to him. He's just the best, and I really look up to him as a lyricist very much. He's been of enormous help in guiding my melodies, the direction my melodies take.

Often when we would write, he might actually sing a melody to me along with his lyrics, and I would probably have taken almost the exact melody he sang and just made it so it was more musical sounding. Cause he's a singer with guts but he's not a singer that you listen to for the melody of it. You listen to him probably, more for the soul of it. Nobody sang "Will You Love Me Tomorrow?" better, ever. But I was able to melodicize what he gave and maybe make it more accessible to people who wanted to hear it sounding like a singer was singing it.

That's interesting, because so many of the songs that you and he wrote together sound like they were written by one person; the words and music fit so perfectly together.

We always talked about marriage. It's not a new phrase; many songwriters talk about it. The marriage of the music to the lyrics is key. And our personal marriage was an outgrowth of that, and it was hard to tell which was which. But the marriage between our words and our music continues to this day.

When we're connected, which is most of the time when we write together, the magic is still there; the marriage of the music and the lyrics is an understood thing that requires very little discussion. It just happens. And there's just a little fine-tuning done between us. But when we write, we write like one person.

An example of that would have to be your classic song "Natural Woman," which doesn't seem like a lyric a man would write.

The title was Jerry Wexler's, which is why his name appears as writer on the song. But Gerry took the title and ran with it.

I know that when Lennon and McCartney started writing songs together for the Beatles that they wanted to be the next Goffin and King—

I was actually told that by them. They were very much aware of us as writers and I was extremely complimented.

I love that process as well because then the Beatles, who having been influenced by myself and Gerry, came back and made such an impact and, of course, left their mark on me as somebody to aspire to and emulate.

Did you like the Beatles' version of your song "Chains"? Yeah!

They were listening to your songs when starting out; which songwriters were you listening to at the start of your career?

Jerry Leiber and Mark Stoller, primarily. They had a huge impact on us, a major influence in our early songs. The idea of taking street rhythm and blues and combining it with classical music, like "There Goes My Baby" with the timpani by Ben E. King; "Spanish Harlem" with the violins and the entire string section arrangement. That was amazing because my background and Gerry's was in classical; it was pretty strong. But we also loved rock and roll and street music. So to have them put together was like, yeah!

Tapestry became one of the biggest selling album of all time. Did you have any idea that it would be that huge? No.

Do you have any idea what made it such a popular album? Right time and the right place.

Is that all?

I think so. I mean, good tunes. But there's been lots of albums before and since with good tunes.

It seems to be one of the few albums in which every song is a potential single.

I like to believe that. *[Laughs]*

So many great singers, from James Taylor and the Beatles through Aretha Franklin, have performed your songs. Do you have a favorite?

Oh, not at all. I love singing my own songs, but I'm always the first one to sing my songs anyway. So it goes to someone like Aretha. One of my highest moments in time is to have heard what the consummate gospel singer did to one of my songs. To hear the Beatles do it, to hear Springsteen sing "Going Back" and James Taylor's versions of "You've Got a Friend" and "Up on the Roof." The Byrd's versions of stuff, the Monkees' versions of stuff which are kind of fun to go back and listen to. What joy to hear what someone else brings to something of mine. I mean, I throw it out there and they run with it.

In a couple of cases, and I will not ever mention a name, there has been a time or two where a singer has interpreted my song in such a way that I was really let down, that I said, "That is so wrong. I hate this." But it's only happened maybe once or twice in my career. And those times it's probably just a misunderstanding; the person just didn't get it, you know? [*Laughs*] For the most part, the joy of being a songwriter is to hear your song interpreted by somebody else.

The other joy is to hear what the musicians do with it. The band, you know? I come in to a session, and I play it down for the band, and the ideas they bring to it make it coalesce and come together because I hear in my head generally what I want it to sound like. But they bring in things that are either true to the vision or not true to the vision. Generally, it takes just a second and they know right where I'm going with it. And that's the magic for me, to have really excellent musicians play on my songs.

So songwriting is still a joy for you?

Yeah! Songwriting is always a joy.

* * *

♪ Part III

Styles Splinter and Classic Rock Emerges

The artistic and creative void left in the aftermath of "The Day the Music Died," Elvis in the army, and Jerry Lee Lewis's meltdown, was filled largely by a pop/rock hodgepodge performed by saccharin-white artists and produced en masse by the recording industry.

However, the British Invasion of the '60s, which reintroduced to American audiences songs originally performed by American black artists, began to appeal to America's youthful consumers. Creative, entrepreneurial producers and artists in the Midwest and on the West Coast began to reassert rock's cutting-edge spirit first found in the mid– to late 1950s. The girl-group pop sound fashioned first by Brill Building song-writing teams was now reborn in Detroit with African-American producers, songwriters, singers, and musicians as Motown's "Music of Young America." Bob Dylan and The Band emerged from the folk revival to electrify folk and help create what is now called roots music. Out of San Francisco's 1967 summer of love appeared an acid fueled, mythical music based on impossibly long songs with nearly endless improvisation.

Sam Phillips's name is forever etched in the lore of rock history. He discovered, cultivated, inspired and ultimately recorded some of the greats of rock 'n' roll's first creative period. There are many stories about Phillips and the way he prodded Elvis to his first regional hit with "That's All Right Mama" and his treatment of Johnny Cash's sound on "I Walk the Line." These stories tend to mythologize Sun Studio and Sam Phillips, but apart from the myth, there is also the human being who ran the studio for a little more than ten years. With his fervor and passion, Phillips could have been a preacher as easily as a record producer.

Peter Guralnick, who comes from the academic side of rock journalism, brings both scholarship and passion to the characters and music about which he writes. He is best known for his two-volume biography of Elvis Presley, and his writing serves as an antidote to the more visceral and personal style of his contemporaries, such as Lester Bangs and Hunter S. Thompson. The excerpt in this anthology comes from the first book of his trilogy on American vernacular music, the 1971 classic Feel Like Going Home: Portraits in Blues, Country, and Rock 'n' roll. Guralnick's treatment of Sam Phillips reflects a journalist who began the interview expecting to uncover a myth and came away with an appreciation of a flawed human being. His writing is a candid look at Sam Phillips that few others have achieved.

There are so many books about Bob Dylan that one could offer a college degree on his output from the 1960s alone. Howard Sounes's biography of Dylan is a relatively recent publication, but he covers ground previously unexplored. Perhaps the most difficult task in writing about Dylan is connecting the dots from the beginning of his art, to the middle (however that is defined), to his current style. Dylan's history, his songs, styles, subject matter, and tours, is too rich to explore without intense effort. Few artists take the risks that Dylan has taken and continues to take. Few artists are as honest in their assessment of their own music as Dylan. Sounes offers what could be a laundry list of facts read as they should—like a story of a life lived on the edge.

"The Sound of Young America," was the slogan describing music from Berry Gordy Jr.'s Motown corporation, and it was first produced in a white house emblazoned with a sign "Hitsville U.S.A." at 2648 West Grand Boulevard in Detroit, Michigan. Gordy had worked numerous jobs in and around Detroit (the motor city — "Motown") including a stint on an auto assembly line, which served as a model for his hit producing company.

In his essay, "Profiles of Record Labels, Motown," Charles Sikes, director of the African American Art Institute and adjunct professor in the Department of Folklore and Ethnomusicology at Indiana University in Bloomington, details Gordy's production genius. He writes about how Gordy combined the talents of almost exclusively African-American singers, choreographers, style coaches and musicians, to create an important regional music center. The recordings made by, and with, inner-city Black artists also appealed to white teenagers and crossed over from the R&B charts to reach the top of the pop charts.

Mikal Gilmore has been a frequent contributor to Rolling Stone magazine since the early 1970s. His essay, "Haight-Ashbury in the Summer of Loss," from Stories Done, Writings on the 1960s and Its Discontents, examines the scene in the San Francisco Bay Area during the late 1960s, and makes an excellent case why pop culture of this time is described as all about "sex, drugs, and rock 'n' roll." LSD ("acid") was still legal in California until October 1966, and Ken Kesey had been conducting experiments with it which he called "acid tests." Kesey and many others were convinced that the drug offered brief and harmless bouts of psychosis. "Acid tests" were often large parties, where The Warlocks (later called the Grateful Dead) served as the house band. Band members, however, were not just musicians brought from the outside to perform; they were also part of the scene. Thus the drugs, the partiers, the music, and the musicians, were all integrated. The lengthy, predominantly improvised, highly amplified songs emerging from these parties became known as psychedelic rock.

♪ Sam Phillips Talking

By Peter Guralnick

Just as I was finishing up this book, the opportunity arose to do something I had dreamt of for what seemed like a lifetime—well, fifteen years anyway. Through a combination of luck, timing, and the good will of Knox Phillips, with whom I had been in touch off and on by letter and phone since 1968, I got to meet Knox's father, Sam, the somewhat reclusive founder of Sun Records (despite the mania for information on Sun, he has given out only two or three interviews since his retirement from the record business over a decade ago), and the man who almost single-handedly authored one of the most remarkable chapters in the history of American popular music. You've got to understand what the prospect of meeting Sam Phillips meant to me. Some kids dream of curing cancer, some of growing up to be President. As for me I dreamt of playing in the major leagues, winning the Nobel Prize for literature, becoming Elvis Presley's adviser and chief confidant, and—as I grew older and only slightly more realistic—meeting Sam Phillips. From the time that we first discovered Sun Records, my friends and I had constructed elaborate fantasies not just about Elvis but about the man who had recorded Elvis, Jerry Lee Lewis, Carl Perkins, and before that the great Memphis bluesmen (Howlin' Wolf, B.B. King, Bobby Bland) who were just as much our heroes. As I got to know Charlie Rich, and other Sun artists to a lesser degree, the way in which they spoke about Sam Phillips—his astonishing persuasive powers and force of mind—the way in which they recalled his ability to inspire, even as they complained about royalty rates and the eventual necessity for their leaving Sun, only fueled my vision of this behind-the-scenes Machiavellian genius who had discovered so many of the unique talents of a generation and seemingly gotten the very best out of them while they were still on his label.

The day I met Sam Phillips was momentous in several respects other than the meeting itself. I was doing a story for the *New York Times Magazine* (momentous for me) on the legendary Million Dollar Quartet, an impromptu session in which Elvis had joined Carl

Perkins, Johnny Cash, and Jerry Lee in the Sun studio in 1957. Sam's new radio station, WWEE in Memphis, where I was due to meet Sam for what Knox said might be no more than a fifteen-minute interview ('With Sam you can't ever tell,' said Knox, to whom the founder of Sun is 'both my father and Sam'), was flooded that day by a frozen sprinkler system, and as a result I spent about nine hours out at the station stacking tapes, sponging off audio equipment, and doing my best to help out. And, it just so happened, the day that I met Sam Phillips was also the day that the first real attempt at a rock 'n' roll film documentary was aired on national TV, with rare early footage of Elvis, Jerry Lee, and other familiar figures from the dawn of rock 'n' roll.

It was a peculiar way to meet a lifelong hero. Almost all the pictures that I had ever seen of Sam Phillips showed a young, slick-haired businessman with a sly, almost foxy smile and the slit-eyed look of one of his most self-aware artists, Jerry Lee Lewis. The man that I encountered briefly from time to time all through the course of that day, padding about on carpeting so saturated with water that it soaked up through your shoes, had the look of an Old Testament prophet in tennis sneakers, his long hair and long reddish beard only matching the oracular tone and language that came out in the cadences of a southern preacher. He was totally in charge, flattering the contractor who had built the studio for him, following the sprinkler system man's explanation of just what had happened with courtly good humor, assigning specific tasks to each of the employees of the 50,000-watt station until they could get back on the air, fending off the good wishes of friends and family who had gathered around for support, dispatching Knox and his other son, Jerry, on various errands to pick up emergency equipment around town, and charming members of the local press corps (TV, radio, and newspapers all had their representatives on the scene of the disaster) with no apparent strain or impatience. With each individual he focused the full force of his personality for just as long as it took to get that individual moving in the proper direction, and—for all the differences of circumstances and setting—I felt for one brief moment as if I were getting a glimpse of the inspired chaos that was Sun.

The radio station, like the original Sun studio, is a testament to Sam Phillips's vision. According to Knox, Sam built 'every square inch' of the old studio with his own hands, installed the acoustic tile, built the speakers, rigged up all the audio equipment, even calculated the precise advantage of a control booth raised to a particular height (with his training as a radio engineer, his intimate knowledge of recording methods and equipment was not as surprising as it might at first seem). Similarly, he personally supervised every aspect of the new radio station's construction, 'like to drove the contractors crazy' with his exacting specifications, alone conceived its unique design—which might best be described as pyramidally modernistic (it features turrets and a brown cedar and stone facade)—and spent nearly every waking moment at the studio while the building was going up. Which was, as everyone remarked, the shame of it all, since the studio had only been in operation a few months, and now much of the equipment and the expensive carpet that Sam had specially ordered from New York would have to be replaced. No one seemed quite sure how Sam was going to react—since it is generally agreed that Sam has always been careful with a dollar—but like the southern diplomat that Chuck Berry has sung about, Sam had nothing but cheerful words of encouragement for everyone and thanks for their kind thoughts. In fact, he seemed almost to thrive on the crisis atmosphere, and his commander's role seemed only to animate him.

During one of our frequent encounters in passing at the coffee machine, he explained briefly the format of his new station (he also owns the largest station in the tri-city area around his hometown of Florence, Alabama, plus several smaller stations), which he hoped would set a new trend in contemporary radio. Basically WWEE follows a Top 40 format, but it mixes in music from all eras as well and seeks to emphasize the *connectedness* that Phillips feels is missing from today's tight Top 40 playlists. 'It's different,' he gladly admits, 'but I never have been one to do the same as everyone else. If I've got to do the same, I'd just as soon not do it.' Then he was off to attend to some fresh problem.

I wasn't sure if I was going to get any more than these occasional nuggets, the unwavering focus of Sam Phillips's gaze, and the opportunity to observe him under somewhat trying circumstances. If it had been no more than that, I think I still would have felt privileged, so compelling was my own vision of Sam Phillips. When we finally sat down at the end of that long afternoon and evening, after things finally seemed to be under control and the maintenance crew had finally succeeded in mopping up most of the water with suction cleaners, Sam Phillips seemed scarcely even winded, and I realized as he talked that he was speaking to every fantasy I had ever had about him, that he was telling the story of how one man, and one group, had made history.

He wasn't much interested in facts and dates, though he seemed secure in the knowledge that these would be noted by future chroniclers. What Sam Phillips was interested in was *feeling* and people—the very variousness of human nature. 'My mission' he said, 'was to bring out of a person what was in him, to recognize that individual's unique quality and then to find the key to unlock it.' As I listened, I heard from him what my friends and I had so carefully constructed for ourselves, and I had a glimmer for the first time in a long time of the unlikely notion that history is not necessarily an accident, that the self-willed individual can affect his environment, and his times, in ways that we cannot even calculate.

Sam Phillips was born on January 5, 1923, on a farm outside of Florence, Alabama, in a family of eight children. This is where he first encountered black music, particularly in the person of Uncle Silas Payne, a blind, elderly sharecropper who used to tell him stories and sing him songs that have stayed with him all his life.

'I was raised by two great Southern parents. They were in the great Southern tradition. They were genuine people. Their beliefs were sustained by generation after generation of acceptance of what, quote unquote, *the norm* is. That's how people, life, circumstances, situations, especially color and the gradation of economic income were judged. Would you believe that that had a lot to do with life, black and white—your economic *income*, whether you had patches on your pants? My father was—and I hate to say this, because my father was probably the truest human being that I've ever met in my life, to the feel that I had—but at the same time he wouldn't break, bless his heart and God rest his soul, with the tradition, other than he would see that no one went hungry, even if we didn't have much more than the poorest sharecropper.

'But I saw—and I don't remember when, but I saw as a child—I thought to myself: suppose that I would have been born *black*. Suppose that I would have been born a little bit more down the economic ladder. So I think I felt from the beginning the total inequity of man's inhumanity to his brother. And it didn't take its place with me of getting up in the pulpit and preaching. It took on the aspect with me that someday I would act on my feelings, I would show them on an individual, one-to-one basis.'

Although, Sam says, he would have liked to have been a criminal defense lawyer, he went into radio when his father died, going to work as an announcer for Muscle Shoals station WLAY, where as a high school student he had set up broadcasts for the Coffee High marching band (Sam played drums and sousaphone and composed the school's drum march, which is used to this day). At WLAY he also met his wife, Becky—a ukeleleist who sang and played duets with her sister on piano—and got his certification as a radio engineer through a correspondence course. He went on to work as an engineer in Decatur, then at WLAC in Nashville, arriving in Memphis at WREC (this was the station whose announcers, Rufus Thomas said, all spoke in an impressively 'big, booming voice') in the winter of 1944-45. Starting in June, he began to engineer live broadcasts of big bands like Glenn Miller, Jimmy or Tommy Dorsey, from the Hotel Peabody Skyway, and the following year these programs started going out nightly on the CBS network. It was a prestigious job, obviously, but it left him feeling frustrated and dissatisfied because 'it had gotten where with stock arrangements and everything, the creativity actually just was not there for those people. Don't get me wrong, I loved the forties bands, but when you're scheduled you just don't have that instinctive intuitional thing, and these dudes—I can remember well—they might have played the damned song 4000 times, and they were *still* turning the pages. Well, in those bands really you were numbered.'

706 Union Avenue. Miss Taylor's Restaurant is on the corner, just to the right of the original Sun Studios, Pat Rainer

What Sam Phillips heard in his head was the black blues he had been listening to from childhood on, the same music that you could hear in Memphis every day on Beale Street, the thoroughfare of the blues. In 1950 he determined to record these blues singers. He built his own studio in a converted radiator shop on Union Avenue, which was so small there was no room for an office aside from the receptionist's area and all business was conducted at Miss Taylor's Restaurant next door ('third booth by the window'). At first he leased sides to the Chess brothers in Chicago and the Biharis in Los Angeles (who owned the Modern and RPM labels), and at the radio station he was frequently met by fellow workers with greetings like,

Sam Phillips, 1978. Pat Rainer

'Well, you smell okay. I guess you haven't been hanging around those niggers today.' By his own account, though, Sam Phillips wasn't fazed in the least.

'I have *never* been conventional. I don't know if that's good, but it set me apart in the sense that I had a certain independence and individuality. And I knew one thing: believe and trust in what you're doing or don't do it. I just knew that this was great music. My greatest contribution, I think, was to open up an area of freedom within the artist himself, to help him to express what *he* believed his message to be. Talking about egos—these people unfortunately did not *have* an ego. They had a desire—but at the same time to deal with a person that had dreamed, and dreamed, and dreamed, looked, heard, felt, to deal with them under conditions where they were so afraid of being denied again—it took a pure instinctive quality on the part of any person that got the revealing aspects out of these people. It took an umble spirit, I don't care whether it was me or someone else. Because I knew this—to curse these people or to just give the air of, "Man, I'm better than you," I'm wasting my time trying to record these people, to get out of them what's truly in them. I *knew* this.'

Phillips knew, too, that he didn't want to spend the rest of his life working for someone else, and so in June of 1951, after recording what many consider to be the first rock 'n' roll hit ('Rocket 88' by Jackie Brenston, which appeared on Chess, had a driving beat, a booting sax, and celebrated the automobile), he quit his job at WREC and some six months later started the Sun label, its distinctive yellow logo designed by a fellow alumnus of the Coffee High School band. For the next two years Sun's roster was made up almost exclusively of black artists (including Rufus Thomas, who gave the label its first hit), and Phillips has nothing but the fondest memories of the blues singers he recorded. Joe Hill Louis, Dr. Isaiah Ross (the good doctor's specialty was the Boogie Disease), and Jimmy DeBerry are names that come up frequently in conversation, but it is the Howlin' Wolf (in real life Chester Burnett) whom Phillips remembers in particular, not only as the most distinctive blues singer he recorded but as the most distinctive stylist, the most unique *individual* whom he ever met in all his years in the record business.

'Ah, Chester—the vitality of that man was something else. Just to see that man in the studio—God, what I would give to see him as he was in my studio, to see the fervor in his face, to hear the pure instinctive quality of that man's voice. Once he felt at home, once you made him feel that he was in his own indigenous surroundings, Chester could not put anything on, there was no way he could be anything other than himself. Also, he had the ability to read people without even letting you know he was doing it. He gave the appearance of being almost totally unconcerned, but this was just a facade that he kept until such time as he knew you were truly interested in what he was all about. Once he knew that, once you broke that barrier, then you had all he had to offer.'

Only with Elvis's breakthrough success in the summer of 1954 did Phillips abandon his black constituency—and then evidently not without a great deal of soul-searching.

'This is a regrettable thing on my part, but I saw what I was doing as not deserting the black man—God knows, there was no way I could do that, because without the black man I don't know if I would have had the thoughts go through my mind that I did—but when I started out there was nobody on the scene recording black music, and by this time there was an awful lot of good black music that was being recorded by Atlantic, Specialty, Chess, Checker, and I felt they could handle it real good. And I saw what I was trying to do with white men was to broaden the base, to try to get more radio stations to play this kind of music, to give it more widespread exposure. I knew we had a hard trip for all of us. The Southern white man had an expression for his basic roots in country music in the Grand Ole Opry, but we didn't have that for the black man—and yet without those people there would have been no idea for us that was free of great encumbrance.'

What he was looking for from the beginning was the same unique quality he had found in Howlin' Wolf, the same *differentness* that he continues to prize to this day. Talk to Sam for any length of time and you will hear countless homiletics on the dangers of conformity ('I could have become a conformist and gone the, quote unquote, *beaten path,* and if that had happened I would have been a very unhappy man'), the glories of individuality ('You can be a nonconformist and not be a rebel. And you can be a rebel and not be an outcast. Believe in what you believe in, and don't let *anybody, I* don't care who it is, get you off that path'). As his son, Knox, says, 'If a guy came into the studio with a unique, distinctive sound and was himself, Sam heard it immediately, where most people would wince at it at first. Jerry Lee Lewis told me—and he had been up to Nashville, and they all said to him, "Man, get you a guitar"—Jerry Lee told me, Sam took one listen to his tape, and he didn't listen but halfway through, and he said, "You are a rich man." And he didn't mean in money, but in talent."

It was with Elvis that the Sun era as we know it really began, and it was Elvis's music, of course, that gained him entree to the Sun studio in the first place, but you wonder in talking with Sam Phillips if it wasn't Presley's unformed personality—his virtually unconsidered strengths and almost equally instinctive weaknesses, the *contradictions* that were never even partially resolved—which fascinated Phillips just as much as the music. 'He tried not to show it.' Phillips told writer Bob Palmer, 'but he felt so *inferior.* He reminded me of a black man in that way; his insecurity was so *markedly* like that of a black person.' There was never any question in his mind, Sam says, of Elvis's gifts, but there was a good deal of question about his acceptance by the public. Phillips recalls accompanying Elvis on his first trip to the Louisiana Hayride after the debacle at the Grand Ole Opry (when Elvis was advised to go back to truck driving).

Sam Phillips and Jerry Lee Lewis, 1958.

'I didn't let anybody know, but when it came time for Elvis and Scotty and Bill to go on stage, I went out and got me a seat in that audience. Because I'll tell you what, we didn't have any idea how this thing was going to turn out—and I was going to do anything I could to help out, but I'll tell you the power of communication. When he got through his first number, and I don't remember what it was, those people were up on their feet. I mean, all types—old people, fat people, skinny people, listen, honey, it was just one of those things that just come up, and you say, "Man, I'm not believing this." Some big fat lady, I mean it took an effort for her to get up, and she got up and she didn't stop talking, right in the middle of the next number, she didn't know who I was, I didn't know who she was. She said, "Man, have you ever *heard* anything that good?"'

And then, of course, Elvis Presley took off, his contract was sold to RCA almost before the world was fully aware of his existence (in all, Phillips put out five singles on Presley in the year and a half that he was on Sun). The $40,000 that Phillips got for his contract—including $5000 in back royalties—provided working capital for the tiny company, and Sam insists to this day that he had no second thoughts in the wake of Presley's massive popular success. 'If I've been asked once,' he told Bob Palmer, 'I must have been asked a thousand times, did I ever regret it? No, I did not, I do not, and I never will.'

What followed in any case was a period of extraordinary ferment and productivity that has rarely been matched in American popular culture, a time when, as Sam Phillips says, it was possible 'to establish something and get the good old capitalist system out of the way just a little bit to let creativity take its place.' With the money provided by the sale of Elvis's contract, Phillips was free to concentrate on the careers of Carl Perkins, Johnny Cash, Jerry Lee Lewis, Charlie Rich, and other lesser-known but equally luminous talents. The effort paid off not only in sales but in the forging of a new style, the creation of a genuinely original, and lasting, body of music.

'I believe so much in the psychological. I think this had an awful lot to do with it. Number one is that caring figure. Number two is knowing what in the hell you're doing. I think at the time of our relationship there was a true trust. It was almost like a father–son or big brother–little brother relationship. And I think that adequately describes the feel, because—and I'll say this without any equivocation whatsoever—good or bad, I was always in charge of my sessions. Definitely in charge. But at the same time, when I say in charge, it was a type of thing that I made them know I was a part of the total effort. Because they didn't *need* anybody else looking down their nose, they'd had *enough* of that in their life. That would have been the one thing that would have kept them exactly where they were—*nowhere.*'

You CAN HEAR an example of Phillips's psychologizing on the Dutch bootleg LP, *Good Rockin' Tonight,* which contains alternate takes of several of Elvis's earliest sides as well as a studio conversation between Jerry Lee Lewis and Sam Phillips that came about in the midst of recording 'Great Balls of Fire,' one of Lewis's biggest hits. Lewis apparently was reluctant to record the song because of what he saw as its blasphemous attitude towards the 'fire' prophesied in Revelations. He and Phillips got into a heated theological discussion, in the course of which Sam declared in measured tones, 'Now look, Jerry, religious conviction doesn't mean anything resembling extremism. You mean to tell me you're gonna take the Bible and revolutionize the whole universe?' It is a revealing exchange—revealing both of the antinomian doubts that fueled rock 'n' roll from the start, and of Sam Phillips's skill as an advocate—and, needless to say, Phillips prevailed.

A similar crisis occurred when Billy Lee Riley, a very talented artist who never quite achieved a fame commensurate with his talents, felt slighted by the attention that Sam was paying to his new artist, Jerry Lee Lewis. Riley came into the studio drunk one night and started tearing it up. Knox Phillips, who is today recording Riley for his own Red Rooster label but was no more than fourteen at the time, called his father—he told Bob Palmer—and 'Sam said, "Lock the studio door, and don't let him leave till I get there."'

'Sam got there,' Riley told Palmer, 'and we went back in his little cubbyhole and talked all night till sun-up. Sam told me, "'Red Hot' [Riley's latest single] ain't got it. We're savin' you for something *good.*" When I left I felt like I was the biggest star on Sun Records.'

Carl Perkins remembers when Sam Phillips showed up unexpectedly for Perkins's first appearance on Dallas's Big D Jamboree. 'I was just about to go on the stage when he said, "Wait a minute, cat"—he always called me "cat"—he had this box under his arm, and he took out a pair of blue suede shoes that he'd had made—well, he didn't have them made, he'd had somebody to put blue sparkles all over them, man, they was good-looking shoes, and when the lights hit them things, that house went wild. And Sam flew from Memphis to Dallas to put them shoes on my feet.

'Sam, he got a kick out of doing things like that. You got to remember that Elvis, Cash, none of us had anything. We were very poor, came from poor people, and it was Sam—I know he did for me—bought me the first clothes I ever had to wear on stage. Well, you see, he really had the knack, he just seemed to know—when we'd be making a record, he'd step out from behind that little old glass window, and he'd say, "All right, boys, we just about on it now." He'd say, "Do it again. Do it one time for Sam." Oh yeah, he did me that way all the time. It was just that type of thing, you just forgot about making a record and tried to show him. It was things like that that'd cause me—I'd walk out on a limb, I'd try things I knew I couldn't do, and I'd get in a corner trying to do it and then have to work my way out of it. I'd say, "Mr. Phillips, that's terrible." He said, "That's original." I said, "But it's just a big original mistake." And he said, *"That's what Sun Records is.* That's what we are."'

And yet one by one they left him. Elvis, of course, was the first. Then Johnny Cash and Carl Perkins went to Columbia. Jerry Lee Lewis eventually signed with Mercury, and Jack Clement and Bill Justis (Sun's chief engineer and arranger) were both fired on the same day for 'insubordination.' Some say all these defections were the normal sort of fallout for any small company; others point to a low royalty rate, problems with distribution, and Sam Phillips's notorious fiscal conservatism.

'Now what happened was that some of the artists—now I'm not a person that's real easy to get close to in certain areas, and I wish I weren't that way, but I know this—and some of the artists later on, I think, felt that maybe I was devoting a little more time to this new artist that needed nurturing like I had tried to nurture the early ones. So there was a little friction, and they got a little mad at me, but I think they trusted me even though they left me when a bunch of bullshitters started talking big money and this sort of thing. It's kind of like a family. Some children can feel that just because you feel this one needs a little more attention—well, they've forgotten that *they* got attention and love. But for that reason I have never felt hard at any of the people that left me.'

Almost without exception, each of the artists went on to a painful history of guilt and inner turmoil, and Sam Phillips has given much thought to just what it was that caused so much unhappiness in the later lives of his protégés. It was not, he is firmly convinced, rock 'n' roll itself that was the culprit.

'Well, to me the entertainment of people—the *ability* to entertain with the spiritual qualifications of these people—is just almost boundless. I'll tell you what, there is a lot of spirituality out on that stage that just like religion—or anything else in church when it's used the wrong way—is going to hurt some people. But that doesn't mean that rock itself was bad. It never was. It's just that people got so wrought up in the idea of making millions of dollars. And the managers and the bookers, they didn't give a damn, man, it's another product, it's another number, milk it for what it's worth. And so it was difficult for these people to undergird themselves, and then, of course, it happened so fast. So the first thing that started in their minds was: when am I going to be rejected?'

Sun sale closing, 1969; Shelby Singleton, center, Sam Phillips, left, Courtesy of John and Shelby Singleton.

Knox Phillips remembers vividly the day when the Million Dollar Quartet was both formed and disbanded (what happened was that Elvis, already under contract to RCA, wandered down to the Sun studio during a Carl Perkins session on which Jerry Lee Lewis was playing piano; it was, as Sam Phillips says, a momentous 'happenstance,' but one which, because Elvis was an RCA recording artist, had still not been heard by the public as of 1979). Elvis hugged Knox and his brother, Jerry, then twelve and nine respectively. 'He said, "Stay with me, boys, stay with me." And at the time I didn't know that had any real significance, because I didn't know Elvis intimately or anything, but evidently he was a very insecure person, and us having long hair and looking a little bit like him represented some kind of reinforcement.'

'Well, he was torn,' says Sam. 'Elvis—if he had had the proper love ratio with someone that he truly loved and felt and trusted—this would never have befallen Elvis. Because Elvis in so many ways was an extremely strong person, but in other ways, without that ability to communicate with somebody that he felt truly felt him and knew him and understood him, this is where Elvis's problem came. Where it comes in with all of us. So

I can tell you one thing. All of the artists that I had, if they had stayed with Sam Phillips, we might have starved to death together. But—and I like a drink as good as anybody, but I'll tell you what—there would have been no great extremes, because I would have shown them one way or the other *that I loved them.*'

EVENTUALLY SAM PHILLIPS, too, lost interest in his creation and then got out of the record business altogether.

With protégé Jack Clement, 1973. Courtesy of Jack Clement.

'I thank myself for having the good judgment to get out of the business rather than trying to compete against certain economic blocs that I just could not control. Number one, I knew I couldn't compete with the giants, and number two, I saw the business falling apart at the seams to where I couldn't live with it and make a living in an honest way. So rather than to lose my respect for myself and to cheat people, instead of just folding my tent and running away and being bitter at anybody and not doing anything, I just proceeded to do something else. We get a little fulfillment day by day.'

Sam Phillips went on to become a wealthy man (he is an original shareholder in Holiday Inns), but he remains a Memphian through and through (Memphis, always a haven for eccentrics and individualists, is the only locale I know that actually boasts of its craziness). He still lives in the same modest house he has inhabited for the last twenty years, busies himself with his radio stations, expresses nothing but contempt for the Nashville establishment, whom he sees as 'a bunch of bullshitters' for the most part, and remains 'as strong in the faith of reason' as he has always been.

When we met, he was waiting for the latest Arbitron ratings to determine if the new radio station format had a chance of catching on. At the end of a long day we sat in a waterlogged office watching rock 'n' roll history on a tiny black and white TV, mostly with the sound turned off. For a moment there was Jerry Lee Lewis, and Sam perked up. 'Ah, Uncle Gerald,' he chuckled appreciatively. 'You think that guy isn't dynamic? That man can play more piano in a minute than anyone I've ever seen!' Then Elvis came on the screen, looking impossibly young, impossibly expectant. The show was called 'The Heroes of Rock 'n' Roll.'

'Ah, wasn't he something. Let me tell you something about him. Elvis—you looking at him now, back then—he looks so clumsy and so totally uncoordinated. And this was the beauty of it, he was being himself. Well, he had that little innocence about him, and yet he had, even then he had a little something that was almost impudent in a way. That was his crutch. He certainly didn't mean to be impudent, but he had enough of that, along with what he could convey, that he was just beautiful and lovely—and I'm not talking about physical beauty, because he was not that good-looking then. Really, by conventional standards he was supposed to have been thrown off that stage, and I—listen, I calculated that stuff in my mind. Are they going to resent him? With his long sideburns? That could be a plus or a minus. But I looked at it as this. When he came through like he did, it was neither. *He stood on his own.*

'Let me say this. I don't want to come off as the poor ole country boy that made good or anything like that. I'm just trying to come over with what I know deep in my heart to be the truth, as I relayed it to myself then. I may have some dates wrong, and some facts and figures, but the material aspects of it is not wrong. Cause I will see it in my mind's eye until the day I die—and then I'm not so sure I won't see it after that. I'm not looking for any heroism or anything at all, but I think that music is a part of a very spiritual aspect of people. And I just think that it has gotten out of hand a little bit today, scientifically trying to analyze everything that you do, and if it doesn't have that stamp, then nobody can peddle it. I don't say there's a thing wrong with disco, but when you drive so much of the same thing and people get into too much of a pattern, I want to tell you that if that is giving of yourself in a way that you can be fulfilled, then I just don't have the ability to interpret it in that way. Listen, they're talking about that you've got to have—well, what is the trend now? Well, *Jesus God,* now if there's anything we don't need, it's a trend.

'One of these days, though, I may not live to see it, maybe you all will, but one of these days that freedom is going to come back.'

Sam Phillips's voice rises, it is like a flood, and you can hear him telling Elvis that yes, his music will prevail. It will.

'Because look, the expression of the people is almost, it's so powerful, it's almost like a hydrogen bomb. It's going to get out.

'Now let me just tell you one other thing, Peter, and I'll get out of here. I'm not just saying go back to the fifties and this sort of thing. But if it could be worked—and it will be worked—to where just a few like Elvis could break out, then I would preach, I would become an evangelist if I were alive, saying, For God's sake, *don't* let's become con-formists—*please.* Just do your thing in your own way. Don't ever let fame and fortune or recognition or anything interfere with what you feel is here—*if you* feel you are a creative individual. Then don't let the companies get this going real good and buy up all the rights of the individual some way or the other. That's not right. We'll go back in another circle. Till it gets so damn boring that your head is swimming. And I'll tell you, I hope it's not too long coming, because of the fact as we go longer and longer into the lack of individual expression, as we go along, if we get too far we going to get away from some of the real basic things. All of us damn cats and people that appreciate not the fifties necessarily but that freedom are gonna forget about the feel. We gonna be in jail, and not even know it.'

Motown

By Charles Sykes

It happened in a White two-story house located at 2648 West Grand. Boulevard in "Motor City," Detroit, Michigan. A sign above the large picture window prominently displayed the words, "Hitsville U.S.A." Its owner, Berry Gordy, a Black songwriter, intended it to be a "factory" where hit records could be "built."[1] Young Black men and women would come and go in shifts, each doing his or her part in an assembly line that operated 24 hours a day, much like those in hundreds of local automobile factories. They were producing a new type of rhythm and blues that would bear the "Motown" trademark. From 1959 to 1972, Detroit was home for Motown Record Corporation, and Hitsville was the company's primary recording studio. Gordy's intention to make hit records was realized as the new local phenomenon called the Motown Sound gained mass appeal.

While based in Detroit, Motown affected the careers of some of the most famous artists in the history of popular music: Diana Ross and the Supremes, Smokey Robinson and the Miracles, Martha & the Vandellas, the Temptations (Figure 16.1), Four Tops, Marvelettes, Mary Wells, Stevie Wonder, Marvin Gaye, and others. Through their voices, and with the talents of outstanding musicians known as the Funk Brothers, Motown's writers and producers gave the world some of the most memorable songs ever recorded. They were songs people could relate to: upbeat, with elements of gospel, pop, and jazz fused and packaged in slick musical arrangements, like the well-coordinated outfits their artists wore when they performed live. Stage routines were choreographed to project an air of "class" and "sophistication," very much within the range of acceptability for mainstream audiences, but with a subtle edge that spoke "young," "cool," "Black," "urban," and "Detroit." And most of Motown's personnel *were* young Blacks born or raised in Detroit. By 1962, Motown would advertise its music as "The Sound of Young America," a slogan consistent with the ages of company personnel and with the large number of young Americans buying Motown's records.

Before Motown, the music industry had no history of a Black owned company seriously competing with White-owned companies at the national level. Motown's record sales and numbers of hit records were competitive with top independent labels and major labels in both R&B and pop categories.[2] Motown produced a product that, although delivered through Black voices and faces, crossed over into the White market at an unprecedented level of success.

In June 1972, Motown closed its Detroit offices and moved to Los Angeles, California. Here the company ventured into movies and television, while continuing record production in the newer, Los Angeles–based Hitsville Studios. The L.A. move disconnected Motown from its hometown, but even the company's later incorporation as an entity within such international media conglomerates as Vivendi's Universal Music Group has not dislodged the Motown legacy from its Detroit 'roots. And the old Hitsville U.S.A., reestablished in 1985 as the Motown Historical Museum, stands as a symbol of that legacy, built during the 13 years the company was based in the "Motor City."

"The legacy of Motown," says Gordy, "is its body of music."[3] Motown's musical foundation was laid in the context of Detroit's Black community. Here, under the leadership of Berry Gordy and his staff of writers and producers, various human, physical, social, and cultural resources coalesced in the Hitsville studio as the Motown Sound. This essay looks at the Motown legacy as representative of Detroit generally, and of the city's Black community in particular. By exploring issues of Black entrepreneurship, local influences, musical eclecticism, and crossover, we uncover the values that underlay the structure and operation of Motown. The final two *sections* offer a description of production processes and works of various artists, writers, and producers, giving special attention to recordings written and produced by Holland-Dozier-Holland (H-D-H) for the Supremes. H-D-H piloted a new R&B concept that became known as the Motown Sound. The Supremes (Figure 16.2), with H-D-H's material as their core repertoire, led Motown's effort to break into the mass market.

Black Entrepreneurship And Community Philosophy

The *Gordy* family epitomized ideals of self-help and social consciousness, values Detroit historian Richard Thomas says represented "the heart and soul of [black] community building" in post–World War I Detroit.[4] Berry Gordy Sr. and his wife Bertha had moved from Georgia to Detroit in 1922, seven years before Berry Jr. was born. Hard work, family unity, and economic prudence helped the Gordys and their eight children progress from the welfare rolls to become one of the most successful families in Detroit.[5] They owned and operated businesses in realty, building contracting, insurance, printing, and groceries, naming their grocery store after Booker T. Washington. As Black entrepreneurs and members of the Booker T. Washington Trade Association, the Gordys were part of a movement to promote economic health and community pride through patronage of Black businesses, which provided convenient access to needed services. In 1965, Berry Jr. received the Trade Association's business achievement award. Motown had become a multi-million dollar operation, one of America's largest Black-owned businesses, and a testament to the ideals of self-help. But Motown's success also represented the thinking of Black Nationalism, which advocated Black economic independence.[6]

With an $800 loan through the family's Ber-Berry Co-op, Gordy became owner of his new Tamla label in 1959. Later that year he established a second label, Motown, a name derived from Detroit's nickname, the "Motor City." Gordy writes: "The Tamla name was commercial enough but had been more of a gimmick. Now I wanted something that meant more to me, something that would capture the feeling of my roots—my home town."[7] The company was incorporated under the name Motown, and the Motown label, bearing a map of southeast Michigan with a star marking Detroit as capital, would become the flagship label.[8]

Sixteen labels created under Gordy's leadership imprinted the company's recording repertoire by the end of 1971. Several affiliated companies, all owned by Berry Gordy, operated the business of Motown. Jobete Music, Stein and Van Stock, ITMI, Gordy Enterprises, Motown Records, and Hitsville together handled recording, sales, promotion, publishing, tours, artist management, and artist development with minimal need for outside services. The company hired its own staff of writers, producers, musicians, artists, and technical and management personnel to take care of virtually all needs. And a number of the Motown's personnel, particularly in the early days, were Gordy family members.

As with earlier Gordy family businesses, good community relations were important to Motown's success. Stage band students from Northwestern High School, located only a few blocks from Hitsville, observed recording sessions to learn about the process.[9] Public appearances by Motown artists helped promote local business and special causes, like Detroit United Foundation's annual Torch Drive, for which Motown permitted the use of "The Happening," the Supremes' latest record, for the campaign's theme song.[10] Motown artists' appearances at DJ record hops would bring crowds, thus increasing income for the DJs, who reciprocated with airplay for Motown's recordings.[11] Detroit was devastated by riots in July 1967. To help quell tensions, Motown released "I Care about Detroit," a promo recorded by Smokey Robinson and the Miracles. A year later, the United Foundation used the record as a theme for "Detroit is Happening," a program that provided summer jobs and recreational activities for the city's youth in an effort to prevent a recurrence of riots.[12]

Motown's presence in Detroit spawned a large local fan base and a sense of local pride. But survival in the record business meant popularity beyond Detroit by reaching the masses. The success that Motown would achieve in the mass market was predicated on Berry Gordy's idea that the company's output should consist of an eclectic repertoire that appealed to a general audience. Detroit provided a cosmopolitan environment in which a broad-based vision like Gordy's could materialize.

Local Music Influences And Musical Eclecticism

Cities offer exposure to a "great diversity of musical behavior within a broad range of events" facilitated by education systems, public and private organizations, business and entertainment, and mass media.[13] Physical and social boundaries that define racial and cultural groups constantly *criss-cross,* fostering the likelihood of diverse musical experiences and eclectic tastes, even within segregated neighborhoods.

Berry Gordy showed an eclectic taste for music at an early age. Uncle B.A., his first music teacher, stimulated his love for classical piano. Radio exposed him to mainstream pop and "race" music aired in small segments on local programs like WJLB's "Interracial Goodwill Hour."[14] At age seven, he created his own "Berry's Boogie" on the family's old upright piano. He loved the Mills Brothers and the Ink Spots, two jazz-pop vocal groups whose recordings would later influence his approach to songwriting.[15] As a teenager, he was listening *to* jazz and dancing *to* the big bands of Duke Ellington and Count Basie at favorite Eastside Detroit nightspots.[16] At age 20 he wrote a song entitled "You Are You" for the famous mainstream pop artist Doris Day. "Thinking of a general audience even then," he writes, "I had written the song with Doris Day in mind. She was America's girl next door."[17]

Berry indulged his love for jazz by opening the 3D Record Mart, a jazz record store, only to find out that the local public was much more interested in blues and rhythm and blues. 3D failed, but Berry began listening to R&B and learned to love its infectious simplicity. Three years working on the Lincoln-Mercury (a division of Ford Motor Company) assembly line gave him opportunity to hone his R&B songwriting craft in moments between assembling parts. By 1957, Berry had become a writer for the famous R&B (rhythm and blues) star, Jackie Wilson. His diverse musical influences congealed during the late 1950s into concepts that would later influence the Motown Sound and the processes by which it was created.

The 1950s marked the "golden age of jazz in Detroit."[18] Some of the world's finest jazz musicians and vocalists—local greats like Barry Harris, Yusef Lateef, Kenny Burrell, and the Jones brothers, Hank, Elvin and Thad; and guest greats like Cannonball Adderley, Billy Holiday, Sarah Vaughan, Mingus, and Miles—could be heard on any night at Klein's, the Blue Bird, the West End, the Flame, and many other clubs. Berry Gordy frequented the Flame Show Bar, one of Detroit's most popular, upscale clubs that hosted acts ranging from jazz to popular. The Flame is where Berry heard and met Billie Holiday, whose life story inspired Motown's first movie production, *Lady Sing the Blues,* released in 1972.

The jazz and R&B businesses intersected at the Flame, and fruitful relationships resulted, especially for Berry and Motown. Club co-owner Al Green also managed a number of local R&B acts, including Jackie Wilson. Berry's sister Gwen, who owned photo concessions at the Flame, introduced him to Green, thus launching his career as one of Jackie Wilson's songwriters. Berry would eventually hire Maurice Ring, the Flame's house bandleader, as music director in Motown's Artist Development department, and

"Beans" Bowles, who played saxophone in King's band, as a musician and road manager for Motown's first tour.

Detroit's club scene was a breeding ground for the Funk Brothers, the musicians who played on hundreds of recordings released during the Detroit era. Their backgrounds included formal training in classical music and jazz. Band, orchestra, and stage band were their training ensembles in school music programs. But even before finishing high school, a number of them played professional jazz and blues engagements in Detroit's club scene. In the nightclub environment, keyboardist Johnny Griffith claimed, the "Detroit Sound," which gave shape to the Motown Sound, was nurtured.[19]

Future Motown artists, writers, and producers, born during World War II, were teenagers during the 1950s and consumer-participants in a new popular culture. American popular music, formally defined by mainstream pop, had become redefined as rhythm and blues or rock 'n' roll. Teenagers were the target market of record companies and broadcast media who disseminated and propagated this new music. Like Berry Gordy, the new generation of Detroit's Black teenagers was exposed to diverse forms of music. In church, they would hear and sing gospel. In Glee Club and other school music classes, they studied European-based classical and folk traditions under the tutelage of White teachers.[20] Broadcast media, primarily radio and to a lesser but growing extent television, provided access to a broad array of musical offerings and was the core source of exposure to the current forms of music that future Motown personnel would listen to, dance to, buy on record, and emulate.

Black radio programming had gained a substantial presence as R&B became integrated into American popular culture. White and Black DJs became leading propagators of R&B through airplay, hosting record hops, and organizing concerts that featured heroes of future Motown personnel WJBK's Ed "Jack the Bellboy" McKenzie began in the 1940s playing blues, boogie-woogie, and R&B records "on what was essentially a pop [radio] show," and continued to do so in the 1950s.[21] Robin Seymour of WKHM and Mickey Shorr of WJBK were key promoters of R&B, although under the rock 'n' roll banner. Their live concert promotions brought to Detroit top R&B acts like Frankie Lyman and the Teenagers, who several Motown artists note as being of major influence, and the Cadillacs, a group whose look and choreography made a profound impression on future Temptations' Otis Williams and whose choreographer, Cholly Atkins, would eventually groom Motown acts for the stage.[22]

While Ed McKenzie, Robin Seymour, Mickey Shorr, and other White DJs included R&B as part of eclectic play lists, WJLB aired all R&B shows with Black DJs LeRoy White, Bristoe Bryant, and Ernie Durham, one of the first Detroit DJs to host record hops. DJs at WJLB would later become important figures for breaking Motown's records in the local market, as would their counterparts at WCHB, Detroit's first Black-owned, all-Black-format radio station, located in the Inkster suburb.[23] Most of the station's airtime was devoted to Black popular music, spun by DJs Joe Howard, Larry Dean, and Larry Dixon. Early morning programming, however, featured gospel music, which during the

1950s included records by the Harmonizing Four, Dixie Hummingbirds, and other gospel groups who planted the gospel roots of R&B groups like the Temptations.[24]

There were hundreds of teenage vocal groups in Detroit: male groups, girl groups, mixed groups. Street corners and school hallways vibrated with the sounds of blow harmonies, falsetto, doo-wop vocables, teen love lyrics, and other remnants of the vocal group tradition. Competition was stiff; talent shows frequently held in high schools provided incentive to be the best, and Ed McKenzie's "Saturday Party" on WXYZ-TV offered opportunities for young Black groups like the Five Chimes (future Miracles) to appear on television and win top talent honors.[25] Members of the Five Chimes, Matadors, Primes, Primettes, Distants, Del-Phis, and other groups would eventually take their talents to the next level as Motown artists, writers, and producers.[26]

The group concept would become central to the Motown legacy. While Motown always carried solo artists on its roster, its legacy was in large part shaped by vocal group. sounds, visual images of three to five people dressed in coordinated outfits with similar hairstyles (processes for men in the early days), synchronized dance movements, and group identity, which was *so* much a part of youth culture in post–World War II urban contexts. As company owner, Berry Gordy faced the challenge of bringing cohesion to the disparate individuals and groups of young talent that would come to Hitsville and positioning the company for success in the mass market.

A brochure printed sometime during the mid-1960s suggests that Motown avoided promoting itself as a Black company, but instead promoted its multiple services and diverse recording repertoire, released on the company's multiple labels. The brochure's cover shows a cartoon-like orchestra conductor image with long straight hair, dressed in tie and tails, smiling and posed as if introducing the title, "This Is Motown Record Corporation" (Figure 163). The text inside boasts that Motown is "one of America's leading independent recording companies" and "a versatile, highly successful producer of single and long-playing records that satisfy a variety of preferences in popular music." Motown's eclectic nature is emphasized:

> There is a Motown record to appeal to every type of audience. The Motown, Tamla, Gordy, Soul, VIP and Mel-o-dy labels feature rhythm and blues, ballads, rock and roll, country and western, and general "pop" music. The company has increased its activity in the jazz field and offers some of the world's finest jazz artists on the Workshop label, and *so* that no taste is slighted, the Divinity label produces religious [gospel] records.[27]

The brochure text gives only a hint of Motown's diverse body of recordings. R&B and soul, musical traditions that are themselves diverse, constitute the core of the company's repertoire. But Motown's recording activities reached beyond R&B and soul. An album entitled *The Great March to Freedom* (1963) featured speeches by Martin Luther King Jr., including his "I Have a Dream" speech. *The Soulful Moods of Marvin Gaye* (1961) consisted of standards like "My Funny Valentine." The *Supremes at the Copa* (1965) album included Broadway tunes. Covers of British pop tunes were recorded on the Supremes' *A Bit of Liverpool* (1964), and the group recorded a Christmas album entitled *Merry Christmas* (1965). The spoken words of Black political figures Martin. Luther King Jr. and Stokely Carmichael and poets Langston Hughes and Margaret Banner were captured and preserved on the Black Forum label, launched in 1970. These are just a few examples of the range and scope of records released by Motown.

Berry Gordy clearly was on a mission to sell to the masses, which for a company peddling R&B records during his time meant capturing a substantial share of the White consumer market while nurturing the Black consumer base from which the music came. He proved by the mid-1960s that his mission could be accomplished by focusing less on promoting Motown's racial identity and more on implementing various means by which Motown could reach a broad audience. Motown's eclectic repertoire, which echoed Gordy's diverse musical experiences and tastes formulated in Detroit, tapped the musical tastes of people across racial, social, and cultural boundaries. Motown's top acts took their eclectic repertoire into mainstream venues—the Palace in Las Vegas, Copacabana in New York—and overseas to Europe and Asia, occasionally performing for royalty. The artist development staff, which included music director Maurice King, choreographer Cholly Atkins, and image specialist Maxine Powell, would groom the artists to "appear in #1 places," far removed from the Black Detroit neighborhoods where most of them grew up and learned their craft.[28]

In 1964, the Supremes made their debut on the *Ed Sullivan Show,* a top-rated TV variety show sponsored by Lincoln-Mercury, broadcast nationally on CBS. The show brought the Supremes into millions of American homes, introducing their well-groomed act to a diverse range of viewers who may not otherwise have seen it and proving that young Blacks from inner-city Detroit singing R&B could be, in the words of a young White female fan, "the epitome of glamour."[29] Berry Gordy strategically scheduled subsequent appearances by the Supremes and other Motown acts on Sullivan's show to promote new releases.[30]

For many Blacks, seeing the Supremes, the Temptations, the Four Tops, and others on national television, or hearing news of their *success* in contexts where segregation still excluded Blacks as patrons, offered a sense of racial pride. For many Whites, the music performed and images projected by Motown's artists helped dispel Black stereotypes, or at least spoke to their musical sensibilities enough to reel them in as consumers. Yet Motown's success across racial, social, and cultural boundaries has often generated criticism narrowly focused on the notion that the company's success came with a compromise of Black roots, as evidenced in both music and presentation style.[31] Compromise or not, it is unlikely that an independent, Black-owned company operating solely on a premise of racial identity within the racially segregated climate of the 1960s would have achieved mass appeal and longevity comparable to that achieved by Motown. Berry Gordy's astute sense of what it took to be successful drove the business of Motown and was very much in tune with

Maxine Powell's opinion that the company's work was not about race: "Honey, that's not Black; that's show business," she says.[32]

Crossover

"Saying you listened to [DJ] 'Frantic Ernie' carried a certain amount of status for white kids who wanted to be ultracool," David Carson writes.[33] Berry was able to get Tom Clay to play Motown's records on WJBK, a pop format station that appealed to local White listeners.[34] While R&B had its roots in the Black community, White teenagers in earshot of Black radio programming were embracing R&B, although under the rock 'n' roll banner. By the time Berry Gordy launched his Tamla label in 1959, rock 'n' roll had become the subject heading of a modern popular music narrative that included diverse forms of R&B recorded by Black artists; covers of R&B recorded by White artists whose stylistic orientations ranged from mainstream pop (Pat Boone) to rockabilly (Elvis Presley, Bill Haley); and original rock 'n' roll songs of similar range and diversity, recorded primarily by White artists and based on Black R&B models. But record charts, the measuring sticks of success in the record industry, were segregated. Black artists routinely faired better on the R&B charts, representing music recorded by Blacks for Blacks, than on the pop charts, representing music recorded by Whites for the larger White market. Optimal success in record sales required selling across defined markets, or "crossing over." Crossover was firmly wedged into the record business before Motown. During the mid-1950s, some Black artists (Platters, Silhouettes, Lloyd Price) scored number-one pop hits, while some White artists—(Johnnie Ray, Elvis Presley) scored number-one R&B hits. By the time Berry started Motown, it was apparent that consumers' record collections might be integrated even while record charts and neighborhoods remained segregated.

Motown's first major step into the crossover market came with the Miracle's "Shop Around" (1960), which hit number one on the R&B charts and number two on the pop charts. A year later the Marvelettes' "Please Mr. Postman" hit number one on both charts, an accomplishment that would be repeated in 1963 with Little Stevie Wonder's "Fingertips—Part 2" and later with other top Motown acts. Mary Wells and Martha & the Vandellas also did well in both pop and R&B charts during the early years of the Detroit era.

Billboard's temporary suspension of R&B charts from November 1963 to January 1965, which meant that popular music would all compete for ranking on the pop charts, paralleled the Temptations, Four Tops, and Supremes' first weekly Top 25 pop hits. More significantly, during this period the Supremes would record their first three of ten number-one pop hits written and produced by Holland-Dozier-Holland. The Supremes clearly held honors as Motown's top crossover act. However, 25 other acts contributed to the company's 107 Top 10 pop hits and 29 number-one pop hit singles charting before 1972, as shown in the table (Figure 16.4). However—if chart rankings have any value in

Dates	Pop		R&B	
	Top 10	#1	Top 10	#1
1959	0	0	1	0
1960	1	1	3	1
1961	1	1	2	1
1962	6	0	11	4
1963	5	1	9	2
1964	6	4	**	**
1965	11	5	27	6
1966	13	3	30	9
1967	13	2	27	5
1968	11	2	22	6
1969	13	3	22	7
1970	16	6	26	8
1971	11	1	20	5
Total	107	29	200	54

Figure 16.4 Motown's Weekly Top 10 and #1 hits on *Billboard's* pop and R&B charts (1959–1971).

measuring success within racially defined markets—Motown's success on the White pop charts did not dilute its sales on the Black R&B charts; in other words, Motown was able to maintain its Black consumer base in spite, of crossover *success,* Cornell West asserts that Berry Gordy "perceived a vacuum in the musical culture of the nation. He was able to convince young brothers and sisters, like me, on the Black side of town that this was my music. And at the same time convince White brothers and sisters on the other side of town listening to the Beach Boys, that Motown was also their music. Nothing like that had ever occurred."[35]

Berry Gordy developed his company around a concept that, through music style, image, and repertoire, promoted the likelihood that non Blacks would like and buy Motown's records. But turning the possibility of crossover into reality depended as much on a company's business networking as it did on its ability to produce records having potential cross-market appeal. Suzanne Smith explains: "In the 1960s black popular music did not crossover to White audiences on the basis of its appeal alone. The transition involved an elaborate system of marketing the artists and behind-the-scenes deal making with distributors, disc jockeys, and record store owners."[36]

In 1960, Barney Ales, one of Motown's first White executives, was brought on board as head of the sales department just in time to push "Please Mr. Postman" to number one on the pop charts. Ales, a former distributor introduced to Berry by DJ Tom Clay, built Motown's sales department primarily by hiring experienced Whites who could get distributors to push for airplay and record sales in White markets, particularly in the racially biased South. On the other hand, Motown's promotion department consisted of industry-savvy Blacks like former DJ Jack Gibson, whose reputations enabled them to wield similar success with Black radio stations and sales outlets.

As Motown's popularity grew and racial prejudice against Black products and their representatives decreased during the mid- to late 1960s, Motown's sales and promotion staffs became integrated, while company marketing practices used to evade racial prejudice, like avoiding use of the artists' faces on record covers (a practice that Motown used early on), became less necessary.[37] But in the process of achieving crossover success, Berry had learned how to negotiate racial prejudice. He not only managed to establish positive working relationships with key industry personnel whose cooperation was crucial to selling his records across markets, but he also hired some of the most talented members of their ranks and placed them in key roles on Motown's management roster, a strategy that helped wedge the company inside the music industry's business network. Berry's astute recognition and employment of talent in key roles would similarly manifest itself in Motown's production process, whose operation created the records his company then so skillfully promoted to the masses.

Assembling The Sound: Production Processes And Role Players

While working at Lincoln-Mercury from 1955 to 1957, Berry was struck by the "pleasing simplicity" and efficiency of the assembly line process: "how everyone did the same thing over and over again," and how cars would "start out as frames and end up brand new spanking cars/"[38] The assembly line concept would become manifested at Motown in two ways. One was Berry's idea that a young artist could come into the company as an "unknown" and eventually become a "star."[39] The second was the process by which various people with clearly defined roles would work collectively to create hit records. Recollections by former Motown personnel help describe the record-making assembly line as it operated during the mid-1960s:

"Usually a producer was assigned to an artist, or an artist was assigned to a producer, and they had the job of coming up with material," says the Miracles' Ron White. The material may be created by a songwriter, but "more times than not … the producer would write the material for the artist."[40] Thus, records were typically generated by songwriter-producers, often working in teams. The producer would teach the song to the artist. Vocal groups, however, would sometimes create their own background parts, as Smokey Robinson confirms: "I would always let the Temptations make up their own backgrounds because they were masters at it."[41] Motown's resident background vocalists, the Andantes, or artist groups were often assigned to sing background vocals for other artists and would create their own parts.

Most songwriter-producers could not read music, so Johnny Alien, Paul Riser, Hank Cosby, and other arrangers would score parts for the musicians. The producer would sing or play basic ideas *so* that the arranger could transcribe them to paper. The arrangement, which might include the arranger's ideas as well as those of the producer, was taken into the studio for the musicians to rehearse and record. The Funk Brothers, in response to the producer's instructions, however, often spontaneously created rhythm section arrangements as on-the-spot "head" arrangements. Once the basic rhythm arrangement was established, recording began.

The rhythm tracks, the "foundation" of the recording, were cut first. After the rhythm tracks were laid down, horn, string (usually played by musicians from the Detroit Symphony), arid vocal tracks were overdubbed. Once all tracks were cut, the master was produced. The producer would work with the engineer to edit, balance, and mix the multiple tracks down to one (mono) or two (stereo) tracks, taking the liberty to augment or cut material based *on* his perception of what was more or less important to the sound of the recording.[42] The master was then taken to quality control, a committee consisting of several artists, writers, producers, office staff, and Berry Gordy, who determined by vote whether a record should or should not be released. Quality control might also give suggestions for additional production work to be done.[43]

Motown also created songs from *tracks—rhythm:* tracks, or generic grooves recorded onto tape by the Funk Brothers without reference to specific songs. Tracks were given to writers to use as raw material from which to write songs. Songwriter Sylvia Moy viewed this method, unconventional at the time, as a "backwards" way of writing a song. She would later recognize that the process saved the company money.[44]

Collaboration, improvisation, and role-playing, processes inherent to Black music-making within or outside of the studio, were key elements of Motown's assembly line. Each participant contributed in unique ways. The Funk Brothers' sense of ensemble, sound quality, musicianship, and creativity, anchored by the revolutionary bass playing style of James Jamerson, provided the musical backdrop for numerous hits.[45] Martha Reeves writes that the musicians **"were** responsible for all of the success of the singers at Motown because it was their music that inspired us to sing our best with excitement."[46] Yet, the vocalists were the stars. The artists—their sounds, vocal styles, names, and looks—branded the records for consumers, arguably more so than those who wrote, arranged, played on, or produced the recordings. But the **songwriters** generated the stories and melodies that gave context and purpose to the **work of others** involved in record-making at Motown. However, the producers, who often wrote the songs as well, held ultimate responsibility for leading the production process and delivering hits that would meet the company's goals.

"We're going *to* make music with a great beat, with some great stories. ... Our stories are going to be such that anybody can listen to them. ... They will not be offensive," Smokey remembers Berry saying when he started Motown.[47] Berry's words provided goals that would, in obvious and subtle ways, connect the entire body of music to the Motown legacy. The assembly line provided a process by which those goals could be achieved.

The Motown Sound: Gospel In A Pop Package

Berry believed that songs should tell stories that people can relate to. And, like stories, "songs need a beginning, middle and end."[48] A song "should be honest and have a good concept," he writes. "Probably the first thing people relate to is the melody." The melody should be memorable and include "hooks" **(phrases of repetition)** that are "infectious," not "monotonous."[49] As the Detroit era progressed, Berry's ideas about songwriting served as a master narrative for his staff writers and producers who worked to get their records released.

The Detroit era evolved in three overlapping phases, marked by musical style and related personnel: Phase I, 1959 to 1963, the formative years; Phase II, 1964 to 1967, the "classic" period, when the Motown Sound crystallized; and Phase III, 1968 to 1972, a period of diversification and transition to the post-Detroit era.[50] I focus here on style features of Holland-Dozier-Holland's songs recorded by the Supremes during Phase II, but make reference to music and **music-makers** that predated, coexisted with, and followed the **H-D-H/Supremes** affiliation.

Phase I

Phase I releases, produced on Motown's two- and three-track recording systems, mirror then-past and current R&B styles. The first Tamla release, "Come To Me" (1959), a Gordy production recorded by Marv Johnson, recalls the doo-wop vocal tradition with its "ooos," "ahhs," and vocal riffs, ingredients that were so **much** a part of R&B through the mid-1960s. Blues elements are present in Gordy productions like Motown's first national hits, **"Money"** (1959), recorded by Barrett Strong; the Miracles' "Shop Around" (1960), cowritten by Smokey Robinson; "Do You Love Me" (1962), recorded by the Contours; and "Fingertips—Part 2" (1963), cowritten by several Motown personnel and recorded live by the "12 Year Old Genius," Stevie Wonder.

Robert Bateman and Brian Holland teamed up as "Brianbert" to write and produce, with A&R head William "Mickey" Stevenson, "Please Mr. Postman" (1961) for the Marvelettes, Motown's prototypical, teenage pop-sounding girl group. Another Marvelettes recording, "Strange I Know" (1962), is perhaps the first recording of James Jamerson's innovative, jazz-influenced, bass playing style, characterized bypassing tones, eighth-and sixteenth-note combinations, syncopation, and deep, full tone quality.[51] But Jamerson also demonstrates skill in playing the shuffle pattern on "old school," boogie-woogie-based R&B pieces like Marvin Gaye's "Pride And Joy" (1963), cowritten by Norman Whitfield and produced by Mickey Stevenson.

Smokey Robinson's Phase-I productions for Mary Wells are distinctive models of how lyricism and narrative can be central elements of R&B. With fellow Miracles Ron White and Bobbie Rogers as cowriters, Smokey generated seven Top 10 hits for Mary, including the Grammy-nominated "You Beat Me to the Punch" (1962). Set in verse-chorus form with a contrasting bridge, Smokers productions for Mary project a calypso feel, which he credits to his listening to Harry Belafonte while growing up.[52]

It was clear in 1963 that something different was coming out of Detroit. Early that year, Martha & the Vandellas recorded their first hit, "Come and Get These Memories."- Martha writes, "The song had a steady beat, great background harmony parts, horns, catchy lyrics, and a *story* line that everyone could identify with."[53] Her comments could apply to several other 1963 hits: Martha & the Vandellas' "(Love is Like a) Heatwave," the Miracles' "Mickey's Monkey," Marvin Gaye's "Can I Get a Witness," and the Supremes' "When the Love Light Starts Shining through His Eyes." These records, all written and produced by Holland-Dozier-Holland, echoed what Berry is reported to have said when he heard "Memories": "That's the sound I've been looking for. That's the Motown Sound!"[54]

By 1963, Lamont **Dozier** and brothers Brian and Eddie Holland had formed the songwriting-production team, Holland-Dozier-Holland, or **H-D-H.** Their work launched a highly successful concept that would transform several Motown acts into hit-makers, provide leadership in reaching the masses, and give definition to a new R&B sound concept which solidified the following year as other developments marked the beginning of a new phase.

Phase II

By 1964, records were made on Motown's new eight-track system, built by Hitsville sound engineer Mike McLean. A revolutionary piece of technology at a time when four-track recording was considered state-of-the-art, the eight-track system activated the assembly-line process and made it possible for important components of the Motown Sound, like Jamerson's bass part, to be isolated, hence better controlled, on separate tracks.[55] Multi-track recording technology provided the technological foundation for the musical concepts at work in defining the character of Mo town's recordings.

Even as the Beatles invaded the top rungs of America's record charts, Motown's arrival as a major force in the popular music industry was evident in 1964. Early that year, Mary Wells hit number one on *Billboard's* then pop-only charts with Smokey Robinson's "My Guy." Martha & the Vandellas recorded their signature piece, "Dancing in the Street," cowritten by Marvin Gaye and producer Mickey Stevenson. David Ruffin joined the Temptations as co-lead singer and the group broke into the charts with Smokey Robinson's "The Way You Do the Things You Do." The Four Tops, previously hitless, made their way into the charts with the H-D-H hit, "Baby I Need Your Loving." And the Supremes recorded three number-one pop hits by H-D-H: "Where Did Our Love Go," "Baby Love," and "Come See about Me." Motown and the Motown sound had come of age.

Two important decisions contributed to the Supremes' success during Phase II. Berry Gordy determined that Diana Ross's "whiney voice" was preferable for their lead.[56] The other was the assignment of H-D-H as the Supremes' writers and producers. H-D-H had piloted the Supremes' first appearance in the top 25 with "When the Love Light Starts Shining through His Eyes," an up-tempo, densely textured pop-gospel-styled production with horns blaring on the chorus, driving rhythmic accompaniment, baritone saxophone assisting with the bass line, handclaps, organ, and tambourine—all the ingredients of the "hallelujah" gospel sound of H-D-H's 1963 productions. But in 1964, H-D-H made a drastic change in the Supremes' material, beginning with "Where Did Our Love Go."

"Where Did Our Love Go" is set in a simple, transparent texture that focuses the sound squarely on Diana's voice. Mary Wilson and Florence Ballard sing a sparse two-part background accompaniment, mostly in call-response, emphasizing key thematic phrases and complementing the melody with lyrics like "baby, baby, oooo baby, baby." The lyrics deal with teenage love and longing, and project innocence. There is a constant pulsation on each beat in the measure, created in the studio (by people stomping on boards placed on the floor) and assisted by piano and bass, which adds a repetitive, syncopated pattern. Guitars are mixed far into the background. A vibraphone shimmers out chord pads on I, V, II, and V changes throughout the tune. The formal structure consists of a series of verses and **choruses,** all based *on* the same chords. There *is* no bridge, but rather an eight-bar baritone sax solo.

In "Where Did Our Love Go," H-D-H seem to have stripped their gospel-pop concept down to bare bones. Mary Wilson comments: "To my ears, 'Where Did Our Love Go' was a teenybopper song. It had childish repetitive lyrics, … a limited melody, and *no* drive. It was too smooth, and I couldn't imagine anyone liking it."[57] But people did like it: the record hit number one in the United States and number two in the U.K.

Subsequent H-D-H releases built upon ingredients used in "Where Did Our Love Go," with handclaps, strings, punctuating horns, tambourine, modulations, and other *stock* H-D-H features selectively added. The Supremes' music matured as they matured. Arrangements became increasingly more sophisticated, with thicker textures and a more rhythmic drive. The teenage Supremes who joined Motown in 1961 had become young women in their twenties when they recorded "Reflections" (1967), a song whose "the way life used to be" lyrics, delivered by a deeper-voiced Diana, suggest experience and maturity. But even through change, all their "classic" period releases illustrate the gospel-pop formula that became "synonymous with the 'Motown Sound.'"[58]

The Supremes/H-D-H recordings use Black gospel elements as their foundation, evidenced in their use of tambourine, call-response, rhythmic repetition, multilayering, and handclaps, and in the ways in which the singers bend tones and anticipate and delay beats. Yet Diana's clear, nasal voice, as well as the simplicity and control placed on vocal and instrumental parts, all suggest a pop orientation. In the Supremes' songs, H-D-H took Black gospel elements and packaged them into a pop production concept.

H-D-H's productions for other artists are technically and structurally very similar to those of the Supremes, but qualitatively very different, adjusting to differences in their artists' vocal styles. Richly textured orchestrations in "Baby I Need Your Loving" (1964) and "Reach Out, I'll Be There" (1966), for example, complement the maleness and maturity of the Four Tops' sound, which is centered on the dramatic, pleading, sometimes preaching *voice* of lead singer Levi Stubbs. Martha Reeves' intense, powerful delivery is appropriately matched with the intense lyrics and driving rhythms of "Nowhere to Run" (1965). H-D-H would periodically break from their stock formula in tunes like the shuffle rhythm-based "How Sweet It Is (To Be Loved By You)" recorded by Marvin Gaye (1965) and Jr. Walker & the All Stars (1966); the slightly funky Four Tops recording "I Can't Help Myself" (1965); the uncharacteristically funky "Roadrunner" recorded by Jr. Walker & the All Stars (1966); and "Love (Makes Me Do Foolish Things)," a slow, 1950s-type R&B ballad and an anomaly among H-D-H's regular pallet of medium- and up-tempo hits, recorded in 1966 by Martha & the Vandellas.

The focus here on H-D-H and the Supremes is not intended to assert their domination over classic Motown, but rather to give definition to a musical concept that fronted Motown's mass appeal during a period in which various artistic, technical, and management phenomena crystallized to epitomize the Motown legacy. The works of other writer-producer-artist combinations made different but no less vital contributions to shaping that legacy.

Smokey Robinson, Motown's most prolific songwriter, wrote or cowrote and produced some of the most important Phase II hits: for Mary Wells, "My Guy" (1964), her last release before leaving Motown; for the Miracles, "Ooo Baby Baby (1965), "Going to a Go-Go" (1965), "Tracks of My Tears" (1965), and "I Second that Emotion" (1967); for Marvin Gaye, "I'll Be Doggone" and "Ain't That Peculiar" (1965); and for the Marvelettes, "Don't Mess With Bill" (1966) and "The Hunter Gets Captured by the Game" (1967). Following "The Way You Do the Things You Do," Smokey produced several hits for the Temptations, but his "My Girl" (1965) is arguably one of the most memorable songs ever released by Motown and a song that defined the classic Temptations. Norman Whitfield, with Eddie Holland as cowriter, eventually gained primary responsibility for the Temptations' material; shifting the group to a more soulful sound, he teamed up with cowriter Eddie Holland to cut "Ain't Too Proud to Beg" (1966) and other hits.

Stevie Wonder had begun writing his own songs with Sylvia Moy, his mother Lula Hardaway, and arranger Hank Cosby, who produced "Uptight" (1965) and "I Was Made to Love Her" (1967).[59] Clarence Paul, mentor for the sightless Stevie and cowriter-producer of records for Marvin, Martha, and the Marvelettes, produced several middle-of-the-road tunes for Stevie, including a cover of Bob Dylan's "Blowing in the Wind" (1966).

Berry Gordy produced "Shotgun" (1965) for the soul label artist Jr. Walker and the All Stars who came to Motown with former Moonglows member Harvey Fuqua. Harvey became head of artist development, but produced records for Jr. Walker & the All Stars and, with Johnny Bristol, duets for Marvin Gaye and Tammi Terrell, including "Ain't No

Mountain High Enough" and "Your Precious Love" (1967), both written by Nick Ashford and Valerie Simpson, one of the premier writer-producer teams of Phase III.

Phase III

As Motown entered the third and final phase of the Detroit era, new sound concepts emerged amidst key personnel changes. Mickey Stevenson, Harvey Fuqua, and Clarence Paul had all left the company by the end of 1967, the same year that Supremes' Florence Ballard was replaced by Cindy Birdsong. In 1968, H-D-H left Motown. With H-D-H gone, Top 10 hits would cease for the Four Tops until 1970, when Smokey Robinson and Frank Wilson teamed up to write "Still Water (Love)," Martha & the Vandellas never returned *to* the Top 10.

Diana Ross & the Supremes, the group's new name after Flo left, recorded three number-one hits by 1970, the most unique of which was "Love Child" (1968). Produced by a new team that called themselves The Clan, "Love Child," in stark contrast to earlier Supremes material, delivers messages against teen pregnancy and illegitimacy. Diana left the group in 1970 for a solo career at Motown, and she hit number one with a dramatic remake of "Ain't No Mountain High Enough," previously recorded by Marvin Gaye and Tammi Terrell, written and produced by Ashford and Simpson. Marvin and Tammi, with Ashford and Simpson as their primary writers and producers, would become the most successful duet ever assembled by Motown, but that all ended when Tammi died in 1970 from a brain tumor.

Dennis Edwards replaced David Ruffin, who in 1968 was dismissed from the Temptations. Barrett Strong joined Norman Whitfield as the Temptations' cowriter, replacing the departed Eddie Holland. Under Whitfield and Strong, the Temptations became Motown's leading hit act at the end of the 1960s. Their "Cloud Nine" (1968), Motown's first Grammy winner, was also the first in a series of "psychedelic soul" records that represented a complete departure from anything Motown had previously released. But Norman had already tested new waters with the mystical sounding "I Heard It through the Grapevine" (1968), recorded by Marvin Gaye, which contrasts with the gospel-based version of the same song released by Gladys Knight and the Pips in 1967. Norman's Phase III work delved; into social themes with songs like "War" (Edwin Starr, 1970), "Ball of Confusion" (Temptations, 1970), and "Smiling Faces" (Undisputed Truth, 1971).

Marvin Gaye and Stevie Wonder were among the few Motown artists who were also writers. Both Marvin and Stevie would reach new levels of independence in 1971 as artist-writer-producers, like Smokey Robinson, with concept albums. For Marvin, it was *What's Going On,* a social theme-based project that became Motown's largest selling album. For Stevie, it was *Where I'm Coming From,* which, although far less successful than Marvin's work, provided a prelude to several Grammy-winning albums produced by Stevie over the next few years.

In 1969, Motown launched the Rare Earth label, named after the White psychedelic rock group signed to the label, a move that expanded its audience base. But the Jackson 5's signing that year was a far more substantial audience development endeavor. With members ranging from ages 11 to 18, the Jackson 5 enabled the company to reach a new generation of teenagers and a new pre-teen audience. Motown formed a songwriter-production group named The Corporation to produce youth-oriented tunes like "I Want You Back," "ABC," and "The Love You Save," all number-one hits released in 1970. The Jackson 5 would become the company's new top hit-making act of the early 1970s, as Motown moved west.

Motown's West Coast operations, based in Los Angeles, actually opened in 1966 as an effort to increase the company's presence in visual media. Movie and TV opportunities certainly did escalate after the move, and so did West Coast recording activities. While Hitsville remained Studio A until it closed in 1972, more and more records were made, sometimes in part, on the West Coast and other locations. Phase III repertoire, then, includes a mixture of records recorded at Hitsville and at other places, some using Detroit musicians and others using musicians from other cities, including L.A. The differences are subtle but significant, especially given my attempt here to define the Motown sound as a Detroit phenomenon.

Conclusion

When Motown announced that its headquarters were moving to Los Angeles, local citizens felt that the company had "abandoned Detroit."[60] Some local DJs boycotted by halting airplay of Motown's records. Motown's presence in its hometown had manifested a sense of ownership among Detroiters. But company vice president and general manager Amos Wilder said that moving into "the creative center of the entertainment world" was "simply a matter of sound business judgment, economics and logistics."[61]

Some members of Motown's Detroit roster chose not to move to L.A.; others were not invited. Jamerson was the only Funk Brother invited, but by the mid-1970s his career ended, primarily due to his problems with alcohol and depression. Top hit-making acts from Detroit Phases II and III made the transition to L.A., but most had left the company by the early 1980s. As examples, only the Temptations, who had just returned after three years with another label, and solo acts Smokey Robinson, Diana Ross, and Marvin Gaye remained to represent the Detroit era in a 1980 roster that included Rick James, Mary Jane Girls, Commodores, High Energy, Dazz Band, and DeBarge. The Commodores did quite well in the hit category, but as a company, Motown's hit-making fervor had diminished. Gordy saw L.A. as a move upward and outward into screen-based media. But he would later admit that while the company achieved some, though moderate, success in the TV and movie business, "we would have been better off with the record thing if we had stayed in Detroit."[62]

In 1988, Berry sold Motown to Boston Ventures and MCA Records, thus ending nearly 30 years of independent Black ownership and beginning the label's trek among several international, media conglomerates. Dutch-owned Polygram bought Motown in 1993. Seagram, which owned Universal Studios, bought Polygram in 1998, and in 2000, France-based Vivendi bought Seagram, making Motown a division of its Universal Music Group.

Throughout changes in music style, personnel, and ownership, Detroit remains the model for what Motown is believed to be about. At the dawn of the Polygram purchase, CEO Jheryl Busby brought Berry Gordy back as chairman emeritus of Motown's board of directors.[63] Andre Harrell, Motown CEO for only one year, proposed to "lead Motown Records back to glory and back to its roots" by reestablishing the assembly line artist development model, recruiting Detroit talent, and opening a Detroit office.[64] "Can the new Motown recapture the old magic?" read a *CNN News* headline amidst the company's fortieth anniversary celebration. Long-time company employee Georgia Ward claims that "you can't recapture that full impact of the 1960s" but "there are things that can be done to remind people what Motown was all about."[65] In 2004, company management seemed to have attempted just that.

In 2004, Motown.com provided two windows, visually situated side by side and linked, into the Motown legacy. The *Classic Motown* site, loosely defined *to* include DeBarge and the Commodores, reminds us of the music and legends who shaped the past. *Motown Now,* subtitled "The legacy continues …," gives us an overview of Motown's activities in 2004.[66] The past and present intersect on this site, as Stevie Wonder, the Temptations, and Smokey Robinson are listed amidst newer acts like Brian McKnight, Erykah Badu, India.Arie, and former Doobie Brothers lead singer Michael McDonald, whose recording output includes classic covers like "Ain't No Mountain High Enough."

The Motown legacy continues, but it is based upon the works of Berry Gordy and his employees during the Detroit era. The body of music that they recorded remains very much a part of the world's mediascape, integrated as sound and subject in numerous movies, used in radio and TV commercials to sell various products to the masses, celebrated in televised anniversary specials, written about in books, covered in live performances and recordings by newer Motown and non-Motown artists, sampled in digitally produced music and hip-hop, and digitally remastered for sale in albums and boxed sets. Music of Motown Detroit, now all representing a broader definition of classic Motown, still has mass appeal.

Berry's vision of Motown was broadly focused on reaching the masses, and he had the ability and resources to make it happen. The seed was planted in his middle-class, Detroit-based family, where he learned skills and values necessary for success in business. Post–World War II Detroit provided a cosmopolitan environment in which Berry and the *next* generation of Black residents could become key members of a vibrant and diverse musical culture and gain *access* to media that would afford others access to their talents and creativity. As a high-profile, Black-owned company whose objective was to sell records to the mainstream in a White leadership-dominated industry, Motown surely faced obstacles. But through image, sound, and marketing strategies, Motown became situated as a company with music for everyone. And while some have questioned the degree to which Motown represents its Black roots, the success that the company achieved bolstered Black representation in the music industry by creating a high-quality product that could be embraced across racial and cultural lines and transcend generations.

Yesterday Is Gone,
But the Past Lives On

By Howard Sounes

The man's walk was weirdly jaunty, like a puppet on invisible strings. His head seemed to move to its own rhythm. He wore ill-fitting clothes, which made him look out of place in a fashionable district of Manhattan, almost the garb of a homeless person. If one looked closely, however, the clothes appeared new. If one looked closer still at the sallow, half-bearded face, this slightly built, middle-aged man seemed familiar. Under the hat there was the distinctive hooked nose, the delicate features framed with wisps of beard. When he went to scratch his nose, his fingernails were very lonwwg and dirty. When he looked to cross the street, his eyes were seen to be vivid blue, bluer than robins' eggs.

"You're Bob Dylan!"

People often recognized him, yelling out excited greetings, not quite believing they were seeing a legend on the street. Bob hated it when they grabbed at him, but he was at heart a polite Midwesterner and he did not mind saying hello. When he spoke—just to say, perhaps, "Hey, man, how are ya *doin'?*"—his voice was so distinctive, with words pushed up from his diaphragm in bursts and then seemingly squeezed out through his almost comical nose, emphasizing the *wrong word* in a sentence and clipping other words short, it could be only Bob Dylan.

Bob came to the corner of 57th Street and Lexington Avenue and entered a small club, Tommy Makem's Irish Pavilion. Tommy Makem was an old friend from the early 1960s when Bob was learning his trade, a soft-spoken Irishman who had performed traditional folk songs with The Clancy Brothers in the clubs of Greenwich Village, New York. Makem had not seen Bobby—as he knew him—in many years. "There was no one with him, no driver, no companion, no nothing. He was just on his own," he recalls.

Makem settled Bob at a quiet table, where he would not be seen by other patrons. Then Makem fetched his banjo and got on stage for the show. He performed the old ballads Bob loved, hearty songs like "Brennan on the Moor" and the wistful "Will You Go, Lassie, Go."

There was a break before the second set and Makem went over to where Bob was having something to eat and drink. "If you feel like singing a song, let me know," he said. But Bob preferred to sit quietly alone. He was enjoying himself greatly. The Irish Pavilion reminded him of his early days in New York and the people he had met there, artists like John Lee Hooker, "Cisco" Houston, and "Big" Joe Williams. These men were monumental in his mind; they had informed and influenced his entire career.

After the audience drifted away, Makem pulled up a chair and he and Bob talked as the staff swept up around their chairs. It was the past Bob wanted to discuss—old friends from the old clubs, people he had not seen in thirty years, and old memories like the evening he ran up to the Irishman on Sixth Avenue excited about a song he had written. "God it must have been 2:30 or 3 o'clock in the morning," says Makem. "Stopping [to] sing me a long murder ballad that he had written to the tune of some song he had heard Liam [Clancy] and myself singing. There would be twenty verses in it, and he would sing the whole lot for you. I thought, God, it's a very interesting thing this young fella's doing."

A Few weeks after Bob's unexpected visit to the Irish Pavilion, in the spring of 1992, Tommy Makem received a letter from Bob's record company, Sony Music. Makem was invited to perform at a concert celebrating Bob's thirty years as a recording artist (although, in fact, he had been making records for thirty-one). Bob had not said a word about it when they met, but that was typical of him; he was never much of a talker. Makem was not sure at first what sort of show this would be. From the low-key way in which Bob padded around town on his own, dressed like a bum, one might think his days as a major star were over, and that a celebration of his career would be held in a modest theater somewhere with a few old friends. "It was extremely glamorous and much more of a huge event than I realized," says Makem. "It was gigantic."

The venue for Bob's "Thirtieth Anniversary Concert Celebration," as it was called, was Madison Square Garden, the huge sports arena in Manhattan. When it was announced that Bob would appear with some of the most famous names in music, eighteen thousand seats sold within an hour. This was despite the fact promoters were charging between $50 and $150 a seat, record prices for a concert of its kind. When Makem arrived at the Rihga Royal Hotel, where the musicians were staying, he discovered that the guest list included not only old folkies but superstars such as Eric Clapton and George Harrison, who were devoted friends of Bob. For ten days prior to the show, limousines ferried the artists between the hotel and the Kaufman Astoria Studios for rehearsals. Bob dressed down, for rehearsals, his sweatshirt hood over his head, muttering that he was not sure the concert was a good idea: "It'll be like goin' to my own *funeral.*"

Still, there was great excitement on the evening of Friday, October 16, 1992, as the lights in the Garden came up to reveal a huge stage in the shape of a Mexican hacienda. The house band, Booker T. and the M.G.s, began the show with one of Bob's songs of Christian faith, "Gotta Serve Somebody." Then, for more than three hours, they backed a succession of stars selected to represent the range of Dylan's influence, from folk artists;

country artists, such as Willie Nelson and Johnny Cash; African-American stars who had covered his songs, like Stevie Wonder and the O'Jays; and younger rockers, including Eddie Vedder and Tom Petty and The Heart-breakers, who toured with Bob in the 1980s. All performed Bob Dylan songs.

At times the concert was a salutary reminder of how many years had passed since the salad days of Dylan and his contemporaries. Carolyn Hester—one of the beauties of the folk revival—now had the white hair of a grandmother. The Band, the extraordinary group Bob toured with in 1965–66, and again in 1974, had been five rugged young men with full, dark beards. In the intervening years, guitarist Robbie Robertson had become estranged from the group, and pianist Richard Manuel had killed himself. The remaining three members now appeared much changed as they walked on stage to perform the song "When I Paint My Masterpiece." The beards of drummer Levon Helm and keyboardist Garth Hudson were gray, and Helm looked frail. Rick Danko, the once skinny bass guitarist, was bloated after years of drug abuse. "It was a shock," says Joel Bernstein, who had worked for Bob and The Band in their heyday. "When the lights came up [you] could hear people go, 'Uh!'"

In comparison, Richie Havens looked much like he had years ago when he and The Band were among the stars of the original Woodstock Festival. He brought the audience to its feet with a tremendous cover of "Just Like a Woman." "I was greatly pleased to be invited and to be able to sing a song I still do on stage," he says. "Bob is one of my mental mentors—an utterly shy person, except on stage [which] is what most people perceive as [his] mysteriousness."

True to form, Bob was secreted in his dressing room, watching the show on closed-circuit television. Numerous celebrities, including John McEnroe, Martin Scorsese, and Carly Simon, were drifting around backstage, craning their necks to catch sight of one of the few people in the world more famous than themselves. Ronnie Wood of The Rolling Stones passed around a 180-proof bottle of vodka. Liam Clancy took a swig. He had flown in from Ireland with his brothers to perform "When the Ship Comes In" with Tommy Makem. "Christ, if we have any more of that we'll never sing tonight," he said.

Outside in the auditorium members of the audience were expressing themselves in a forthright way if anybody came on stage that they did not like. Singer Sophie B. Hawkins got short shrift. The president of Sony Music was booed. Kris Kristofferson nervously introduced an artist whose name, he said, was synonymous with courage. Irish singer Sinead O'Connor, stick-thin with head shaved, stepped up to the microphone. She had recently been embroiled in controversy over a television appearance during which she denounced the Pope. There was fierce booing. Booker T. repeatedly played the opening chords of "I Believe in You," the song she had rehearsed, but she froze.

"Get off!" people shouted.

O'Connor made a cutting motion with her hand, ordered her microphone turned up, and spat out the words of the song "War." It was a genuine act of protest and, for a few moments, she silenced the hecklers. Then it dawned on the audience that she was not singing a Bob Dylan song at all. "War" was by Bob Marley. She was howled off stage; she was so upset she threw up. Artists watched her humiliation with surprise. "It was outrageous," says blues artist John Hammond Jr., son of Bob's first record producer. "I couldn't believe the New York audience would be so unopen to her view."

Neil Young came on after the Sinead O'Connor debacle, seeming a bit nervous. But the crowd loved him, especially when he performed "All Along the Watchtower" in the incandescent style of Jimi Hendrix, who had had a hit with it in 1968. (Curiously, many of Bob's songs were more familiar to a mass audience as cover versions than in their original recordings.) "This song's for you, Bob," shouted Young. "Thanks for having *Bobfest.*" Roger McGuinn of The Byrds also received a warm reception when he performed "Mr. Tambourine Man." The Byrds had a number-one hit with the song in the summer of 1965, and the distinctive sound of McGuinn's twelve-string guitar and his tremulous, slightly spacey vocal invoked a profound nostalgia. He sounded just like he had all those years ago. "It was joyful," he says. "I was singing to God."

When the stage was cleared, George Harrison made a long-overdue announcement. "Some of you may call him Bobby. Some of you may call him Zimmy. I call him Lucky," he said in his distinctive Liverpudlian accent, recalling their brief-lived band, The Traveling Wilburys. "Ladies and gentlemen, please welcome BOB DYLAN!"

The audience shrieked and whistled, straining to catch their first glimpse of the legend. A little man trotted out into the converging violet spotlights, appearing to many surprisingly short and skinny. The applause grew even louder. Dressed in a black silk suit, his white shirt done up tight, Bob looked like a disheveled waiter. He had not shaved, or maybe even slept, for several days. His skin was pale and his face was deeply lined. His once luxuriant curly hair was lank against his sweaty forehead. He moved to the microphone and began strumming his acoustic guitar with his long, nicotine-yellow fingernails. It might be a $5 million show, but he was going to perform solo, as he'd done in coffeehouses decades ago. The tune he strummed was rudimentary and he did not attempt to converse with his audience, other than to say a casual "Thanks everybody." When he started playing, though, the attention of all eighteen thousand people were locked onto this extraordinarily charismatic man. Beyond the front rows of special guests—which were all the nearsighted singer could make out—was a vast cavern of people, a cavern studded with the rapid flashing of camera bulbs.

He began with "Song to Woody," the first important song he wrote. It was a tribute to his first hero, Woody Guthrie, the father of American folk music. When he wrote it, Bob was nineteen, affecting a world-weariness beyond his years. At fifty-two, his battered features and weary voice betrayed a man who had been on an extraordinary journey. Woody's daughter, Nora, sat in front. She began to weep as Bob sang about her father, who died in 1967, worn away by Huntington's chorea. "If dad was on a river, there were a lot of streams and estuaries coming in and out of that river. That was a very big river that he was on," she explains. "Bob went right in and he then became captain of that same river. My father faded, and Bob took it over, and I've always felt that he's always been a pretty true captain."

After "Song to Woody," Bob ripped into "It's Alright, Ma (I'm Only Bleeding)," bending at the knees and twisting his body as he thrashed the steel strings of his guitar. Guest artists crowded around the perimeter of the stage to watch him. Ronnie Wood and drummer Anton Fig peeped from behind the drum riser. "He was just on fire," says Fig.

Roger McGuinn, Tom Petty, Eric Clapton, Neil Young, and George Harrison joined Bob for a singalong version of "My Back Pages." Then everybody crowded onto the stage for "Knockin' on Heaven's Door," recently a hit for Guns N' Roses. At the end, Bob stood center stage, applauded not only by the audience but also by the great stars clustered around him. Ronnie Wood and George Harrison sang "For He's a Jolly Good Fellow." Bob stood awkwardly, apparently not knowing quite what to do with his hands, not knowing what words to say. Carolyn Hester picked up a small spray of flowers that had been thrown on stage and, encouraged by Neil Young, gave them to Bob, hugging him quickly and pecking him on the cheek. She feared he might not like it, even though they were old friends. "I thought, I'll be thrown out for that, but nobody threw me out. I was so glad. And he smiled. He gave a little smile. Everybody was amazed." It was the first time Bob had smiled all evening.

It was clear during the planning of the event that there had to be an after-show party, somewhere Sony could entertain Bob, celebrity guests, and music-industry people. The Waldorf-Astoria hotel had been a possibility early on. But then Bob said, "I don't want to go there. I'm going to Tommy Makem's place." So plans were changed and the little folk club was hired for the night. It held only a hundred and fifty people, and first priority went to Bob's friends and notable guest stars. Fans and press watched them arrive. Then there were the band musicians, their wives and girlfriends. There was little room left for record-company executives and the remaining celebrities who wanted to get in. In fact, there was no room for anybody else. "You can't come in unless you have a ticket," Tommy Makem was told when he returned from the show.

"I own this pub," Makem informed the security man. But he still had to find his ticket.

Inside, Bob was ensconced like a gypsy king at a long rectangular table in a corner of the Irish Pavilion, a glass of white wine in front of him. Around him, at smaller tables, sat his courtiers—close friends including George Harrison, who was drinking tea, Ronnie Wood, and Eric Clapton, who was learning to play the Irish tin whistle. Others were escorted to Bob's table one at a time to pay their respects. "Bob Dylan, King of Rock 'n' Roll, was what was going on that night," says Carolyn Hester. "He would summon various ones of us."

When Liam Clancy came up to thank Bob for inviting The Clancy Brothers to perform, Bob asked him to sit awhile. Clancy said he and his brothers were thinking of making an album of Bob's songs, in traditional Irish folk style. It would be a way of giving the songs back to him. "Man, would you do that? *Would* you?" asked Bob.

"Would you object?"

"Liam, you don't realize, do you, man?" asked Bob, who had relaxed a good deal. He was alternating white wine with Guinness, and was drinking steadily. "You're my fucking hero, man." Bob's acceptance by the folk artists he looked up to when he first came to New York from Minnesota was the fulfillment of a lifelong dream, and he beamed at the portly, fifty-six-year-old Irishman. "He ceased being the star and he was the insecure little boy I first knew," says Clancy. "He was looking for affirmation [then], and he was still looking after all these years, after all the stardom and acclaim and everything. … I thought it was lovely that, at that stage of his life, he could admit it."

Clancy told Bob he had not looked comfortable on stage. He had heard persistent rumors that Bob had a drug problem. Bob's strange behavior in recent years—performing in hooded sweatshirts and hats that hid his face, and singing songs in ways that made them almost unrecognizable—seemed to indicate something was wrong. But his reply was surprising. "Hey, man, I suffer from claustrophobia," he said. "I just wanted to be out [of there]. I can't stand that much time indoors anymore."

"You were breaking out in a cold sweat."

"I don't want to be in that situation anymore, but I have to do it."

Clancy then plucked up the courage to ask a question that had bothered him for years. When they were young men in Greenwich Village, the Irishman had a girlfriend named Cathy. He suspected Cathy had had an affair with Bob, who had always been an incorrigible womanizer. "Bobby, were you screwing Cathy?" he asked.

Bob looked at him and Clancy knew he was going to get the truth at last. "Man, she loved you," he replied, apparently unable to tell a lie. "But she was so lonesome. I gotta admit, man, I did comfort her."

Clancy was hurt. It was painful to think that the love letters Cathy had sent him when he was on the road with his brothers were written when she was snuggled up in New York with baby-faced Bobby Dylan. But they were both too old to fight. Instead, Clancy picked up a guitar and thrust it at Bob, reminding him that in the old days, at the Lion's Head or the White Horse Tavern, they always passed a guitar at the end of an evening. "Come on, here's a guitar. Sing me a song."

"I can't do that anymore, man."

"Are you too big a fucking star for that? Don't pull that shit with me, Bobby. Sing a fuckin' song now, because that's what we've done, always."

Reluctantly, Bob took the guitar and began singing "Roddy McCorley," a traditional song he had learned from The Clancy Brothers. But when it came to his friend's turn to sing a verse, he dried. "Jesus, would you believe it, I was so drunk I couldn't remember it?" From the other end of the table, Ronnie Wood piped up:

> *Up the narrow street he stepped*
> *Smiling, proud and young*

The guitar was passed to George Harrison who sang the next verse. Keyboard player Ian McLagan, who toured with Bob in 1984, jerked awake and contributed a lewd ditty he had learned from Steve Marriott, of The Faces, when they were playing pubs in London:

I love my wife
I love her dearly
I love the hole she pisses through

Before long, everybody was laughing, singing songs, reciting snatches of poetry, and slapping one another on the back. "Drink is a great leveler and we all had our arms around each other, and we were in a huddle, like we were when we were young," says Clancy. "We could have been a rugby team at the end of the evening." They drank until morning light came through the windows. At seven A.M. Tommy Makem's sons announced it was time they were all off home to their beds. Fans and press were gone. So were the limousines, the chauffeurs sent home hours ago. They would have to get taxis.

With his custom-made stage suit crumpled and smelling of beer and cigarettes, Bob looked relaxed, much happier than the embarrassed figure on stage at the Garden. When the cabs came, he hugged his friends, thanked them for coming, and allowed himself to be guided to a car. He was smiling broadly as he was driven away into the early morning traffic.

He would sleep until late afternoon. When he woke, in the dusk of a missed day, he would have to turn his mind back to his tour, the so-called Never-Ending Tour of a hundred or so shows a year. He was due to give a concert at the University of Delaware in a couple of days. After that, there were concerts booked until Christmas. They were mostly small theaters, and the people who came to see him probably would not buy his new album; nowadays people came to the shows, like they visited museums, to experience history. His personal life was in ruins. He was getting divorced for the second time, from a marriage he had managed to keep hidden. He was concerned for the future of the daughter he had fathered by his secret, second wife, and mindful of the large sums of money he would have to hand over for the settlement. The show at the Garden would help, but there was a massive overhead and he was not sure how the CD and video spin-offs would sell. Judging by the performance of his recent albums, they might sink without a trace. Maybe it would help if he could talk about his problems, but he was an inward man, with no confidants. Having been famous all his adult life, he felt he could trust only himself.

These were the peculiar pressures of being Bob Dylan. Yet for one night he had been Bobby again, the carefree boy who had come out of the Midwest to make his fortune in New York, the boy who had hung out in the Village with Tommy Makem, Liam Clancy, and Carolyn Hester. He had been happy then, as happy as he has ever been. "A very lonely man," says Clancy, of his old friend. "So few people left in the world, I suppose, that he [can] talk to."

Haight-Ashbury in the Summer of Loss

By Mikal Gilmore

On the unseasonably clear morning of January 14, 1967, American poets Allen Ginsberg and Gary Snyder led a prayer march in a clockwise circle around the polo field in Golden Gate Park. They were preparing the field as they walked—blessing it in a Hindu rite of purification—for an assembly of pilgrims to be known as the Gathering of the Tribes for a Human Be-In, the first major gathering of the hippie counterculture. By the early afternoon, the grounds were filled with twenty thousand celebrants, moving to the sway of loud electric music, the throb of LSD, the entrancement of newly discovered fraternity. The planners of this event—mainly the editors of San Francisco's underground newspaper *The Oracle*—intended the event for anyone who cared to attend, though primarily it would draw the psychedelic community from the Haight district and the nearby San Francisco State College. The organizers recruited the Bay Area's best bands—among them the Grateful Dead, Jefferson Airplane, Country Joe and the Fish, Big Brother and the Holding Company, Quicksilver Messenger Service and the Loading Zone—all playing for free. They also invited several of the counterculture's best known figures, such as philosopher and psychologist Alan Watts, antiwar activist Jerry Rubin, poets Ginsberg, Snyder, Michael McClure and Lenore Kandel (whose poem "To Fuck with Love" was at the heart of an obscenity charge she was facing in San Francisco), and controversial psychedelic gurus Timothy Leary and Richard Alpert. *The Oracle* also extended a special invitation to radical activists at the University of California at Berkeley, who for some time had regarded hippies and their fast-emerging alternative culture as passive and hedonistic, and too withdrawn from political interests. This gathering, its heralds believed, would show that these two disparate but sympathetic clans could meet on a common plane in mutual accord. Allen Cohen, *The Oracle's* editor, anticipated the day in these terms: "A union of love and activism previously separated by categorical dogma and label mongering will finally occur ecstatically ... so that a revolution of form can be filled."

Mikal Gilmore, "Haight-Ashbury in the Summer of Loss," *Stories Done: Writings on the 1960s and Its Discontents*, pp. 84-103. Copyright © 2008 by Mikal Gilmore. Reprinted with permission by Free Press, a division of Simon & Schuster, Inc.

The Diggers, a Haight-Ashbury–based loose collection of street-theater provocateurs and community guardians, served turkey sandwiches spiced with LSD, with both the meat and the drugs supplied by Stanley Owsley, maker of the most powerful and most refined psychedelics commonly available. He also provided "White Lightning" acid in large quantities, for the occasion. The musicians played loud and commandingly; the Bay Area's notorious Hell's Angels looked after, and played with, the children who had wandered off in the crowd; the spiritual and inspirational leaders held forth to little real attention; and through it all, two policemen sat on horseback calmly watching, as various illegal drugs were in open use around the field. The Be-In ran from 1:00 to 5:00 p.m., and when it was over the organizers and volunteers swept the field of all debris. They were glowing. The Gathering of the Tribes for a Human Be-In had demonstrated that America's outsiders were considerable in their numbers and peaceful in their intent. It showed that new mind-sets were finding a footing in the land, that there was a future to be lived in a collective dream. Foremost, the Be-In announced that San Francisco was again a frontier town, this time for an unanticipated kind of frontier.

Watching it all unfold throughout the day was Emmett Grogan, the Diggers' best-known doctrinaire and idealist. All he saw was a sham and massive trouble to come. In his autobiography, *Ringolevio,* Grogan wrote that he was angry with the Be-In's organizers for "drawing a disproportionate number of kids to the district … who fell for the Love Hoax and expected to live comfortably poor and expected to take their place in the district's kingdom of love." Though Allen Ginsberg had a brighter disposition, there was a moment, he later remembered, when looking at the Be-In's multitudes in their seeming incorruptibility, a shudder passed through him. Ginsberg turned to fellow poet Lawrence Ferlinghetti, who ran San Francisco's City Lights bookstore, and said: "What if we're all wrong?"

It was only the first month in a year of expected miracles.

In 1967 the San Francisco Bay Area would be the epicenter of a cultural and political upheaval that challenged not just how people viewed America's purposes and standards, but also how they understood the meanings of life, art and the mind. California had long been the American location, in myth and history, where the bold and the hopeful migrated to realize ultimate visions—that luminous shore where they might find new starts or dead ends, the place where the American dream hit its last edge. San Francisco was the twist in that dream—a city with opium, whores and outlawry in its past, an image as alluring as it was notorious. It was there, in the 1950s, in the city's North Beach district, that Allen Ginsberg wrote *Howl*—an epic poem about the discarded people and promises of America, and the fears that lay behind and ahead for all—and it was there he first read the poem aloud, at a gathering that included Gary Snyder and Jack Kerouac, author of the not yet published novel *On the Road. Howl* was a shocking poem, a monumental piece of resistance but also of new prospects: It opened not just new doors in America's literature and public arts, it also pounded at the nation's ideals of civilization. Nobody had ever said anything like it before; as a result, it changed what could be said. It also helped make

North Beach the putative home for the Beats—the hard-living literary and philosophical movement that Ginsberg, Kerouac and William Burroughs had helped define in the late 1940s. North Beach remained largely an enclave of poets and Beats until the mid-1960s, when a younger bohemian crowd—more colorfully dressed, with longer hair and affection for the rock & roll that followed in the wake of the Beatles—began mingling in the area. The Beats called these newcomers, somewhat derisively, "hippies," which is to say diminutive hipsters. The hippies drew certain traits from the Beats—including looser attitudes about sex, plus predilections for marijuana and improvisational music—though they were decidedly more optimistic about the potential of the era. Around that same time, as strip joints and new restaurants drove up rents in North Beach, the hippies began moving to Haight-Ashbury, a largely once black but now moribund neighborhood with plenty of affordable Victorian houses, near Golden Gate Park and not far from San Francisco State College.

Two key exploits—both born outside San Francisco—had decisive bearing on how the Haight would develop its character and purposes. The first took shape in the South Bay, in La Honda and Palo Alto, where in 1965 author Ken Kesey was conducting psychedelic group events known as the Acid Tests. In 1959 Kesey had volunteered to take part in a local Veteran Hospital's experimental program studying the effects of psychomimetic drugs—that is, drugs believed to induce brief and harmless bouts of psychosis. The experiments familiarized Kesey with LSD, a drug that delivered what he believed to be a radical way of looking at life with a new hallucinatory and ecstatic perspective. For the next few years, Kesey made himself a pioneer for LSD, and with his crew of cohorts, the Merry Pranksters, he began staging large parties to see what would happen when people took the drug in settings where there were no rules. The Warlocks—later called the Grateful Dead—became the house band for these events. In those hours, Jerry Garcia would later say, the Dead's music "had a real sense of proportion to the event"—which is to say that sometimes the group's playing would seem to overshadow the event, and at other times it would function as commentary or backdrop to the action of the event itself. Either way, neither the Pranksters nor the Dead were the stars of the party. Instead, the parties' central force was formed from the union of the music and musicians with the audience, and the spirit and shape of what was happening from moment to moment—which meant that there was a blur between the performers, the event and the audience.

Kesey conducted the Acid Tests at various sites over the next year (LSD was still legal to consume in California until October 1966). Then, in late 1966, as he was facing marijuana possession charges (Kesey eventually served six months in prison), the outlaw author announced that it was time for the emerging counterculture he had helped foster to stop taking psychedelics. Along with the Pranksters, he conducted a Graduation Day event for LSD users on Halloween 1966, at a San Francisco warehouse. Most of the San Franciscans now involved in psychedelics felt that Kesey was trying to control something he could no longer control. LSD was now a vital part of the burgeoning Haight-Ashbury community.

The other development that helped form the Haight's early temperament took place at a Western-style dance hall, the Red Dog Saloon. In June 1965 a San Francisco band, the Charlatans, took up residence at the saloon. Their easygoing attitude and meandering performances, as they played sometimes under LSD's influence, set another model for public psychedelic gatherings, one much less tense and sardonic than Kesey's. In San Francisco in October 1965 a couple of Red Dog veterans, now calling themselves the Family Dog, staged an evening of dancing and bands at the Longshore man's Hall. The event, called A Tribute to Dr. Strange, featured the Charla tans, Jefferson Airplane and the Great Society. The event spontaneously fused the lenient spirit of the Acid Tests with Red Dog's focus on dancing and proved a pivotal occasion in the psychedelic scene's history. Over the next two years, San Francisco dance ballrooms—primarily the Avalon and the Fillmore—became not merely a central metaphor for Haight-Ashbury's reinvention of community, but also a fundamental enactment of it. "In the early days," Big Brother and the Holding Company's Sam Andrew later said, "the audience and the bands were on the same plane … It felt like everyone was joined by this electric current, and they were all part of it." In *Beneath the Diamond Sky: Haight-Ashbury: 1965-1970,* by Barney Hoskyns, Haight-Ashbury community leader David Simpson expanded on this idea:

> "It is very important to know how closely the alternative community of San Francisco identified with the music of specific musicians . … They were our bands, they were our musicians. Neither they nor we felt the distinction between the artists and the people, and it gave the music great strength . … It was a wonderful inspired sense of oneness."

The bands that emerged in this setting—including Jefferson Airplane, Big Brother and the Holding Company, Quicksilver Messenger Service and Country Joe and the Fish—were made up largely of musicians who had come up playing in the Bay Area's numerous folk music venues. The folk crowd had been notoriously dismissive of rock & roll; they saw it as unserious and decadent, not at all committed to social or political concerns. But after the arrival of the Beatles in 1964 and Bob Dylan's transition to electric music in 1965—and after the Los Angeles band the Byrds exhibited a mellifluent and rousing example of folk rock that also included such disparate elements as Indian ragas and John Coltrane–style modal jazz—Bay Area folk musicians began to see how electric music could incorporate substantive themes and poetic language. "Rather than being some drug-induced thing," said Country Joe and the Fish guitarist Barry Melton in *Beneath the Diamond Sky,* "it was really a bunch of serious folkie musicologists who played bluegrass and blues joining forces with guys who played at the edge of town, chewed gum and couldn't put two sentences together—the rock & roll players." But as psychedelics made their way steadily into the music scene, bands couldn't help but adapt to the drugs' effects as they played together. LSD changed musicians' sense of continuity—a player could follow a melody wherever it might lead, altering the shape and function of the music's harmonic structure, transforming it into a background of reverie for improvisations—a process that the Grateful Dead's Jerry Garcia once described as "something like ordered chaos." LSD could also alter one's sense of time: The perceived moment, and not its true measurement, mattered most. In performances that sometimes meant a single song's exploration might stretch for a half hour or even much longer.

The best circumstance for hearing this new daring music was in the ballrooms. Promoter Chet Helms had taken over the Family Dog and was presenting shows regularly at the Avalon, and Bill Graham—a gruff organizer resented by some, but who fought fiercely for the community's rights to gather and hear music—ran the Fillmore. In these venues' darkened and large spaces, loud and propulsive sounds combined with vivid and kinetic images, making for an immersive environment. In particular, the dance hall scene's famous light show displays—in which artists and technicians mixed colored liquids in glass pans and swirled the blends in overhead projections, in improvised motions that fit the music—were an indispensable part of the inclusive experience.

This new music, and the life it found in the concert halls, played a considerable part in the Haight-Ashbury's early growth, and that success rapidly became a problem. In the late 1960s rock & roll was more than a powerful and strange form of music—it was a sign of an unprecedented cultural divide, marked largely along generational lines. The parents of the nation's youth had expected their children to affirm the values of a post–World War II America that was intent on expanding its prosperity and overcoming the threat of communist empire—even though it was the youth who would pay the bloodiest costs for the nation's war in Vietnam. But the youth were forging their own ideals of peace, tolerance, politics, aesthetics and community. Those ambitions were manifest in a grow- ing opposition to Vietnam involvement and in the desire to form a new culture—the counterculture—with its own ethics and practices.

San Francisco's city hall and media saw Haight-Ashbury foremost as a society of drug users and dealers, draft evaders and indolent freeloaders—a place to be watched, contained and deprecated. Two local headlines in 1967 declared: "Mayor Warns Hippies to Stay Out of Town" and "Supervisors Back War on Hippies." The police ratcheted up pressures, shutting down dances at the Fillmore and other locales when possible, while various other city officials tried to revoke dance hall licenses and succeeded in forbidding the attendance of youth under eighteen. Meantime, the press reported often and disapprovingly on what they saw as the hippies' weirdness. Finally, in October 1966, possession of LSD became illegal. San Francisco's youth culture—and others like it—had to take its central ritual underground.

It made for a paradox. San Francisco—in the case of both the Haight and the new music emanating from the city's ballrooms—was forging a model for a freewheeling, beneficent culture. "Let me see you get together." Love one another right now," Jefferson Airplane sang on its first album, and it wasn't an orgiastic bid. But because this new ideal of commonality worked outside received notions of civic duty and the sanctions of authority, it was seen as an ominous uprising. The community's only significant public advocate was

San Francisco Chronicle jazz critic Ralph J. Gleason (later a cofounder of *Rolling Stone*), who began covering the new music and the counterculture knowledgeably, and reported on the police harassment of Fillmore promoter Bill Graham as he tried to cope with the new under-eighteen rule. Gleason wrote: "Since the dances have started—almost exactly a year ago—the only trouble at the dance halls has been the police. … The trouble is, this society is terrified of youth, so it has been made illegal."

It certainly felt that way to many at the time. Haight-Ashbury and its integral psyche-delic community was an experiment, on a scale that had not been seen in America since the Mormons turned Nauvoo into a city-state in 1840s Illinois. Of course, the Mormons were driven from the state for their beliefs, and by the time 1967 rolled around in Haight-Ashbury, there were many who wanted the hippies to come to a similar end.

Truth be told, there never was a Summer of Love in 1967 San Francisco. If there was such a season, it was in that spring and summer stretch of 1966, when Haight-Ashbury was taking on the aspects of a town within a city, when shops like Ron and Jay Thelin's Psychedelic Shop were opening on Haight Street and an increasing and creative population was giving new life to a once fading district. As Charles Perry wrote in *The Haight-Ashbury: A History,* "To the people involved in psychedelics … a whole world now revolved around the Haight-Ashbury, and was plainly growing. … What was happening was so big it would wash … imperfections away or perhaps engulf them and transform them into unexpected benefits."

But by 1967, it was a different story. It's true the year had begun with the large and peaceful Human Be-In, but it had also started with the inauguration of a new governor, Ronald Reagan, who won election largely for condemning recalcitrant youth and promis-ing to come down hard on them. These two events were promises running in opposite directions, but what eventually happened to the Haight had nothing to do with promises. Dreams simply hit hard limits and bad faith. Indeed, Haight-Ashbury became a village of arguments after the Be-In. Already, in the year's early months, the district's population was denser, and an alarming amount of the new faces appeared to belong to high school–age runaways. But that was nothing compared to what was now anticipated. Both community leaders and police were predicting an influx of anything from fifty thousand to two hun-dred thousand visitors to the Haight by summer's end—numbers that, no matter how they finally tallied, could amount to a disaster.

The Diggers—the Haight's contrarian conscience—had been at odds with many of the Haight's leaders for some time. Police had stepped up drug arrests in Haight-Ashbury recently, and *The Oracle* and the hip merchants believed that opening a benevolent dia-logue with the police chief and patrolling officers would increase mutual empathy and help assuage the problem. One shop owner posted a sign in his window, urging people in the neighborhood to "Take a Cop to Dinner." The Diggers saw this as a message of useless appeasement. They issued a broadside through the Haight, stating: "And so, if you own anything or don't, take a cop to dinner this week and feed his power to judge the morality of San Francisco." The Diggers were now leveling much of the blame for the impending surge at the Haight Independent Proprietors (HIP), a merchants' association that had formed in November 1966. They also aimed disapproval at the psychedelic community's newspaper, *The Oracle,* and at some of the new culture's self-appointed spokesmen, such as Timothy Leary, whose resounding call to youth to drop out of social obligations and tune in to LSD's enlightenment, they believed, was irresponsible and intentionally guileless. The Diggers believed that all these contingents' various interests were commodifying the community and despoiling its original promise. Emmett Grogan and the other Diggers had envisioned Haight-Ashbury as a self-sustained local village with its own economy and with an ethos of self-invention. *The Oracle,* by contrast, envisioned little short of a global transformation (indeed, the paper enjoyed a worldwide readership of over one hundred thousand), with an event like the January Be-In serving as a lure to a nationwide immigration that would, in the Diggers' estimation, destroy Haight-Ashbury and everything it had been trying to achieve.

Some of what happened in the months leading up to the Summer of Love took on curious, even absurd, aspects. That was because the new psychedelic vogue not only could make money but was in fact changing how marketers were responding to trends. In *The Haight-Ashbury,* Charles Perry notes an advertising executive's comments to the *Washington Post:* "People all of a sudden are becoming aware of a segment of the population having an almost controlling effect on what is bought and not bought—as though it didn't exist last year. Industry is jumping up and down and saying, 'How can we get with it? What can we put in or copy?'" Which perhaps explains why the Gray Line Bus Company began a "San Francisco Haight-Ashbury District 'Hippie-Hop' Tour"—"the only foreign tour within the continental United States." At first the Haight's residents took the tour with good humor, but they soon began to resent tourists gawking rudely, as if hippies were a zoo exhibition. Early on, the Diggers commandeered one of the buses and drove it over to the Grateful Dead's house on Ashbury—a stop that Gray Line made a regular feature of the tours. Finally, residents began following the tours, sometimes holding up mirrors to the sightseers, sometimes pelting the buses with tomatoes. In May, Gray Line canceled the tours.

But the problem of how to handle the flood of newcomers and tourists that the Haight would unwittingly invite to its streets come summer was still pressing. In early February, the Diggers and the hip merchants met to discuss how to prepare for the incursion. The Diggers had already been working to establish spaces for overnight shelters—crash pads— for runaways and itinerants, and they were surprised to learn that all that HIP had planned was access to free legal advice and a job co-op. That set off the Diggers' Emmett Grogan, who launched into an invective, charging that HIP wasn't serious about their accountability. The Diggers, though, weren't alone in trying to prepare for a mass arrival. In the spring, Episcopal ministers asked the park commission to allow temporary camping in Golden Gate Park to avert a crisis. San Francisco Police Chief Thomas Cahill (the man who had first named the new movement the "Love Generation") shut down that possibility, saying, "Any encouragement … tending to attract still more undesirables to the problem areas of

San Francisco is a disservice to the community." The following day, San Francisco mayor John Shelley said he wanted any arriving hippies declared officially unwelcome.

Digger Peter Cohon (actor Peter Coyote) felt that though the young people arriving in the Haight that year were already encumbering the Diggers' resources, the collective felt they had no choice but to continue in their efforts. "The city" Coyote later said, "was ... telling all these kids—our age, a lot of them younger—to get lost. And our feeling was that they were our kids. You know? This was America; these were our kids." Certainly, the Diggers understood the hazards of sheltering runaways: It might expose the neighborhood to even greater police scrutiny, running the danger of more drug arrests. But nobody—not the Diggers, not the merchants and not the Haight's residents—was about to cooperate with the authorities in their hunt for runaways. Radical activist Abbie Hoffman, who for a time saw himself as a Digger, once likened runaways to "escaping slaves." Turning them in would undermine every principle that the hippie community had built itself on.

In May a twenty-four-hour resource, the Haight-Ashbury Switchboard, opened to help people find places to sleep or eat, and to guide them through crises. The following month, the around-the-clock Free Clinic opened, staffed by thirty volunteer doctors. Still, worries persisted. In mid April, Haight watchdog Chester Anderson had issued the most famous and disturbing broadside in the community's history:

> Pretty little sixteen-year-old middle-class chick comes to the Haight to see what it's all about & gets picked up by a seventeen-year-old street dealer who spends all day shooting her full of speed again & again, then feeds her 300 mikes [a high dosage of LSD] & raffles off her temporarily unemployed body for the biggest Haight Street gang bang since the night before last.
>
> The politics & ethics of ecstasy.
>
> Rape is as common as bullshit on Haight Street.

On an earlier occasion Anderson wrote: "Are you aware that Haight Street is just as bad as the squares say it is?"

It would still be weeks until the Summer of Love.

Despite this growing sense of crisis, the ballroom scene and San Francisco's new generation of bands continued to flourish. Jefferson Airplane—comprising folk and blues players assembled by lead singer Marty Balin, who was eager to craft a folk-rock band—was the first truly popular sensation to emerge from the Haight and would consistently prove one of the Bay Area's most exhilarating live bands. In May, their second album, *Surrealistic Pillow* (their first to feature Grace Slick, from the Great Society, as a soaring co-lead vocalist, and along with *Bless Its Pointed Little Head,* the band's best album), rose to Number Three on the album chart, and yielded two remarkable singles, "Somebody to Love" and "White Rabbit" (the latter, in part, an outright paean to psychedelics). By contrast, the Grateful Dead—the band that had played Ken Kesey's Acid Tests—recorded a debut that many believed fell short of their already renowned live performances (later captured memorably on *Live Dead)*. Even so, that first album, *Grateful Dead,* included a number of songs that would remain in the band's concert repertoire for the duration of its lifespan, and it was also the only brash rock & roll album the Dead ever made. Other bands were also forceful presences. Berkeley's Country Joe and the Fish was the only prominent band on the scene to put radical politics out front, and their first album, *Electric Music for the Mind and Body,* remains one of San Francisco psychedelia's most rewarding works. Though Quicksilver Messenger Service wouldn't appear on an album before 1968, the band on its best nights was the fiercest of any of the San Francisco bands, featuring long-ranging song suites and mesmeric instrumental passages, driven by John Cipollina's fleet and sinuous guitar lines and Greg Elmore's impelling drum thrusts. (In almost all cases, dynamic and inventive drummers were essential to the success of the San Francisco bands' music.)

But the Haight's dark horse proved to be Big Brother and the Holding Company, with singer Janis Joplin, as became powerfully evident at the June Monterey Pop Festival. Monterey Pop was conceived by the Mamas and the Papas' John Phillips and record producer Lou Adler as a showcase for the new sensibilities in folk and popular music and avant-garde rock & roll, but the San Francisco bands were wary of the Los Angeles–based organizers' intentions.

At first, most Bay Area artists refused to sign a release form that would grant the festival worldwide rights for the use of their performances in a film, until they understood that the film was the only way for the enterprise to recoup some of its expenses, since it was a nonprofit affair. Before it was over, most of the artists signed the release, and in the case of Big Brother and the Holding Company, that decision led to an historic moment. Though the band's musicians carried a reputation for somewhat ungainly performances, their appearance in D. A. Pennebaker's film *Monterey Pop* is searing and riveting, and Joplin's rendition of Big Mama Thornton's "Ball and Chain," in which she merged deep-felt pain with an overwhelming eroticism, was perhaps the high point of the festival—a febrile moment that instantaneously made Joplin the Haight's single biggest star. The funny hitch in this development was that Joplin herself despised psychedelics; she and some of the other members of Big Brother preferred alcohol (they referred to themselves as "alkydelics") and heroin. Later, Joplin more or less disavowed the community that had embraced her. "They're frauds," she said, "the whole goddamn culture. They bitch about brainwashing from their parents, and they do the same damn thing."

Monterey Pop took a lot of blame for spoiling the virtues of the San Francisco rock scene by fomenting stardom in what had once been a community of peers, but the judgment was neither fair nor accurate. Several of the artists—in particular Jefferson Airplane and Janis Joplin—already had ambitions that reached beyond hometown success, plus most were growing discouraged by the increasingly corrosive atmosphere in the Haight. In the end, it is the music that the scene produced that remains the single most palpable legacy of the whole experiment. It still has effect, it still has verve and life, a sense of confidence in the untried.

Indeed, that music was powerful enough in its time that it helped create and spread the vision of the Haight as a hub for epiphany to an outside world that was unaware of the neighborhood's impending crisis. For that matter, the Haight's darkening realities didn't particularly intrude on the rest of San Francisco, where many other young people felt they were in fact living the Summer of Love dream. The main venues for the new rock & roll, the Avalon and the Fillmore, existed outside the Haight, and they drew audiences from all over the Bay Area. The experience inside those dance halls was blissful, and it was what inspired Ralph Gleason, in describing the Fillmore and the Avalon, to write: "The kids and the adults there are outstanding for their peacefulness." This impression also reached young people outside of California. The national media was rendering Haight-Ashbury and San Francisco's music-centered scene as something both deplorable and fascinating, but the other, more meaningful medium—the music itself—was spreading sounds and images of transformation. It was hard for many to hear the music emerging in 1967 and not want to go to San Francisco, with its apparent promise of community founded on ideals of hope and concord—where the war didn't reach—and the possibilities of amazing psychedelic and sexual adventures. This was a new world, there for the journey

In the final days before summer 1967, folksinger Scott McKenzie's hit single "San Francisco (Be Sure to Wear Flowers in Your Hair)," written by John Phillips of the Mamas and the Papas, was everywhere on pop radio. The naïveté of its sunshine promise was maddening—"For those who come to San Francisco / Summertime will be a love-in there / In the streets of San Francisco / Gentle people with flowers in their hair"—and yet there was something undeniably lovely, even haunting, about the song. McKenzie's voice, the way the music opens into a space of gravity as a bass pulse grounds the song's reverie, now seem to anticipate a heartbreak past the serene ideal described in the lyrics. The Utopia the song envisioned was, like all Utopias, illusory, but its myth was now an inexorable allure.

Truth be told, the idea of an LSD-bound community was, as much as the music, an essential part of that allure. LSD was foremost a drug that facilitated remarkable encounters with the self and other selves. In the Haight, LSD became a bonding instrument—a way of declaring a new fraternity and forging a new paradigm that stood apart from old precepts. This outlook could make the drug's effects feel like a shared insight—especially in a dark room full of music and dancers—but all of acid's peregrinations came from inside the user and for the most part ended there. Timothy Leary understood this, and advocated preparing the LSD user with the proper mind-set and providing reassuring surroundings, for a healthy psychological experience. Of course, Ken Kesey also appreciated LSD's intense inner reality, but his idea of the right set and setting was to foment perplexity (or worse) in relatively unrestrained environments. A fair number of people came away from various Acid Tests deeply unsettled, and it seemed to some that for Kesey that was the ideal.

Kesey's model is the one that had greater bearing in the Haight, though using psychedelics in public settings—even friendly ones—always entailed a certain jeopardy. This became notoriously apparent on the day summer began, June 21, when the Diggers staged their own version of a gathering, a summer solstice festivity that would "leave Be-Ins to the college students, ad men and news medea [sic]." By the time the Summer of Love actually started, harder drugs had begun to pervade the Haight. According to Martin Torgoff's account in *Can't Find My Way Home: America in the Great Stoned Age, 1945–2000,* the Diggers' solstice observance was far worse. A new drug, STP, produced by Owsley Stanley, had come into circulation at a June 21 summer solstice festival. STP stood for Serenity, Tranquility, Peace, though the drug provided no such experiences. Instead, it kept users in a psychedelic state for up to three days, and it wasn't a pleasant experience for many. Torgoff claims that five thousand people took the drug at the solstice gathering, and for three days San Francisco's emergency rooms were filled with people undergoing bad experiences with STP. There was nothing that could be done for them. Thorazine, an antipsychotic with a tranquilizing effect, had been widely given to LSD users in emotional and mental trouble, but Thorazine wouldn't work with STP. Instead, it only made the psychedelic's effect horribly worse.

The event seemed to correspond to a declining interest in psychedelics in the Haight. As it developed, with the flood of newcomers also came different drug preferences. Many people in Haight-Ashbury were now shooting methedrine, an amphetamine. Numerous others were trying heroin, sometimes as a counteragent to the high-wired, agitating effects of amphetamines. All of these drugs had one thing in common: They were ways of managing the apprehension and the desolation that now filled Haight-Ashbury's streets and many of its homes as well. They were also inherently dangerous. Injecting drugs always ran risks of infection and overdose, and amphetamines—that is, speed—might also induce psychosis, even violence, far more readily than the use of psychedelics. "The criminal element was growing, and it got harder to deal with," Carolyn Adams (known as Mountain Girl in the Haight, and once married to Jerry Garcia) told Nicholas von Hoffman in *We Are the People Our Parents Warned Us Against.* "The freedom thing was being turned into the freedom to fuck up in public—the freedom to break a bottle, the freedom to hit somebody, the freedom to step on somebody who was on the ground. These powerful elements of destruction had suddenly entered this beautiful street party that had been going on ever since the Be-In." Soon, the Grateful Dead began scouting new locations to base themselves and their families.

In that same June that "San Francisco (Wear Some Flowers in Your Hair)" was a hit, *The Oracle* published an editorial that tried to defuse the imminent Summer of Love predicament. In March the paper had posed the question, "Will success spoil the Haight-Ashbury?" The writer answered: "Maybe. Probably. … But not if we're very, very good. And careful." Now *The Oracle's* editors admitted that they and others had been unable to garner the help of the city's resources in caring for the young people who were about to swarm not just the Haight but much of the rest of San Francisco. They urged readers to create their own alternative communities, but not in San Francisco. If the suggestion had any effect—and perhaps it did—it wasn't at all apparent. Bad things had started, and they weren't about to stop.

In the heart of the summer of 1967 in Haight-Ashbury, there were bad drugs—drugs that weren't what they were purported to be—being sold and consumed, there were street beatings, and there were confrontations with the police. On an early July evening, a police attempt to clear a blocked intersection turned into a serious hourlong clash. It ended in nine arrests and four bad injuries, including a girl who had her jaw broken twice by a policeman's nightstick. A man attempting to walk his sheepdog was arrested, and a policeman beat the dog to death with a nightstick. The Haight was like a tinderbox, but instead of blowing up, the neighborhood steadily burned itself down.

In early August, a drug dealer was found dead in his apartment near the Haight. He had been stabbed a dozen times, and his right arm—the arm he was known to chain his briefcase to—was severed and missing. The man later arrested in the murder still had the arm with him but claimed he wasn't sure why, due to his prolonged bad history with LSD. Three days after the first murder, another slain man was found, this time in Marin County. He was a black LSD dealer who had been a familiar figure in Haight-Ashbury. In between the news of the two murders, something else happened: Beatle George Harrison and his wife, Pattie Boyd, paid the Haight a brief visit. Harrison, who was on LSD when he arrived, strolled up Haight Street to the Panhandle. It wasn't long before he was noticed and was asked to sing a song. He strummed a guitar somebody handed him, trying to find his way through "Baby You're a Rich Man," but found the experience disconcerting and made a fast retreat. Harrison later said that he had expected something a bit more urbane, like London's psychedelic scene. Instead, he felt appalled by the "hideous, spotty little teenagers" he'd found in Haight-Ashbury, and before leaving San Francisco he resolved not to take any more LSD. (Despite his experience, Harrison donated $66,000 to the Haight-Ashbury Free Clinic in 1974 and saved it from closing down.)

By the time the Summer of Love was finished in September, more than seventy-five thousand people had visited Haight-Ashbury, then left the place. There are numerous statistics and subjective claims about how many people had bad drug or health experiences during that time. For example, the Free Clinic treated more than twelve thousand patients in three months, and San Francisco's General Hospital reported a fivefold increase in acute drug episodes from February to July. Other organizations' figures vary widely; accurate research on drug use in a nomadic and suspicious community is an elusive feat. It's clear, however, that multi-thousands took LSD in San Francisco in the mid- and late 1960s (according to one commonly quoted figure, four million Americans had already taken the drug by 1964, which seems implausible beyond belief), but what the quality or results of those incidents might have been couldn't be determined. Haight-Ashbury may have been the largest laboratory for drug experimentation in America's history, but nobody was monitoring it with anything close to objectivity. Perhaps the worst of it could never have been quantified. In Joan Didion's account of the Haight during 1967, "Slouching Towards Bethlehem," she told of meeting a five-year-old girl, Susan, reading a comic book, stoned on LSD. The girl's mother, Didion wrote, had been giving her child both LSD and peyote for a year. It was an unbearable glimpse at a dream that didn't even know when it had passed into nightmare.

Come October, Ron and Jay Thelins closed the Psychedelic Shop and left a sign in its window: "Nebraska Needs You More." By then, residents were continually leaving the district for safer homes, for communes and country life. The Grateful Dead, though, didn't move quite fast enough: On October 2, police raided their house on Ashbury Street and arrested two band members (Bob Weir and Pigpen) for drug possession. Four days later, the Diggers and others led a Death of Hippie/Birth of the Free Man funeral march, bearing a cardboard coffin, to the corner of Haight and Ash-bury. Not many Haight locals joined in. Some wondered why a group that attacked anybody seen to be in leadership positions was still trying to determine the community's viewpoints. Nobody much thought that the hippie movement was truly dead.

Both the Grateful Dead's arrest and the Death of Hippie procession were covered in the first issue of a new magazine, *Rolling Stone,* dated November 9, 1967. *Rolling Stone* was started by Jann Wenner, who had been a student at the University of California at Berkeley. Earlier in the year, Wenner had approached his friend Ralph J. Gleason, the *San Francisco Chronicle* columnist who been reviewing the city's new music, with an idea: He wanted to launch a new-style music magazine—one that would give rock & roll its cultural and revolutionary due. *"Rolling Stone"* Wenner wrote in the magazine's first issue, "is not just about music but about the things and attitudes that the music embraces." The magazine would cover the San Francisco scene definitively. It would also write about the news and attitudes surrounding illegal drugs, and about the new culture that was burgeoning in—and disturbing—America. This was terrain that the Haight made promising for years to come.

The Haight itself, though, was clearly finished. "It was like somebody had come through it with a flame-thrower," poet Michael McClure later said. A number of the district's more devoted inhabitants moved on to life in self-sustaining communes, some in or near cities, others in rural locations throughout California and America. (In 1968 Stewart Brand, who had been associated with Ken Kesey and the Merry Pranksters and who organized the pivotal 1966 Trips Festival, created *The Whole Earth Catalog,* which proved an imaginative and widely influential resource for the rural movement.) Many others moved across the Bay to Berkeley and areas around Oakland, where cheap rents could still be found. Berkeley—which had been a focal point for civil liberties activism and radical politics since the 1964 Free Speech Movement at the University of California—also witnessed extraordinary events in 1967, peaking in fierce October antidraft demonstrations in Oakland that proved the tipping point in America's burgeoning antiwar movement. In time, Telegraph Avenue became the new Haight Street, though Berkeley police—who conflated longhairs with the city's fervent antiwar movement—proved even more relentless in the harassment of hippies and students. Tensions turned bitter and ugly, finally culminating in May 1968, in an argument between the University at Berkeley and students over a piece of contested land, People's Park. Police ended up seizing the land in a violent confrontation. Governor

Ronald Reagan praised the raid and sent in two thousand National Guard troops to suppress any further reaction. In essence, it was the final stand of what had become of the Haight-Ashbury movement.

Still others from Haight-Ashbury—musicians, former community leaders, merchants—moved north across the Golden Gate Bridge, to the spacious, largely undeveloped terrain of Marin and Sonoma counties. The most notable of these émigrés was the Grateful Dead, who had been known as the "people's band" in Haight-Ashbury—the band that cared about the following it played to, and that often staged benefits or free shows for the community's good. Long after the Haight's moment had passed, it would be the Grateful Dead—and the Dead alone among the original San Francisco bands—who would still exemplify the ideals of camaraderie and compassion that most other 1960s-bred groups had long relinquished and that many subsequent rock artists repudiated in favor of more hard-bitten ideals. Though the band left San Francisco for the pastoral relief of Marin, they also took something about the Haight's best spirit with them as they traveled the world for three decades. By and large, the people who gathered to see them weren't simply an audience, but rather a dispersed society that, by gathering, reenacted the ideal of the San Francisco ballrooms of 1966 and 1967—a possibility that still existed as long as the Dead lasted.

When Jerry Garcia died in August 1995, a tie-dyed flag was flown on the middle flagpole at San Francisco's city hall, and the surrounding flags were lowered to half-staff. It was a fitting gesture from a civic government that had once feared the movement and social changes that the Haight represented, and that now acknowledged not just the passing of a great musician and bandleader, but that the seasons of the Haight-Ashbury adventure proved one of the most notable chapters in the city's modern history. Over the years, San Francisco had come to embody some of the best of what that neighborhood had handed down.

What went wrong in Haight-Ashbury? How did an adventure that began in exploring new forms of creativity and the life of the mind turn into an environment of dread and decay? Or was it all wrong from the start, a journey in bad values and bad judgment, leading to a place of bad ends? People have been arguing over these questions for over forty years now.

Part of the Haight's rise and fall was always psychedelics and how they drew the people there into extraordinary shared experiences. "In places as public as the Haight-Ashbury and as private as farms in the Kansas countryside," wrote David Farber in *The Age of Great Dreams: America in the 1960s,* "young people dropped acid, imagined the impossible, and then tried to bring it to life." That was the drug's miracle, but also its curse: LSD's effects, in the moment, could seem life changing, rich in boundless potentials that might turn the world upside down. But in the end, the LSD experience couldn't function on the scale that the Haight had facilitated. It wasn't so much because of the damage the drug purportedly caused; despite all the media hysteria and horror-stricken anecdotes, LSD did only limited injury. Millions of people took it, and the lives the drug hampered were certainly in far smaller numbers than those destroyed by the harder drugs that took over the Haight or by the legal ruin of heavy drinking.

LSD, it has to be said, was an amazing experience. It could be great fun and it could be edgy, even frightening. But almost all of us weathered those mind storms—we recovered and went on. Whether we got much from it, that's another arguing point. Still, LSD was radical. Its greatest hazard wasn't insanity nor even upheaval, but breaking the bounds of permitted possibilities, not all of them beneficial, as Carolyn Adams noted when she was speaking about "the freedom thing" that went awry in the Haight. On communal and mass levels, LSD stood to transmute familiar notions of order—and in late-1960s America, disrupting social conventions often proved constructive. But the nation's dominant culture wasn't willing to abide hallucinogenic disruptions that would reach into their homes and schools, and into the recesses of the rational mind. LSD was just too damn scary to America to survive as a social currency, and Haight-Ashbury's identity with the drug inspired abhorrence among many. It seems long ago now, that time when an urban village could disturb and excite an entire nation. What happened in San Francisco in those seasons was seen as a fissure in modern certainties—as a blight or as a wonder. In the years since, the transformations that took place in the Haight and in similar neighborhoods, towns and college centers across the country have been denounced as the source for many subsequent social dilemmas, including varying drug problems and youth's endemic sexual activity. The hippie movement of the 1960s, we have been told time and time again by conservative critics, injured—even corrupted—American civilization: It unleashed frightening and empowering specters that continue to haunt and harm us, say those detractors, and the permissions that resulted need to be resisted and, where possible, overturned. The 1960s counterculture became a scapegoat, blamed for a social changeover that was, in some ways, already ongoing and that developed from a complex mesh of conditions. The truth is, legal narcotic addictions were a mainstream American societal scourge long before the illegal use of marijuana and psychedelics became popular, and freedom of sexual activity became more permissible after the availability of birth control pills. In any event, an increasing open-mindedness about sexuality, as well as about the public communication of controversial ideas, were significant improvements.

There were other effects that were also clearly enriching. The powerful sense of connectivity that motivated the Haight at its best—of people being of one place and of like mind—and a growing belief among the counterculture in the primacy of the natural world over modern materialism, soon led to a keener sense of connection to the environment humanity depends on yet has steadily spoiled. To be sure, environmentalism was already an important concern, but the counterculture helped advance it as a global movement that has never lost its urgency. In March 1970, after a campaign around the nation and in the UN, San Francisco inaugurated an Earth Day observance that grew massively in dimension over time.

The hippie movement also had great influence on how Americans (and others in the Western world) viewed, judged and tolerated one another—though this change developed in fitful and complex ways. Initially, much of this transpired over issues of appearance. More and more men, for example, now wore their hair much longer. This fashion had started, of course, with the Beatles' arrival in America in February 1964, inspiring a trend of longer hairstyles for men over the years; high schools fought to ban the style, and countless American businesses refused to hire males with longer hair. By 1967 hair length often reached to a man's shoulders or longer. This progression incurred both public hostility and sometimes violence. Men's long hair was no small break with twentieth-century style—to some it heralded a suspicious feminization, and to many others it was an emblem of radical beliefs and practices that were seen as affronts to longstanding values. That is, long hair—along with more ornate and flowing types of clothing among young males and females alike—was seen as a deliberate flouting of more uniform postwar standards, as a breach in accepted public manners, as a disavowal of American values. (This is partly what the film *Easy Rider* was about: People could risk their lives over these differences.) But within seasons, more people gradually adopted these styles, until by the 1970s, long hair often meant little more than personal preference—even conservatives and reactionaries could look hip without danger. More significantly, mass numbers of people began experimenting with marijuana, even though many of them had no particular devotion to what they saw as hippie or radical ideals. Plus, they grew more accepting of changes in sexual morality and political convictions. (By 1972 this developing new world-view largely remade the Democratic Party, after the debacle of the 1968 Chicago Convention.) Was all this progress? If not, it was certainly major change, and though various instances of deviance and nonconformity are still frequent objects of derision, open-mindedness and social liberalization made some worthy advances that have never been overturned.

This is how the spirit that is identified with 1967—or more accurately, the combined effect of the hippie movement, the changing rock & roll scene and social and political activism—spread into the world. This is how it changed the possibilities for how life and community could be lived, as well as how new forms of democracy might come from the streets and from the peripheries in American society. The Haight and the culture it represented initially bore influence through its music and its impact on similar-minded communities throughout the nation, then later—more lastingly—through its effect on ideas, attitudes and social and personal practices. This process didn't end up remaking institutions as some in the counterculture expected would happen, nor was it an unambiguous, sweeping break with the world of the past. However, to a remarkable degree it vastly reconfigured America's culture and manners for the next forty years—and, of course, it ignited a mean-witted conservative backlash that owes much of its being and fervor to the purpose of annulling the forces set free in that time.

What happened in San Francisco, and throughout much of youth culture in that time, is still with us, whether we like it or not. Now, much of it is assimilated, but in that year, in that summer, radical transformation seemed everywhere—in the music, in the streets, in the news, in our homes—and it felt startling and provoking. That atmosphere formed the central dynamic of a war of values that became the story of America in the late 1960s and early 1970s. Each side felt as if it were playing for big stakes—nothing less than the fate of the nation's soul. The story of our times since then has been a reaction, an effort to roll back the spirits of transformation and resistance of that time, and to make sure that nothing like it might happen again. But it can never be completely undone. The resonance of that disruption still informs almost every major political dispute and cultural rupture of our times. In one way or another, the arguments of San Francisco in 1967 will never end.

♪ Part IV

Rediscovering the American Voice: The Singer/Songwriter

The 1960s were the era of classic rock. As the era of the professional songwriter declined, bands loaded with performers who wrote their own songs began to emerge, including The Beatles, The Rolling Stones, The Who, The Grateful Dead, and The Band. The 1970s was a relatively calm decade, without the drama of the 60s and its heavy social/political turmoil—such as Kent State—providing subject matter for songs. Songwriters of the 70s, without such galvanizing social issues, embraced a more personal style of writing.. The most accomplished of these included Paul Simon, Randy Newman, Bob Dylan, Billy Joel, Jackson Browne, James Taylor, Bruce Springsteen, and Jimmy Webb, among others. Some of the artists had achieved fame in the 1960s and either shifted gears or reinvented themselves for the next decade. Dylan, of course, has never stopped reinventing himself, but he is an anomaly. The writers in Part IV—James Miller, Nick Hornby, and Barney Hoskyns—focus on this more personal style of songwriting.

James Miller writes about the rise to fame of Bruce Springsteen. Rock fans and critics had been looking for the next Dylan at a time when Dylan wasn't interested in being Dylan, and for them, Springsteen seemed to represent the future. Jon Landau, first as a writer for *Rolling Stone* magazine, and later as Springsteen's co-producer (*Born to Run*), was the first to sing his praises, but it didn't take long for rock audiences to catch on. Part of Springsteen's allure was his live show. His energy and emotional range were precisely what '60s rock fans were seeking. His acceptance wasn't immediate, but by the time Springsteen delivered *Born to Run*, fans knew he was the real thing.

Nick Hornby, the English novelist and essayist, is best known for his literary contribution to rock and roll. His book *Hi Fidelity* was adapted to film, a movie that captured the book's excitement, despite the fact that it changed the setting and embellished the main character. (See Jack Black.) Hornby is certainly a knowledgeable fan of rock 'n roll that often identifies with the artists.

The key message of his essay on Jackson Browne is the idea that listeners must move past the constraints of "good taste" (what's currently popular) to embrace the music that moves them. Hornby uses himself as an example: In the late 1970s when he was actively following the music that rebelled against big arena acts such as Led Zeppelin, The Who, and the Rolling Stones, the "in" music of the day was Punk. In the process of listening to what he was supposed to like, Nick Hornby later discovered that he was missing out on great artists such as Jackson Browne.

Hornby didn't realize what he was missing until he had reached his mid-40s. He takes the reader on an exploration of lyrics and music that he had rejected as a younger man. While rock music is generally a young person's art form, Hornby makes a strong case for keeping an open mind, well into middle and old age. He writes beautifully about beautiful music, and characterizes the essence of pop music:

By the mid- to late 1960s, singer-songwriters born and raised on the east coast such as Bruce Springsteen, Paul Simon and Billy Joel, were turning inward to present more personal, introspective examinations of the life around them. Happy Traum, editor of *Sing Out* magazine in a 1999 *Rolling Stone* article observed:

> As if an aural backlash to psy-ky-delick acid rock and to the all-hell-has-broken-loose styles of Aretha Franklin and Janis Joplin, the music is gentle, sensitive, and graceful. Nowadays it's the personal and the poetic, rather than a message that dominates.

In his essay *Hotel California, New Kids in Town*, British music critic and editor of the on-line music journal *Rock's Backpages*, Barney Hoskyns describes the journey of other folk-revival songwriters to Southern California. By the mid 1960s the folk revival popularity was beginning to fade, and successful east-coast folk artists, including Brits Graham Nash and Allan Clarke of Hollies, Canadians Joni Mitchell and Neil Young, and Americans David Crosby, and Stephen Stills were lured to the Southern California scene in Laurel Canyon. There a "small circle of friends," and others including Randy Newman, John Sebastian, and Eric Clapton, often in gatherings at Mama Cass's house, played and sang for one another, honing ideas for songs.

Legendary producers David Geffen and Russ Titelman also became part of that scene and produced hit records for many of these artists. David Geffen, through his success in elevating the careers of Joni Mitchell and Neil Young, established his own label signing numerous artists including The Eagles, Linda Ronstadt, John David Souther, and later Donna Summer, Asia, and Sonic Youth.

Beginning in the late 1960s and culminating in the mid '70s, most notably in lyrics from Don Henley and Glenn Frey of the Eagles, the turn inward from the California Laurel Canyon scene presents a less burnished view of the California Dream. The '60s depiction by surf bands, including Jan and Dean and the Beach Boys—surfing, girls, cars, be-true-to-your-school—is now considered naive, superficial and hollow. The sun-drenched gloss has dulled, revealing the reality of aging, unfulfilled individuals still trying to act out the carefree excesses of their adolescence.

October 1975

Rock and Roll Future

By James Miller

It had begun with a rare surge of spontaneous enthusiasm for a new performer, shared among a handful of club-goers on the East Coast. By the spring of 1974, the euphoria had spread to a small but influential group of rock critics, wired into the infrastructure of media outlets that had sprung up, after the Summer of Love, to report on happenings in America's hip youth culture. And finally, one and a half years later, in the fall of 1975, the cause of the commotion became a focus of national attention.

In the eyes of some, it was very glad news: a savior had appeared. His name was Bruce Springsteen. And he was going to be America's greatest pop music hero since Elvis Presley, never mind the Beatles.

Almost every aspect of the Springsteen phenomenon was remarkable. The unrestrained enthusiasm of a small coterie of admirers became the basis for a calculated outpouring of exaggerated praise that, in its intelligence and sustained intensity, made the coverage of Ziggy Stardust seem amateurish by comparison. The performer himself aware of the mounting hubbub, had spent endless hours in the studio, trying to craft a transcendent musical masterpiece. Executives at the performer's record label, Columbia, invested tens of thousands of dollars in a marketing campaign of unprecedented sophistication. Critics chimed in with rave reviews. And by the fall of 1975, with his album in stores and the star on his first national tour, Springsteen was being widely hailed as a rock and roll Messiah: not a pretend one, like Ziggy Stardust, but a real one—a figure blessed with the miraculous ability to lift up people's spirits (and drive their blues away).

That was when the mass media took over. By the end of October, *Time* and *Newsweek,* magazines read by millions of Americans, had both run major pieces—in the same week!—examining the Springsteen phenomenon.

Never before in the history of rock and roll had a single performer been featured simultaneously on the cover of America's two major news magazines. Never before had concerted public proclamations about the significance of a rock and roll performer played such a central role in creating the impression that he was, in fact, significant. Never before had there been such obvious reason to wonder whether the proclamations were actually true.

Springsteen, twenty-six, had been playing in rock bands since the Sixties. Signed to Columbia in 1972 by John Hammond, he had quickly recorded two albums, *Greetings from Asbury Park, NJ.*, released in January 1973, and *The Wild, the Innocent and the E Street Shuffle*, released nine months later. Neither album sold many copies. Critics in the United States, writing in newly influential pop music publications like *Rolling Stone* (the mass-circulation biweekly founded in 1967), nevertheless expressed guarded admiration for both discs, especially the second, a roller-coaster ride through a variety of riffs more or less familiar to anyone steeped in the rock and roll of the Sixties, but elaborated in long, breathless songs about an urban frontier peopled with romantic tramps and outlaws, each one with his or her own mock-heroic stage name: Rosalita, Big Balls Billy, Kitty, Weak-kneed Willie.

In the winter of 1974, Springsteen barnstormed up and down the East Coast. What on record had seemed overwrought on stage became overwhelming. The reason had only partly to do with the quality of the music. Springsteen was a rudimentary guitarist, and his baritone was a raspy instrument. His band, too, though tightly rehearsed, was little more than a glorified bar band, which was not surprising, since Springsteen had recruited its five members (bassist, drummer, organist, pianist, and saxophonist) from bands playing in various New Jersey bars. But if the music was sometimes rough-hewn, and if the band (especially compared to British rivals) was so casually outfitted as to make almost no visual impression at all, Springsteen himself projected a strong aura of blue-collar authenticity, and the band's gritty performances were rarely less than exhausting. Fiercely committed to putting on a memorable show, he and the band made a practice of playing marathon sets that routinely lasted over two hours, until he, or his audience, or both, seemed on the verge of collapse. That was what, finally, provoked wonderment and joy: the sheer do-or-die *spirit* with which Springsteen played his music, night after night, week after week.

"Rock and roll came to my house where there seemed to be no way out," he said to one reporter in these years, explaining his own sense of having been "saved" by rock and roll. "And it came into my house—snuck in, ya know, and opened up a whole world of possibilities. Rock and roll. The Beatles opened doors. Ideally, if any stuff I do could ever do that for somebody, that's the best. Can't do anything better than that. Rock and roll motivates. It's the big, gigantic motivator, at least it was for me. There's a whole lot of things involved, but that's what I think you gotta remain true to. That idea, that *feeling*. That's the real spirit of the music"—and it was that spirit that came across in his performances in these months.

In April 1974, prompted by the buzz on the streets, two young writers—Dave Marsh, then the music editor of a Boston alternative weekly, *The Real Paper*, and Jon Landau, a columnist for *The Real Paper*, and also, as music editor of *Rolling Stone*, perhaps the most influential rock critic in America—went to check out a Springsteen show in a Boston-area bar. "Both of us had seen a lot of music performed in a lot of bars," Marsh later wrote, "but never with an effect like that." In the first of his two books on Springsteen, *Born to Run*—a surprise best-seller in the United States—Marsh described his reaction in frankly religious terms. "The advent of Bruce Springsteen," he wrote, "seemed nothing short of a miracle to me."

And so it seemed as well to Jon Landau: "On a night when I needed to feel young," he wrote a month later, "he made me feel like I was hearing music for the first time."

Landau was one of several writers who had risen to prominence in the Sixties by analyzing the significance of rock and roll. Unlike most of his peers, he knew how to play an instrument, the guitar, and (at the invitation of Jerry Wexler at Atlantic Records, who doubtless saw in Landau a younger version of himself) had gotten involved in producing records, working among others with the MC5, a quintet of self-avowed rock and roll revolutionaries. Appreciating though he did the broader cultural ramifications of the music, Landau was far more interested in how essentially unschooled performers could flourish as showmen expert in the enigmatic art of thrilling large audiences with feats of musical magic. College-educated and bookish, he was fascinated by musicians who were neither. Otis Redding, for example, he praised for being "openly and honestly concerned with pleasing crowds," and also for being "truly a 'folk' artist," unwilling to modulate his music according to passing trends. In an essay published in 1968, he expressed his distaste for the Dionysian posturing of the Doors, and wondered out loud why "it wasn't good enough just to sing about cars, balling, dances, school and summertime blues."

It's small wonder, then, that Bruce Springsteen struck a chord with Landau. He did after all just sing about cars, balling, dances, school, and summertime blues. The world that Springsteen evoked was not, finally, all that different from the one depicted in *American Graffiti*. Even better, Springsteen seemed like the real thing—he was a paragon of populist musical virtues, evidently as untainted and pure in his own way as Robert Johnson or Otis Redding, despite growing up within earshot of Alan Freed's radio show.

"He has far more depth than most artists," Landau explained to *Newsweek* in 1975, "because he really has roots in a place—coastal Jersey, where no record company scouts ever visit." (It was true that John Hammond had not had to leave Midtown Manhattan in order to discover Springsteen—but that was because the singer had come to him.)

In May 1974, after seeing Springsteen live for the second time, Landau—knowing that his words carried uncommon weight within the American music business—wrote an impassioned essay, declaring "I saw rock and roll future and its name is Bruce Springsteen."

Though written for a local Boston weekly, Landau's sentiments were soon enough blazoned in advertisements, paid for by Springsteen's record company. Landau's imprimatur had three immediate effects. The first was to set Springsteen himself a daunting, and perhaps impossible task—to fulfill Landau's prophecy. The second was to force every self-respecting rock critic in America to sit up and take notice. Last but not least, Landau's emphatic words of praise convinced Springsteen's record label to embark on an intensive, and expensive, new effort to market his first two albums.

These were months in which it was clear, certainly to Jon Landau and his peers in the critical community, that the explosive growth of rock and roll had produced paradoxical consequences. More people than ever before were listening to the music—on radio, on television, on film, and not least on recordings, which were selling in larger quantities than ever. But the more pervasive rock and roll became, the less it seemed to matter.

The key problem was simple. As the appetite of younger listeners for rock music had continued to grow, the companies and media outlets competing to satisfy their appetite had begun to specialize, offering different kinds of rock to different target audiences, splitting apart a market that had been unified as recently as 1967, when the Beatles released *Sgt. Pepper.* In the mid-Sixties, radio stations around the world, when they played rock and roll, had generally played more or less the same handful of songs, insuring that the music, when it became popular, reached a large and diverse cohort of listeners. A decade later, the situation was entirely different. In America, rock was easy to hear—indeed, it had all but driven most other forms of music off the radio—but stations rarely played the same songs. Some, sticking with Top 40, played only current hits. Others specialized in oldies but goodies, sometimes concentrating on music from the Fifties, sometimes on music from the Sixties. Some played only "urban" or primarily black artists, while still other stations played only "progressive" artists like David Bowie and Led Zeppelin, acts that sold large numbers of long-playing albums without having a number one single on the Top 40. (By the Nineties, the rise of alternative rock would leave the market even more fragmented.)

In this situation, no one could any longer reasonably expect one radio station to air all the rock music that was worth hearing, just as no one of sound mind would actually wish to hear all the rock and roll records that were now being released. A rock act of real cultural consequence in one country—David Bowie in England, for example—might well become moderately popular in another country, but without having any cultural consequence there at all (such was Bowie's fate in America).

For anyone weaned, like Jon Landau, on the sentiments of shared self-discovery unleashed first by Elvis Presley and then by the Beatles, the new regime was hopelessly frustrating. Motivating his personal quest for "The Next Big Thing" was an inchoate but powerful yearning—for a new rock hero as real and mythic (and as popular) as Elvis and the Beatles. It was precisely this need that Bruce Springsteen seemed to meet. Even better, he seemed to meet it instinctively, spontaneously, without coaching or self-conscious theatricality (unlike Bowie), and also without (as the press duly noted) the use of illegal drugs. He seemed, in short, a throwback to rock's golden age of innocence.

Once Columbia had renewed its publicity campaign for Springsteen in earnest, over the summer of 1974, the singer was in a strange sort of box. Asked to deliver the "future" of rock and roll, he was also now widely expected to function as if he were a " 'folk' artist" (to use Landau's rubric), by using inspiration and intuition to create a fresh new music as ostensibly uncontrived and primordial as that widely believed to have been produced by the first heroes of rock and roll.

Trying to rise to the challenge, Springsteen wrote a new song, "Born to Run," which would become the title track of his next album. Composed like an old-fashioned teen anthem from the early Sixties, Springsteen and his band spent weeks working up an elaborate arrangement in the studio, using multiple overdubs to create a cavernous, majestic, quasi-orchestral sound without actually using an orchestra (though Springsteen had played with that idea, too, cutting an early, rejected version of the song with strings).

Given an advance tape of "Born to Run" by Springsteen, Landau shared it with writers he trusted to be helpful. But as the pressure mounted to produce nothing less than a masterpiece, and his own self-confidence began to falter, Springsteen anxiously reached out for someone who could offer him expert musical advice, the kind of advice that George Martin had given the Beatles. (Up till then, Springsteen had produced his own music in conjunction with his manager, a burly ex-Marine of limited musical talents named Mike Appel.)

The person that Springsteen turned to was Jon Landau—who, having foreseen the future, was now asked to help make his prediction come true.

As 1974 turned into 1975, Springsteen and his band, working with Landau, concentrated on the task at hand. Exploiting the singer's natural aura of artless honesty, Landau implicitly cast his leading man as a new kind of star-spangled superhero, doing with a rock star what filmmaker John Ford had done with John Wayne: taking a minor artist and turning him into a major symbol, a larger-than-life personification of America, Land of the Free.

By the start of summer 1975, the songs for the next album were written, and the recording was largely finished. Executives at Columbia loved what they heard, and decided to invest still more money in promoting Springsteen. "You don't go right to the public to sell a new performer," remarked Bruce Lundvall, the man in charge of Columbia's marketing efforts, speaking to a reporter from *Business Week:* "You sell him to your own company first, then to the trade, then to the record buyers."

At the end of August, on the eve of the album's release, Springsteen and his band were booked into the Bottom Line, a 400-seat nightclub in Greenwich Village that functioned at the time as an industry showcase for new talent. Columbia filled the house night after night with record label staffers, and also made certain that elite tastemakers were on hand to witness the event. Springsteen's appearances also drew long lines of ordinary fans, frantic to obtain one of the artificially scarce tickets, reinforcing the impression that history—real history—was being made. (The atmosphere was not unlike that generated three years earlier when David Bowie had debuted Ziggy Stardust in London at the Royal Festival Hall.)

Since one of the Bottom Line shows was recorded for broadcast, and subsequently circulated widely as an unauthorized album, it is possible to verify some of what was happening musically, and take some measure of the bizarre disproportion between the mood of frenzied excitement communicated by the press coverage and the modest but real charm of the performance at issue.

As Dave Marsh described one show, accurately enough, "the songs invariably build from a whisper to a scream"—subtlety was not one of Springsteen's gifts. Drawing material from all three of his albums, the singer turned several of his songs into epic sagas. One of them, "Kitty's Back," routinely lasted more than eighteen minutes. The music, as it survives on the broadcast recording, is notable for its nervous, unrelenting drive—and also for its unblushing exploitation of crude musical devices, such as the wildly rushing tempo used to climax the song "Rosalita."

These devices were amplified on stage by a host of stunts that dated back to the era of vaudeville and blackface. At the end of one show, described by John Rockwell, a *New York Times* rock critic assigned to profile Springsteen for *Rolling Stone,* Springsteen feigned fainting into the arms of his most important stage foil, Clarence Clemons. A pawn in what had become a quintessential rock and roll mise-en-scène, Clemons was Springsteen's designated "Superspade" (to borrow the charged term used by Robert Christgau in his critique of the Monterey Pop Festival). A modestly talented saxophonist, Clemons had one priceless asset: he was a big, burly black man who was quite willing to clown around for white folk, just like Louis Jordan or Louis Armstrong.

"I don't think I can go on, Clarence," Springsteen croaked at this point in the show. "It's cholesterol on my heart. My doctor told me if I sing this song once more, he wouldn't be responsible. But I gotta do it, Clarence, I gotta." With that, Springsteen hurled himself into the last chorus of "Twist and Shout"—the very same ersatz gospel song that the Beatles had used a decade earlier to bring down the house.

It was a gesture of breathtaking bravado, and, in the view of Rockwell, it epitomized Springsteen's genius: "It was pure corn, of course, but a perfect instance of the way Springsteen can launch into a bit of theatricalized melodrama, couch it in affectionate parody, and wind up heightening his own overwhelmingly personal rock & roll impact." (The reader was left to wonder what, precisely, distinguished a "rock & roll impact" from any other sort.)

The furor over *Born to Run* was an eye-opening experience. For the first time, the key players—music critics, record executives, publicists, disc jockeys, editors in the mainstream media—gained an appreciation for the marvelous circularity of the process of rock star-making as it had evolved: if it was declared loudly enough that a musician had wider cultural significance, it was feasible to manufacture, however briefly, at least a simulacrum of wider cultural significance, insofar as this could be measured by the attention paid to a performer by the mass media. "Is it all publicity?" asked Bruce Lundvall at the time. "Some of it is, sure. But Springsteen has to be good enough to sell records over the long haul."

As the passage of time would show, Bruce Springsteen was in fact good enough "to sell records over the long haul." Indeed, in 1984, his seventh album, *Born in the U.S.A.,* became the object of an even more intensive marketing blitz that, before it was finished, completely overshadowed what Columbia had done with *Born to Run,* and turned it into one of the top-selling records of all time, with over fifteen million copies sold worldwide.

Yet Springsteen's triumph was in some ways Pyrrhic, since it had some perverse and presumably unintended consequences. Like David Bowie as Ziggy Stardust, Bruce Springsteen as "Bruce Springsteen, American Superhero" was widely perceived as a quasi-religious, larger-than-life medium of spiritual uplift. Both Bowie and Springsteen nurtured this impression by shrewdly manipulating the whole range of mass media that had grown up around rock and roll since the Beatles. But by shrewdly manipulating the media, both artists—Bowie did this deliberately—turned the public image of themselves, and their music, into fetishized commodities, prefab tokens of a rapturous transcendence, producing a variety of goods that could be purchased and (for the truly idolatrous) reverently collected. With the successful mass-marketing in the United States of Bruce Springsteen, American Superhero (the very image of redemptive innocence), following on the heels of the successful mass-marketing in England of Ziggy Stardust (the very image of redemptive self-destruction), the age of innocence in rock was well and truly over—probably forever.

In 1997, music historian Fred Goodman justly summed up the larger meaning of the Springsteen phenomenon. "His ultimate embrace of music as business made it impossible to separate the acts of faith from the acts of fortune or to tell which one was pursued in the service of the other. As a business strategy it was superb. … But as an action, its meaning was completely different from that of the protest movement, to which it owed so much of its persona."

Fiercely committed though his stage performances showed him to be, Bruce Springsteen in 1975 didn't challenge the supremacy of crass commercialism in the music business. He unwittingly consummated it—and so revealed, just as Jon Landau had promised that he would, "rock and roll future."

♪ Jackson Browne

Late for the Sky

By Nick Hornby

What was I listening to in 1974, when "Late for the Sky" came out? Not Jackson Browne, for a start. I wasn't really aware of him until 1977, when my musical microclimate was way too ferocious to accommodate delicate Californian flowers; the ubiquity of "The Pretender" in all the record collections of the girls I met at college confirmed my suspicion that when it came to music, girls didn't Get It. And then, a couple of decades later and going through a marriage breakup, I found that *Blood on the Tracks* and *Tunnel of Love,* having been mined exhaustively during peacetime, didn't have much left in them, and meanwhile, The Clash and the Ramones, the people who, I felt, had wanted me to turn my nose up at "The Pretender," had long since ceased to be much use to me. (Which is not to say that the college girls had, after all, Got It back then. We were nineteen—we should all have been listening to punk, not listening to songs about marital discord and early midlife crises, although considering that the boys were listening to punk while studying English literature or law at the University of Cambridge, you could argue that either option involved an element of make-believe that young adults should have grown out of.) So, after taking advice from my friend Lee (q.v.), I returned home with a couple of Jackson Browne albums, and found within minutes that I had made a new friend.

I didn't know any of the great songs on those first three or four albums, apart from "Doctor My Eyes" and "Take It Easy." I'd never heard "Late for the Sky," or "These Days," or "For a Dancer," or "From Silver Lake," or "Jamaica, Say You Will." It was almost like discovering a writer I'd never read—except we discover writers we've never read all the time, and only rarely, as adults, do we stumble across major pop artists with a decent back catalog: it is usually prejudice rather than ignorance that has prevented us from making their acquaintance, and prejudice is harder to overcome (indeed, much more fun to maintain). And, yes, of course it was prejudice that had stopped me from listening to Jackson

Browne. He wasn't a punk. He had a funny pudding-bowl haircut that wasn't very rock 'n' roll. He wrote "Take It Easy" at a time when I didn't want to take it easy. And though I hadn't heard any of the songs, I knew they were wimpy, navel gazing, sensitive—American in all the worst ways and none of the best.

And suddenly, there I was, aged forty-plus, lapping it all up, prepared to forgive all sorts of lyrical infelicities and banalities in the sad songs; prepared to forgive, too, all the limp, hapless, thankfully rare attempts to rock out (although I would have been much less forgiving in vinyl days, when I had no access to a remote control and a skip button). I'm prepared to forgive the bad stuff because the best songs are simply beautiful, and beauty is a rare commodity, especially in pop music, so after a while anything that stops you from embracing it comes to seem self-injurious. I can't afford to be a pop snob anymore, and if there is a piece of music out there that has the ability to move me, then I want to hear it, no matter who's made it. I used to have a reason not to like Little Feat (too polite, as far as I can recall, and maybe too musically precise) and Neil Young (overlong guitar solos) but no one can nurse those kinds of quirks in taste now. You're either for music or you're against it, and being for it means embracing anyone who's any good.

The pop snob's dismissal of people like poor Jackson would be forgivable if everything we spent our snobbiest years listening to was of comparable worth, but of course most of it was the most terrible (and ephemeral) rubbish. Recently, *Mojo* magazine ran their list of the 100 Greatest Punk Singles, and it would be fair to say that probably eighty of them were and remain simply awful—derivative, childish, tuneless even within the context of punk, nothing I would ever want to hear again. And yet at the time I would have taken Half Man Half Biscuit or The Users over Jackson Browne any day of the week. (What am I talking about? I did take Half Man Half Biscuit over Jackson Browne, every day of the week.) I didn't hear David Lindley's hymnal, soulful guitar solo in "Late for the Sky" for a quarter of a century because I was a bigot, as narrow-minded and as dumb as any racist. (And speaking of which: I was old enough to vote, and yet still I made excuses for "Belsen Was a Gas" by the Sex Pistols, while simultaneously finding myself unable to absolve a man for an iffy haircut and a touch of introspection … It was all pretty scary back then, now I come to think about it.) Now I feel far more belligerent about Jackson Browne than I ever did about the Pistols: "You don't like 'Late for the Sky?' Well, fuck you, because I don't give a shit."

This may simply mean that I have become old, and so therefore Jackson Browne's sedate music holds more appeal than punk—that all this is a long-winded way of saying that I'm forty-five (today, as I write!), and so I listen to folky singer-songwriters now, not bratty and loud guitar bands … kids … lower-back pain … a nice night in watching *The West Wing* … blah blah. And yet I still appreciate, and recognize the value of, noise, as my partner would no doubt unhappily concur. None of my friends likes The Strokes as much as I do (although admittedly this is because they feel they've heard it all before, whereas I like having heard it all before, so this might not be the incontrovertible evidence of hard-rockin' eternal youth I'm looking for); Marah's recent live shows, the volume of which reminded Lee of Ted Nugent at his most terrifying, simply made me realize that I should allow my ears to ring more often. So I don't think that my newfound love for Jackson can be explained away by my advancing years.

He would have been wasted on me at the time, though; I wouldn't have understood. I'm not referring to the lyrics, which, after all, are hardly opaque (my late-seventies singer-songwriter Elvis Costello made me work much harder at my practical criticism); I'm referring to the soul. And that's where being older helps, because just as I was mistrustful of any melody that didn't come wrapped in a heavy-metal riff when I was fourteen, I was at twenty-one unable to distinguish between soft rock that expressed pain, and soft rock that expressed a smug stoner's content with his wife, his dog, and his record-company advance. There are so many bits in Jackson Browne's music that I don't think I could have responded to as a young man, because their delicacy and fragility I would have mistaken for blandness. The fragment of chorus in "The Times You've Come," when he sings, in a climactic harmony, "Everyone will tell you it's not worth it," the piano intro to "I Thought I Was a Child," the first few bars of "Late for the Sky" itself, when Lindley's guitar, Browne's piano, and an organ create a breathtakingly somber beauty (and how many record labels would allow a major artist to kick off an album with that now?) … You have to have lived a little, I think, to be able to recognize the depth of feeling that has shaped these moments, and these songs, and if "Late for the Sky" is perfect accompaniment to a divorce, it's not just because its regretful lyrics fit; it's because divorce peels away yet another layer of skin (who knew we had so many, or that their removal caused such discomfort?), and thus allows us to hear things, chords and solos and harmonies and what have you, properly. I should add that I'd rather not hear things properly, that part of me wishes that I had all those extra layers of skin, and I was still in a position to dismiss the music as Californian piffle. But I'm not, and I'll have to make the best of it, and to tell you the truth, the best of it is much, much better than I could possibly have imagined. And isn't that just like life?

Hotel California

New Kids in Town

By Barney Hoskyns

> The mountains and the canyons start to tremble and shake
> The children of the sun begin to wake
> **—Led Zeppelin**

A New Home in the Sun

Joni Mitchell was a stranger in a strange land—twice removed from her native Canada, new to California from America's East Coast. She was strange-looking, too, willowy but hip, with flaxen hair and big teeth and Cubist cheekbones. Men instinctively knew Joni as a peer. They also sensed a prickliness and a perfectionism.

In tow with Mitchell was Elliot Roberts, and Rabinowitz, a rock and roll Woody Allen with an endearing devotion to his single cause— Joni Mitchell. "Elliot pitched being my manager," she recalled of him. "I said, 'I don't need a manager, I'm doing quite nicely.' But he was a funny man. I enjoyed his humor." This odd couple had come out to Los Angeles from New York, where the Greenwich Village folk scene was petering out before their very eyes. Roberts, a Chartoff- Winkler agent, was a graduate of the legendary William Morris mailroom. He'd worked there with the even more ambitious agent, David Geffen. Elliot decided to give up in the world of agenting after Buffy Sainte-Marie, a client, dragged him to see Joni perform in l October 1967.

Joni had already crammed a lot into her short life. She'd been married to a fellow Canadian singer, Chuck Mitchell, and had given up a daughter for adoption—an abandonment that ate at her like a wound. Songwriting served as therapy for her pain. "It was almost like she wanted to erase herself and just let the songs speak for her" reflected her friend the novelist Malka Marom. Joni's unusual open guitar tunings also set her songs apart from the folk balladry of the day. "I was really a folk singer up until 1965, but once I crossed the border I began to write," Mitchell says. "My songs began to be, like playlets or soliloquies. My voice even changed—I no longer was imitative of the folk style, really. I was just a girl with a guitar that made it look that way."

"Elliot became wildly excited about Joni, and he introduced me to her and I became her agent," recalled David Geffen. "And it was the beginning of her career—it was the beginning of our careers. Everything was very small time." Established stars were lining up to cover songs from the Mitchell catalog. "When she first came out," said Roberts, "she had a backlog of twenty, twenty-five songs that most people would dream that they would do in their entire career ... it was stunning." One artist to pay close attention was Judy Collins, folk's ethereal blue-eyed queen. For her 1967 album Wild- flowers Collins chose "Both Sides, Now" and "Michael from Mountains." Tom Rush and Buffy Sainte-Marie both sang Mitchell's "The Circle Game."

Joe Boyd, who produced the English folk group Fairport Convention, met Mitchell at the 1967 Newport Folk Festival and brought her to London that summer to open for the Incredible String Band. Both in America and in England, people sat up and noticed the blonde with the piercing prairie soprano, the idiosyncratic guitar tunings, and the wise-beyond-her-years lyrics. When Roberts and Mitchell went to Florida to play the folk circuit there, David Crosby came to see her at a club called the Gaslight South. "Right away I thought I'd been hit by a hand grenade," he reported later. There was something about the way Mitchell combined naked purity with artful sophistication that shocked Crosby—the sense of a young women who'd seen too much too soon. He set Joni in his sights, bedding her that week. The affair was never likely to last. "We went back to L.A. and tried to live together," Crosby said. "It doesn't work. She shouldn't have an old man. She's about as modest as Mussolini."

"These were two very willful people," says Joel Bernstein. "Neither was going to cave in. I remember being at Joni's old apartment in Chelsea in New York and I heard this commotion on the street. And it was Crosby and Joni screaming at each other on the corner. It gave me a real sense of the volatility of their relationship." The volatility did not obscure David's deep admiration for Joni's talent, nor his awareness of the obstacles she and Elliot were encountering. "Everything about Joni was unique and original, but we couldn't get a deal," says Roberts, who took tapes to Columbia, RCA, and other majors. "The folk period had died, so she was totally against the grain. Everyone wanted a copy of the tape for, like, their wives, but no one would sign her."

Roberts touched down at LAX in late 1967, knowing few people in the city but using Crosby's endorsement as a calling card. Joni followed close behind. Immediately she was received with open arms. Epitomizing the hospitality of Laurel Canyon was B. Mitchel Reed, the KPPC-FM disc jockey whose radio show was the pipeline of all cool sounds in L.A. Reed put Roberts and Mitchell up in his rented house above the Sunset Strip on Sunset Plaza Drive.

Joni wasn't sure about Los Angeles. She was used to crowded sidewalks, teeming urban life—the bustle and commotion of Toronto and Manhattan. She didn't like it that people went everywhere in their big gas-guzzling cars. But once she and Elliot got into Laurel Canyon, up among the cypresses and eucalyptus trees that lined the bumpy, snaking roads, she started to see the City of the Angels as the new golden land that had seduced so many outsiders: the land of David Hockney's painting A Bigger Splash, of exotic palms and dry desert air and the omnipresent vault of blue sky. "Driving around up in the canyons there were no sidewalks and no regimented lines like the way I was used to cities being laid out," she recalls. "And then, having lived in New York, there was the ruralness of it, with trees in the yard and ducks floating around on my neighbors' pond. And the friendliness of it: no one locked their doors." As for Elliot Roberts, well, he'd grown up in the Bronx—how bad could this paved paradise be?

"Elliot would sleep on my couch at 8333 Lookout Mountain," says Ron Stone. "At the same time, Crosby had been tossed out of the Byrds and was mooching off me. We'd smoke a joint and play chess. We were both obnoxious brats. He was my entree to all of this." Crosby urged Roberts to try Reprise Records. "Go see Andy Wickham," he counseled Elliot, who found David inspiring and radically different from anyone he'd known in New York. "Because Crosby 'hangs out' so much," Jerry Hopkins wrote in Rolling Stone, "there's a tendency to think he isn't producing much. In a sense this is true. Yet he is an integral part of the L.A. scene—thanks largely to his track record but also because he is so volatile and opinionated."

When Roberts officially left Chartoff-Winkler, he asked Ron Stone to work for him. To Stone it looked more exciting than selling used leather jackets to the socialites of Beverly Hills. Together they found an office farther down Santa Monica Boulevard, in a building with the fanciful name "Clear Thoughts." "Right away it was like Elliot and Ron could take a New York entrepreneurial viewpoint on the whole thing," says Joel Bernstein, who would soon be taking photo¬graphs of Joni for Elliot. "I think it was really eye-opening to these guys that you could come out here and live up in Laurel Canyon in little wooden houses where you didn't even need heating or air- conditioning . . . and you could still do business." With Ron Stone as his new aide-de-camp, Roberts duly trotted off to see Wickham. The young Englishman loved what he heard. "In his heart, Andy was a folkie," Roberts remembers. "His best friend during that whole period was Phil Ochs."

With Wickham as her first label champion, the twenty-three-year-old Joni had a demo session green-lighted by Mo Ostin on condition that Crosby produce it. "David was very enthusiastic about the music," says Mitchell. "He was twinkly about it. His instincts were correct: he was going to protect the music and pretend to produce me. I think perhaps without that the record company might have set some kind of producer on me who'd have tried to turn an apple into an orange." The sessions that eventually became Joni Mitchell could not have been more auspicious. Recording at Sunset Sound, Mitchell and Crosby kept things stripped and simple: in the main just Joni, her guitar, and such well-worked songs as "Marcie" and "I Had a King." The two of them had now officially split up. "They each described to me crying at the other through the glass in the studio," says Joel Bernstein. Sitting in on occasional guitar and bass was Stephen Stills, who was across the hall with his group Buffalo Springfield. His bandmate, the dark and brooding Neil Young, was known to Mitchell from her apprenticeship on the Canadian folk circuit. Sharing a uniquely dry Canadian humor, Young and Mitchell had always gotten along. Neil's coming-of-age song "Sugar Mountain" had indirectly inspired Joni's similarly themed "Circle Game." "You gotta meet Neil," she told Elliot. "He's the only guy who's funnier than you are."

Roberts wandered down the hall to meet Joni's enigmatic compatriot. Having heard stories about the ongoing friction within Buffalo Springfield and specifically about Young's moodiness, Elliot was pleasantly surprised when the singer turned out to be approach¬able and affable. Joni and Neil compared notes on their respective musical journeys. If Joni's tastes didn't stretch to the febrile rock the Springfield played, she could sense the electricity in the air— the vibrancy of the scene and the exploding of talent on and off the Sunset Strip.

Mitchell divided her debut album into two loosely autobiographical sections—a conceit easier to bring off in the days of vinyl LPs. The first side ("I Came to the City") commenced with "I Had a King," a song detailing—with more than a trace of self-protective bitterness—the breakup of Joni's marriage to Chuck Mitchell. Part Two ("Out of the City and down to the Seaside") found the heroine in the country, by the sea, settled in rustic Southern California. "The Dawntreader" was a gushing homage to Crosby and the boat he tethered at Marina Del Rey. "Song to a Seagull" summarized the theme of the album, with Joni recapping on her urban adventures and subsequent departure for the sea. The song played perfectly into the image of Mitchell as a kind of a fairy maiden striving to float free of human need. The final song, "Cactus Tree," pointed forward to deeper themes in the singer's subsequent work: themes of romantic love, of female autonomy, of commitment versus creative freedom. Describing three lovers—the first almost certainly Crosby—Joni "thinks she loves them all" but fears giving herself completely to any of them. These were important issues for liberated women in the 1960s, rejecting a society where women had tended to live somewhat vicariously as caretakers to men. A self-proclaimed "serial monogamist," Mitchell would struggle for years with the conflicts between her desire for love and her need for independence.

Listening to Joni Mitchell again decades later, it's difficult to ignore how earnest and worthy she sounds on it—yet the power of her swooping, pellucid vibrato and idiosyncratic, questioning chords is right there. "Joni invented everything about her music, including how to tune the guitar," said James Taylor. "From the beginning of the process of writing she's building the canvas as well as putting paint on it."

In March, with the album about to be released, David Crosby presented his protégée to his peer group. Crosby's favorite gambit was to host impromptu acoustic performances by Joni, usually at the Laurel Canyon homes of his friends. "David says, 'I want you to meet somebody,'" recalls Carl Gottlieb. "And he goes upstairs and comes back down with this ethereal blonde. And this is the first time that everybody heard 'Michael from Mountains' and 'Both Sides Now' and 'Chelsea Morning.' And then she goes back upstairs, and we all sit around and look at each other and say, 'What was that? Did we hallucinate it?'" Eric Clapton sat spellbound on Cass Elliot's lawn as Joni cooed "Urge for Going," a song inspired by the death of the folk movement. Crosby was at her side, a joint in his mouth and a Cheshire-cat smile of satisfaction on his face. "Cass had organized a little backyard barbecue," says Henry Diltz. "Because she'd met Cream she invited Clapton, who was very quiet and almost painfully shy. And Joni was there and doing her famous tunings, and Eric sat and stared at her hands to try and figure out what she was doing."

The following day Joni performed on B. Mitchel Reed's KPPC show in Pasadena and answered questions that whetted L.A.'s appetite for the new neofolk star. So much did Reed talk her up that her first live dates in town were all sellouts at the Troubadour. Not that the local attention made much difference to the commercial prospects of Joni Mitchell, which peaked on the Billboard chart at the lowly position of No. 189. As she often would in her career, Joni felt at odds with her record label, whose Stan Cornyn promoted the album with flip irreverence. "Joni Mitchell is 90% Virgin," Cornyn's copy read in the ads he furnished to the new underground press— Crawdaddy!, Rolling Stone, and company. Joni was irked by the line. "She got me on the phone and said it drove her crazy," says Joe Smith. "I said, 'Sleep on it and think about it tomorrow. Anybody who knows you or of you would never associate "virgin" in the same sentence with you.' And she laughed at that."

"Like Neil, Joni was quiet," says Henry Diltz, who photographed her soon after her move to L.A. "A lot of these people were quiet, which was why they became songwriters. It was the only way they could express themselves. It was very different from the Tin Pan Alley tradition, where guys would sit down and try to write a hit song and turn out these teen-romance songs about other people."

Joni found a perfect place of retreat in Laurel Canyon. In April 1968, with money from her modest Reprise advance, she made a down payment on a quaint A-frame cottage built into the side of the hill on Lookout Mountain Avenue. Soon she filled it with antiques and carvings and stained Tiffany windows—not to mention a nine-year-old tomcat named Hunter. Within a year her songs were setting the pace for the new introspection of the singer-songwriter school.

On July 5, 1968, Robert Shelton wrote a New York Times piece about Mitchell and Jerry Jeff Walker titled "Singer-Songwriters Are Making a Comeback." In it he noted that, while the return of solo acoustic performers had at least something to do with econom- ics, "the high-frequency rock'n'roar may have reached its zenith." Nine months later, folk singer and Sing Out! editor Happy Traum came to a similar conclusion in Rolling Stone. "As if an aural backlash to psy-ky-delick acid rock and to the all-hell-has-broken-loose styles of Aretha Franklin and Janis Joplin," Traum wrote, "the music is gentle, sensitive, and graceful. Nowadays it's the personal and the poetic, rather than a message, that domi-nates." It was time to turn inward.

Outside of a Small Circle of Friends

The Los Angeles scene that Joni Mitchell and Elliot Roberts found in the early months of 1968 was in a state of transition. The departures of Gene Clark and David Crosby from the Byrds were symptomatic of a general fragmenting. "Groups had broken up over 1967-68," Ellen Sander wrote in her 1973 book Trips. "Everyone was wonder¬ing what was next, a little worried, but grooving nonetheless on the time between. Days were permeated with a gentle sense of waiting, summer blew up the hills, past the painted mailboxes and decorated VW buses, and musicians were floating about."

Crosby, outside whose Beverly Glen house Cass Elliott's dune buggy was often spotted, was struggling to land a solo deal. His new best friend, Stephen Stills, offered consola-tion. To Paul Rothchild, Crosby touted such new songs as the beautiful "Laughing" and the brooding "Long Time Gone." The Lovin' Spoonful's John Sebastian, killing time in L.A., helped Crosby demo tracks for Elektra. But, as with Jackson Browne, Jac Holzman couldn't make up his mind.

Now Stills's band, too, was unraveling. Neil Young's on-off membership of the Buffalo Springfield was perplexing to some but understandable to those who saw how Stills bullied him. "It would make me really angry, because Stephen pushed Neil back con¬stantly," said Linda McCartney, who photographed the Spring-field. "Neil was painfully shy. I thought, 'Well, he just doesn't stick up for himself.'" Jack Nitzsche, who'd worked closely with Young on the Springfield's "Expecting to Fly" and "Broken Arrow"— orchestral epics inspired by the Beatles' "Day in the Life"—was among several people encouraging Neil to go solo. Young was over at Nitzsche's house in Mandeville Canyon one night when they heard a hammering at the door. It was Stills, hunting for his errant bandmate.

According to Denny Bruce, Stills sneered when Nitzsche answered the door, "I know that baby is here and you're hiding him." Finding Neil in Nitzsche's living room, Stills seized him by the lapels and yelled, "Listen, you fuckin' pussy, this is a band!" He reit¬erated to Neil that Richie Furay was the lead singer, and that he himself was "the second lead singer," and that Neil was merely "a guitar player and occasional vocalist" whose songs had already failed to crack the Top 40 three times. Then he stormed out of the house.

"The Springfield had started to dissolve," Elliot Roberts recalls. "By the time I was around them, Neil and Stephen were never in the studio at the same time." At a band meeting to discuss a motion to replace Charlie Greene and Brian Stone with Roberts— rooming with Young at the time—Young rose to his feet and left the room. Roberts was devastated, so shocked by Young's brusqueness that he moved out of the singer's Laurel Canyon pad and found his own place. Two weeks later, after the Springfield's final live performance, on May 5, 1968, Young showed up at Roberts's new place and asked if he would manage him as a solo artist. "Oh, he'd plotted it all out," Roberts reminisced years later. "I thought, Wow, cool—this guy is as devious as I am."

Young's decision to fly solo was a pivotal moment. In time he would become rock's ultimate loner, partnering with his peers only when it suited him. "Everyone thought of the group as the strongest unit for success," Dickie Davis said. "And Neil didn't. In the end, of course, he's right. The managers, the professionals—they know those groups aren't going to stay together. Jack [Nitzsche] knew. But we didn't."

"I think Neil always wanted to be a solo artist," said Richie Furay. "And I can't hold that against him. It just seems there may have been a different way to make that point clear, rather than just not show up." The tendency to avoid confrontation would be one of the themes of Young's long career. "I just had too much energy and so much creative flow coming out," Young told Cameron Crowe; "when I wanted to get something down, I just felt like, 'This is my fucking trip and I don't have to listen to anybody else's.' I just wasn't mature enough to deal with it."

Matters accelerated still faster for Roberts when Graham Nash came to Los Angeles at the start of July 1968. Struggling to make things work with Brit invaders the Hollies, Graham urgently needed to recharge his musical batteries. The first port of call was Casa Crosby and a big hang with Crosby, Mama Cass, John Sebastian, and—most significantly—Stephen Stills. Nash had gotten to know Crosby slightly during a Byrds tour of England. "I'd never met anybody like him," Nash said. "He was a total punk, a total asshole, totally delightful, totally funny, totally brilliant, a totally musical man."

Already intrigued by Los Angeles, where the Hollies had played several times, Nash also was the archetypal Cass Elliott pet. "Cass showed me many wonderful things in a very gentle way," he told writer Dave Zimmer. "She was the person who introduced me to grass. I'd always been curious." Cass wasn't alone in warming to this personable guy from Manchester, England. Five months before, Joni Mitchell had had a fling with the married Hollie when their touring schedules coincided in Canada. Now Mitchell accompanied Roberts and Steve Stills to see the Hollies play at the Whisky a Go Go. After¬ward they took Nash back with them to Joni's new house on Lookout Mountain.[1]

"Joni's place was a little different from Cass's," says Mark Volman. "It was not so much maternal but about holding court in terms of songwriters who could find themselves there on any given night and would present their music to a kind of inner circle of people. If Joni did drugs it was pretty well hidden."

At the Mitchell gathering, Stephen started fooling around with a new, country-flavored song called "Helplessly Hoping." Crosby joined in with a tentative harmony vocal. As he listened, Nash heard a top-layer falsetto harmony in his head. When Stills and Crosby came back in with the second verse, Graham laid his high harmony over their voices.

---

1 *Over the years there has been much hazy dispute about the exact location of this impromptu gathering on the night of July 3, 1968. Stills thought it took place at Cass Elliott's house, Nash wasn't sure, and both Crosby and Roberts insist it was chez Joni.*

Everyone in the room beamed simultaneously: it was as though three angels had been reunited in space and time. "I was in there on top," Nash told B. Mitchel Reed, "and we all fell down laughing. It was really joyous."

Although he wouldn't officially leave the Hollies until November of that year, Nash was now deeply smitten with Laurel Canyon. For a man who'd grown up on the rainy streets of northwestern England, Lookout Mountain was simply idyllic. "I can only liken it to Vienna at the turn of the century, or Paris in the 1930s," Nash reflected many years later. "Laurel Canyon was very similar, in that there was a freedom in the air, a sense that we could do anything."

"There really was an ethic of peace and love and art and poetry among that crowd," says Elliot Roberts. "Poetry, even more than musicality, was revered, and Joni was the best poet at the time. She had a lot to say, and everybody wanted to hear it." Nash, in particu¬lar, was all ears: he and Joni were falling in love. When he got back to England he made plans to leave his old life—and wife—behind. "England was boring me," he told author Ritchie Yorke the following year. "I decided to leave everything there, every single thing, every penny I earned is still there, and I brought $500 with me and my suitcase to start a complete new life."

Both Sides, Then

With Joni Mitchell established at Reprise, Elliot Roberts now capitalized on his relation-ship with Andy Wickham and Mo Ostin to bring them Neil Young. "It's hard to define that period," Roberts says. "It wasn't a money market yet—everyone was just shooting craps. Warners got more of the folk/writer-oriented end of it: the James Taylors and Van Morrisons and Van Dyke Parkses. All these people reflected Andy Wickham's taste in par-ticular." But it was really Jack Nitzsche, one of Mo's most trusted ears, who got Young in the door at Reprise. Young, for his part, felt immediate trust in Ostin. "Warner Brothers," he later told his biographer Jimmy McDonough, "was making music for adults rather than children."

"Warners was a big standard-bearer for the hip Hollywood frater¬nity," said Bob Merlis, later the company's head of publicity. "It said that you didn't have to be in the Village to be hip, and I think that was one of the reasons a person like Joni Mitchell was prepared to risk leaving New York for Hollywood Babylon." For Lenny Waronker, the fact that sensitive, introspective artists such as Mitchell and Young were signing to Warner-Reprise was vindication of the label's artist-friendly approach to the music business. "Neil and Joni were coming at it from a less trained place than Randy Newman or Van Dyke Parks," Waronker says, "but it was basically the same. There was a line that connected everybody."

Newman claims, affectionately, that Waronker exploited their boyhood friendship to get him cheap. Lenny's father and Randy's uncle had worked together in the 20th Century-Fox orchestra, and the two boys—Lenny was two years older than Randy—played together constantly. "I told Lenny that A&M were offering me $10,000," Randy says. "He said, 'How can you do this to me? Don't you understand that money isn't important now?' But Warners matched A&M's offer and I went with them."

Artists such as Newman and Parks posed problems for Reprise. Scholarly, almost nerdish writers, they weren't part of the counter¬culture in the way that Young, Mitchell, or the Grateful Dead were. But then neither were they Top 40 hacks. "Randy and some others weren't joiners," says Waronker. "Their goals were a little different. It was almost self-consciously trying not to join the game. But every¬body wanted to be the best. That was a big deal—'Who's the best?'" Newman did not aspire to rock credibility. One glance at his hope¬lessly square, polo-necked appearance on the cover of his 1968 debut album makes that clear. Nor did Randy hang out with the Laurel Canyon crowd: by now he was married, with a son. "There was marijuana but I never liked it that much," he says. "I'd see Harry Nilsson sometimes. But I wasn't part of anything. If they had a club I wasn't in it."

"Randy was sadder than I was," says Van Dyke Parks. "He'd seen the dark side of the moon, for some reason that I couldn't figure out. He got more nervous and upset about it all." Randy Newman, coproduced in 1968 by Parks and Waronker, was an astounding debut. The jump from the attractive but insubstantial material Randy had written at Metric to the wry satire of "Laughing Boy" and the bleak self-pity of "I Think It's Going to Rain Today" was clear to anyone paying attention. Sadly, just as Joni's debut had done, the album struggled to find an audience. More specialized still was Parks's own Song Cycle, a highbrow concept album about Southern California that included the track "Laurel Canyon Boulevard" ("the seat of the beat"). "I was trying to ask questions like, 'What was this place? What does it mean to be here?'" Parks claimed. "I wanted to capture the sense of California as a Garden of Eden, a land of opportunity."

"Warners was comfortable," says Russ Titelman, a guitarist/ producer whom Waronker brought into the Burbank fold. "It was people who knew about music and had a lot of fun making it. The signings were incredibly hip. Lenny turned Arlo Guthrie into a pop act, which wasn't easy, and he made hit records with Gordon Light- foot. It created a certain vibe and a certain perception. In a way—a good way—it was all things to all people." One Warner-Reprise insider who could not have been described as comfortable was Jack Nitzsche. If his unhappy adolescence had been alleviated by a worship of James Dean, his mind now wandered to darker places of comfort: alcohol, cocaine, the occult. "Jack's mother was a medium and Jack believed in all that stuff," says Judy Henske, who often visited him in George Raft's old house in Mandeville Canyon. "If you went around with Jack for long enough, you believed in it, too. One time, Jack and I were playing with a ouija board and his mother came in and snatched it away, saying, 'That's a pipeline to the devil!'"

It was no coincidence that Nitzsche was so infatuated with the Rolling Stones, on many of whose mid-1960s albums he had played. In the summer of 1968 the English band was flirting heavily with Satanism and the occult, as "Sympathy for the Devil"—lead track on that year's Beggars Banquet—made only too clear. At the same time they were delving deep into their love of the root American music forms—blues and country—and spending a lot of time in Los Ange¬les. The song "Sister Morphine," which derived from a lyric by Mick Jagger's girlfriend Marianne Faithfull, was written at Nitzsche's house. "That was quite a summer," Denny Bruce recalls. "Everyone was listening to Music from Big Pink, and Marianne and Anita Pallen- berg were swimming nude in Jack's pool."

When Jagger agreed to play Turner, the debauched rock star in Donald Cammell's and Nic Roeg's Performance, Nitzsche was asked to create the film's sound track. That he did so with the help of Lenny Waronker's Burbank "team"—Ry Cooder, Russ Titelman, and Randy Newman—didn't change the fact that the Performance sound track was sonically the antithesis of the cozy Laurel Canyon vibe of 1968. Indeed, one would have to say that, like Beggars Banquet, the Performance music was a lot closer to the Zeitgeist than the debut album by Joni Mitchell. Acoustic introspection was less a response to race riots, protest marches, and assassinations than a retreat from them.

Composed in a witch's cottage in the canyon, with Donald Cammell—godson of infamous occultist Aleister Crowley—plying Nitzsche with cocaine, Performance remains one of the scariest collections of music ever: a brilliantly creepy mix of malevolent Moogs, graveyard gospel vocals, and voodoo blues guitar that fit Cammell's dark vision perfectly. "Death is always part of the music I make," Nitzsche once said. No wonder Warner Brothers shelved the film for two years after an executive's wife freaked out during an advance screening.

Neil Young, a Stones fan, loved the Performance music. The very things that alarmed others about Nitzsche were what fascinated Neil, who asked Jack to help him with his first solo album. In August 1968 he moved from Laurel to Topanga Canyon, putting more distance between him and the Hollywood scene in which Stephen Stills and David Crosby were so engrossed. Tellingly, the first vocal track on Neil Young was called "The Loner." "Neil wasn't as social as other people," says Henry Diltz. "He wasn't as out-there, getting buzzed and drunk. He wasn't partying. He was more serious about his life and music. Unlike Crosby, he never had a big entourage of people partying around him."

Young's flight to Topanga was in one sense a flight from the shock of the 1960s. Shy and still prone to epileptic fits, Neil was ill equipped to deal with the sexual and narcotic adventures of the time. According to Henry Diltz, he was also the victim of a shaming, invasive mother who'd profoundly affected his ability to relate to women. Neil tended to become passive in the presence of girls. He felt marginally safer living off the beaten track in Topanga. Neil Young was the logical extension of songs he had written in the Buffalo Springfield—songs such as "Mr. Soul," "On the Way Home," and "Out of My Mind," that spoke of his struggle and disorientation within the swirling Sunset Strip scene of 1966-1967. "Here We Are in the Years" was a statement about rejecting the smoggy city for "the slower things/That the country brings."

Assisting Young with the record was another Topanga outcast, producer David Briggs. Like Nitzsche, Briggs was a macho misfit—the kind of truculent outsider whom Young adored and fed off. Along with Elliot Roberts, a front man masquerading as a manager,

Nitzsche and Briggs formed a human shield that protected and insulated Young from the outside world. Behind this shield he began to write from a deeper, more intuitive place. "When I was very young and first came in contact with these musicians, I thought that the ones whose lyrics I loved must be really smart," says Nurit Wilde. "And I found out that some of them really weren't smart, they just seemed to have some sort of instinctive feel for words. Neil was one of those."

Released in early 1969, *Neil Young* wasn't quite the album Young had intended to make. When he listened back to it, it was over- arranged and overproduced. But it was shot through with distinctive riffs and passages of spooked beauty that made it a minor landmark. "The beginnings of the singer-songwriter school were the first albums by Neil and Joni," says Jackson Browne. "After that you started to get songs that only the songwriter could have sung—that were part of the songwriter's personality."

An Elf on Roller Skates

With everything heating up around him, Elliot Roberts felt over¬whelmed. When Graham Nash quit the Hollies and moved to L.A. in December 1968, Roberts couldn't see a way to free him or Crosby and Stills from their contractual obligations. He turned to the one man he knew who was sharp enough to find a solution: his old colleague from William Morris in New York.

David Geffen had already provided free advice on how to nego¬tiate Neil Young's contract with Reprise; Roberts had gotten $15,000 out of Mo Ostin as a result. Now Elliot really needed David's formi¬dable brainpower. "I knew he could get this done," Roberts says. "By now he was in television at the Ashley Famous agency, but he was making a lot of side deals for everyone. You could hire David to make deals without having the involvement of David. He preferred it that way, because it gave him a broad spectrum of people from movie stars to rock stars to producers."

Geffen had grown up in blue-collar Brooklyn, a skinny kid with dreams of mogulism. He was seventeen when his pattern-cutter father died and left him with an adoring mother who sold girdles and referred to her son as "King David." He first visited Los Ange¬les in 1961, staying with his brother Mitchell, a student at UCLA. "From the day I arrived," he says, "California seemed like an enchanted land."

Back in New York in 1964, David landed a mailroom job at William Morris. After lying about UCLA references of his own, he steamed open a letter from the university denying that he'd ever studied there. He regularly embellished his resume to enhance his standing. Elliot Roberts was an agent who witnessed Geffen steaming open other letters to get jump starts on what was happening in the company. The guy's drive and ruthlessness, appalling to others, thrilled Roberts. It didn't take David long to rise from the mailroom.

As pop music became bigger business in the mid-1960s, William Morris opened its doors to long-haired musicians it might have dis¬dained two years before. Geffen was perfectly placed to deal with this emerging talent. "Stay with people your own age," senior agent Jerry Brandt counseled him. "Go into the music business." In truth, Gef¬fen knew little about music. When television director Steve Binder turned him on to a remarkable singer named Laura Nyro, he'd never heard of her. Nyro was a Gothic Cass Elliott, a boho Barbra Streisand in black. Her swooping voice and street-operatic songs were starting to be covered by successful pop/MOR acts. Geffen eagerly seized the opportunity to offer his services. Nyro was quickly won over by his infectious enthusiasm, especially after she bombed at the Monterey Pop Festival and he rushed to her side to comfort her.

"She was a very strange girl," Geffen told Joe Smith. "She had hair down to her thighs. She wore purple lipstick, Christmas balls for earrings, strange clothes. But very talented." David Crosby believed that Laura was "a window into something in [Geffen] that was not primarily about money." The fact that Nyro and Geffen were both primarily gay helped: those who weren't in the know even thought they'd become a couple. "People said, 'You know he's gay,'" says Judy Henske. "And I thought, 'Well, you don't get a really gay hit from him, but whatever.' In any case he was great, and the reason that he was so great was that he was so smart. He was really, really fun and really, really smart." Journalist Ellen Sander, who'd written about him in the New York press, also failed to get "a gay hit" from Geffen. She even seduced him one night in her apartment on East Twentieth Street. According to his biographer Tom King, "[David] credited Sander with helping him to conquer his fear of sex with women."

For at least two years, Geffen was jetting between New York and Los Angeles. A fast-rising star, he lived in a chic apartment on Central Park South and stayed at the Beverly Hills Hotel when he was in L.A. On one trip he pressed a demo of Laura's songs into the hands of Bones Howe, producer of the pop-soul group the Fifth Dimension. Subsequently they recorded several Nyro tunes, notably the smash hits "Stoned Soul Picnic" and "Wedding Bell Blues." To Geffen's delight, the value of Laura's catalog increased exponentially as a result. Brazenly disregarding rules governing conflict of interest, he worked as both her agent and her publisher, forming Tuna Fish Music in partnership with her. "David was an opportunist," says Joe Smith. "He was very quick and very smart."

Geffen's energy was formidable. "He never stopped," says Essra Mohawk, an aspiring singer-songwriter adopted by Nyro. "I called him the Elf on Roller Skates. He seemed gay to me, so I never bought that he and Laura were a couple. I liked him a lot. He was very friendly." In May 1968 he quit William Morris and joined Ted Ashley's agency. His responsibilities were now almost entirely musi¬cal. When he wasn't in California himself he would receive at least one phone call a day from Elliot Roberts. Usually it involved the careers of Joni Mitchell and Neil Young.

Before a year was up, Geffen was tiring of Ashley Famous. He began scheming to form not just his own agency but his own label and personal-management firm, too. With unprecedented audacity he suggested to Clive Davis that he leave his job as president of

Columbia and partner him in a new label. Davis declined. In Febru¬ary 1969, turning twenty-six, Geffen resigned from Ashley Famous and launched David Geffen Enterprises. First, however, came a major challenge: the disentangling of Crosby, Stills, and Nash so they could form a new group.

Taking a break from L.A. in early 1969, Crosby, Stills, and Nash honed their new material in a house that Paul Rothchild kept on Long Island. While there they went into New York City to formalize their relationship with David Geffen. Elliot Roberts flew out from L.A. to be present. What CSN proposed in Geffen's Central Park South apartment was a straight no-paper handshake deal. Geffen hesitated for a split second, then agreed. Clive Davis, who thought highly of Geffen's talent, released David Crosby without a whimper; if anything, he was delighted to be rid of "the Bad Byrd." In exchange Davis would get the Buffalo Springfield's Richie Furay and his new group Poco. A tougher sell was producer Jerry Wexler, who fiercely resisted Geffen's request that Atlantic release Stephen Stills. When Geffen came to see him, the meeting sparked a decade of bad blood. Jerry, a well-read jazzophile who scorned agents as parasites, physically threw the smaller man out of his office.

"I knew [Jerry's] accomplishments and went to him with great respect," Geffen later protested. "I'm not saying I was completely in control of my emotions, because I wasn't. But Wexler wouldn't even listen to me. He treated me like dirt. He screamed and yelled and acted like I was looking to rob him." Altogether wilier was the response of Ahmet Ertegun. The legendary cofounder of Atlantic thought a few moves ahead of Wexler. What, he asked himself, can I get out of this arrogant kid? "I saw in him a potential genius entertainment executive or entrepreneur," Ertegun said in 1990. "He was very bright, very fast. He was younger than me and he had a keen sense of where youth was going in America."

Turning on all his Park Avenue charm, Ahmet seduced Geffen, who left thinking that the goateed Atlantic prez was "the most sophisticated, amusing, and encouraging man I had ever met in my life." Within weeks, Crosby, Stills, and Nash was an Atlantic act. "Later I saw [Geffen's] devotion to his artists," Jerry Wexler would concede. "His group of California rock poets worked for him without a contract—that's how deep their trust ran." But the two men were to clash even more unpleasantly.

With the CSN deal inked, Geffen decided to make Los Angeles his base. "There was so much going on in California that it was the only place to be," he says. With Elliot Roberts already based there and building a stable of talent, David knew it was the right time to strike. The two men cemented their partnership as they drove to Carl Gottlieb's house on Gardner Street one afternoon. "David stopped the car," says Roberts. "Then he turned to me and said, 'Listen, let's just do this.'" When Elliot faintly protested that he'd done most of the hard work himself, David told him to shut up. "You know you'll make twice as much money with me," he said.

Installed in a fancy new office at 9130 Sunset Boulevard, the two men plotted to shape the destinies of the canyon ladies and gentle¬men. "The word got around that there were these music-industry guys who were also human beings," says Jackson Browne. "Crosby told me that Geffen was really brilliant but you could also trust him. And you could. David and Elliot would have done anything for their artists. In an industry full of cannibals, they were like the infantry coming over the hill."

"[David] had a description—he said these people were significant artists," Bones Howe recalls. "The significant artist is an artist who creates his own music, records it, and produces it. These people created and crafted themselves. And he was fascinated with that process." "By 'significant artists' I really meant singer-songwriters," Geffen says. "People who were self-contained."

Geffen-Roberts was a fearsome double act, like Charlie Greene and Brian Stone with credibility and Levi's. Elliot was the people person, emotional caretaker to the sensitive stars; Geffen was the financial wizard behind the scenes, outsmarting the industry's cleverest titans. "We were both very involved with the artists, but in different ways," Geffen says. "Elliot would go on the road with them but I would not. I did most of the business for the artists and Elliot did most of the hanging out with them."

"Elliot in some strange way was the vehicle for David to be so suc¬cessful, because in some regard it was his musical taste that defined all of this," says Ron Stone, hired to help manage the Geffen-Roberts acts. "Elliot had this amazing sensitivity to this kind of music and made some incredibly insightful choices. I forgive him all his other foibles, because there was a touch of genius there."

"In the Laurel Canyon and Topanga areas, Elliot was the rare manager who actually lived there rather than Beverly Hills," says photographer and architect Joel Bernstein. "The whole vibe of Elliot's office, with a rolltop desk, told you they'd got into the whole canyon vibe—this whole updated Western fantasy." Geffen-Roberts's clients were under no illusions about the duo's master plan, however. "Elliot Roberts is a good dude," David Crosby told writer Ben Fong- Torres. "However, he is, in his managerial capacity, capable of lying straight-faced to anyone, anytime, ever." And if Roberts didn't rob you blind, the grinning Crosby continued, "we'll send Dave Geffen over: he'll take your whole company. And sell it while you're out to lunch, you know."

But it wasn't all about money for Geffen. There was a part of David that fed off the egos and insecurities of his stars, compulsively trying to make everything perfect for them. David stayed sober and focused while the talent indulged.

"David may have wanted to have a successful business," said Jackson Browne, "but he also wanted to be part of a community of friends. He became our champion, and years later—after a lot of therapy—he finally got over his need to caretake people to the detri¬ment of his own life." In the meantime there were plenty of fragile egos to care-take—and much remarkable talent to exploit.

 Part V

Back to the Basics: Rock Returns to the Garage

In the mid to late 1960s, the British Invasion, Psychedelic Rock, and Motown had rescued rock from the saccharine sound of the recording industry that dominated the decade following "The Day the Music Died." The '70s, however, were characterized by many of the musical excesses of rock: jazz-rock horn bands in the U.S., prog-rock from the U.K., and extreme virtuosic instrumental prowess, especially among guitarists. Almost all genres experience cycles of simplicity and complexity, and by the '70s, rock had moved away from the raw energy of "Louie, Louie," "Good Golly Miss Molly," and "You 'Aint Nothin' But a Hound Dog." For many who considered themselves purists, by the early '70s, rock 'n' roll had deviated too far from music with energy, three chords, and attitude. From this return-to-basics backlash emerged the roots of punk, funk, and metal.

With the exception of disco, pop music had once again become segregated. And disco itself was simply black dance music with its funkiest elements removed. Punk groups from the early era were primarily white, but that doesn't mean that black music had waned in popularity. Funk had taken what it needed from James Brown and moved in entirely new directions with Parliament-Funkadelic, Earth, Wind and Fire, The O'Jays and many other groups.

Funk and punk, with a few exceptions, were not played on the radio. They should have been, but only disco was regularly played. American listeners only experienced the innovative sounds of these styles by purchasing albums. In the case of funk, an element of racial discrimination certainly influenced the decision of radio stations to exclude artists that embraced the style. But more importantly, funk and punk were largely regarded as threats or perversions. We seemed to be back in the early days of rock and roll once more. The music in Part V is the music of rebirth; rock 'n' roll had reinvented itself once again!

Soul music has its roots in gospel music and R&B. "I Gotta' Woman," Ray Charles's 1954 hit, is often considered the first song of the soul genre. James Brown, dubbed the "Godfather of Soul," often claimed that he had always been an R&B singer. Black jazz musicians described soul as music with a slow groove and a hard-driving rhythm—riff-oriented and sexy.

Ann Danielson is in the Musicology Department at the University of Norway, and in her essay "Two Discourses on Blackness" from Presence and Pleasure, The Funk Grooves of James Brown and Parliament, she presents two distinct perspectives for understanding black culture. One she describes as "the Western way of understanding and represent-ing blackness." The other perspective, "the primitivist reading of black culture" rose out of 1960s political movements, and is essentially the African-American account of black music and culture.

Punk meant different things in the United States than it did in Britain. The scene in the U.S. was older and was primarily about the music. The British version of punk had more to do with the ideas that Malcolm McLaren brought back from his visits to clubs like CBGB in New York. For McLaren, punk revolved around fashion and marketing, including the marketing of the musical product in the form of the Sex Pistols. Back in the United States, in 1973 Hilly Kristal opened his club CBGB in the Bowery section of New York. CBGB offered a venue for bands such as The Ramones, Misfits, Television, the Patti Smith Group, Blondie, and Talking Heads to develop their music and perform. It was a low-stakes affair, but that fact allowed groups to take chances and perform original songs along with covers. It was the antithesis of Top 40 radio. Bands were back to three chords and a shout. In retrospect, it was a moment (a long moment) that likely saved rock 'n' roll from its own excesses.

Craig O'Hara is a contributor to AK/PM Press, an independent publisher specializing in Marxist and anarchist literature. It also publishes graphic novels and crime fiction, and produces CDs and political documentaries. O'Hara's essay, "Why Punk: Background Comparisons with Previous Art Movements; Some Defining Characteristics of Punk," in The Philosophy of Punk, More than Noise!, describes the punk movement as a major voice of "out-groups"—Blacks, homosexuals, HIV positive—those alienated and isolated from society. For the disenfranchised, rock 'n' roll has always served a larger purpose than to entertain. Although rock in the '50s and early '60s did address racial barriers, as O'Hara says, "it was not until the late '60s that distinct politics were carried in rock music. It was at this time that Rock showed its power and the sub-culture became a counter-culture."

As the music by and for youth exploded from the late '50s through the '60s, women became more prominent in rock 'n' roll. Jacqueline Warwick's essay, "Rebellion and Girldom," from Girl Groups, Girl Culture, Popular Music and Identity in the 1960s, traces how images of girls — their equality (or not) to boys — was both reflected by, and changed through, a number of early rebel songs from The Shangri-Las, The Angels, The Crystals (Darlene Love and the Blossoms), and The Marvelettes. She notes: "Against the backdrop of an association of girls with domestic, closed spaces and an emphasis on passive, meek behavior with only the nicest boys, so strong in communities with middle-class values, it is clear that songs about outcast boyfriends, and songs wherein girls took the initiative to act on their own desires, must be understood as resistant to the rigid boundaries that confined girls."

By the early '80s, rock in popular culture was both widespread and diverse. Rock had fragmented into so many genres and sub-genres, that in 1980 Billy Joel was prompted to write a song called "It's Still Rock and Roll to Me." MTV, a network established to broadcast music videos, was launched on August 1, 1981, in New York City, and for quite some time the network heavily influenced both the music industry and popular culture. Shortly after the Buggles's "Video Killed the Radio Star" was broadcast as the first music video, rock artists began to clamor to air their videos on MTV.

Gillian G. Gaar, a Seattle-based author of several books about rock music, has also written liner notes for music collections by Laurie Anderson, Judy Collins, and Pat Benetar. In "Smile for the Camera" from She's a Rebel, The History of Women in Rock & Roll, Gaar argues that MTV promoted sex as well as music: "But the performer—male or female—who turned out to be the most skillful at capitalizing on the potential of video, especially its capacity to comment on and challenge conventional perceptions of sex and sexuality, was undoubtedly Madonna." Accused herself of flaunting her sexuality and setting the feminist movement back several years, Madonna replied: "They don't get the joke. The point is I'm not anybody's toy."

Metal emerged as a rock genre between1968 and 1974, largely in the U.K. and the U.S. Its roots lie in blues-rock and psychedelic rock, but heavy metal carved out its own sound with highly amplified distortion, extended guitar solos, and overall loudness. Although heavy metal lyrics and performance styles are generally associated with masculinity and machismo, by the 1980s a number of sub-genres began to appear. Mötley Crüe and Ratt enjoyed major commercial success with a style that became known as glam metal. Metallica and Megadeath broke into the mainstream with a more aggressive style called thrash metal.

Glenn T. Pillsbury, a recent Ph.D. in musicology from UCLA and a rising star in the field of popular music studies, is also the author of the "Metallica" chapter in the Encyclopedia Britannica. He cites 1983 as the beginning of thrash metal because some of the most successful bands associated with that style—Metallica, Anthrax and Slayer—released their first albums that year. Metallica, he argues, exemplified the genre's musical style through its "consistent treatment of tempo in a rhythmically intense manner and as a distinctly aggressive musical element."

♪ Two Discourses on Blackness

By Anne Danielsen

> True "objectivity" where race is concerned is as rare as a necklace of Hope
> diamonds.
>
> —Hoyt W. Fuller

How funk is experienced—and how these experiences are explained and described, thereby gaining meaning in social discourse—varies considerably. As R. Radano and P. V. Bohlman point out, listeners may now acquire recorded musics, formerly bound up within a racial framework, and give them specific, local, alternative meanings. Nevertheless, this process takes place "within a global economy that provides, free of charge, matrices of meaning articulated, if not regulated and controlled, by the transnational institutions of mass-marketed entertainment."[1]

One such matrix of meaning is the Western historical way of understanding and representing blackness. This primitivist reading of black culture is contrasted by the African American account of black music and culture, which arose from 1960s political movements. I will now introduce these two related but very different discourses, both of which link otherness and black music to one another and both of which represent important aspects of the 1970s context of funk. I will then conclude with a discussion of may choice of groove as a primary perspective on funk.

The Primitivist Representation of Black Culture

How, or rather why, has funk taken on the meanings it has within the Anglo-American field of popular music? A starting point for an answer to this question is the common opposition of nature and culture, and by extension the West's historical linking of black culture to nature. The representation of African or black culture as barbarian in this sense has been part of the Western understanding of itself for centuries. Over one hundred fifty years ago Hegel, for example, characterized the African as follows: "All our observations of African man show him as living in a state of savagery and barbarism, and he remains in this state to the present day. The negro is an example of animal man in all his savagery and lawlessness, and if we wish to understand him at all, we must put aside all our European attitudes."[2] According to Hegel, the African had not progressed beyond his immediate existence to an awareness of any other substantial and objective existence; he had not yet attained "the recognition of the universal." As a consequence, the African is not even considered to be at an early stage in the development of our civilized world but instead represents a threshold to history: the African becomes a negative limit for what humanity can be.[3] As James Snead has pointed out, the African comes to represent "an absolute alterity to the European"; the African works as an other against whom we define ourselves.[4]

As postcolonial theorizing has brought to the fore, this othering process—characterized by Hay den White as "ostensive self-definition by negation"[5]—has resulted in a very particular lens through which the West has seen others and made them almost the same, regardless of their striking diversity. Others have all, in short, become what we are not. Others—including other places and other times—have been used as a way of identifying ourselves, thus ending up in a metonymic relation with all of the features structurally glued to the other pole of the culture-nature axis, such as (mind-)body, (intellect-) emotions, (complexity-)simplicity, and so on.

The features linked with such a position of otherness have in turn been considered bad (see Hegel) or good. While the former may be characterized as an instance of a modern affirmative primitivism, the latter should be considered as a critique of modernity. In it the same features are attributed to the other, but they now represent a more natural, more authentic—in short, more human—way of life than the alienated modern world. In line with A.-B. Gran (2000), we may paraphrase White and call this turnabout a process of *critical self-definition by negation.*[6] In this version of primitivism, which is often labeled romantic primitivism, nature is good, culture is bad.[7]

The case of blackface minstrelsy in the United States supports the assumption that this *ambivalent attitude* seems to have always characterized white people's encounters with black culture. Blackface roles became increasingly important to minstrel shows during the nineteenth century, representing an image of black people as they were seen and portrayed by whites. Although the stereotypes changed somewhat over the years, the main features of the image remained constant: blacks were strongly infantilized, presented as simple, happy people who were unable to cope with the freedoms and challenges of a modern "adult" world (and consequently best off in the safer world of the slave plantation). According to Christopher Small, blackface minstrelsy was met by a double-sided response in its white audiences, showing how affirmative and romantic primitivism may often be at work simultaneously. On the one hand, there was the envy that the white person, caught up in a formidable work ethic and overarching Puritanism, felt about the black person, who was perceived as irresponsible, sexually potent, and devoted to the pleasures of the moment. But there was also a genuine admiration of certain qualities in the black community, its communality and soul, or "emotional honesty," as Small puts it. It was the need to make sense of this complex of feelings that lay behind the popularity of blackface minstrelsy, according to Small: "The minstrel show articulated with precision these attitudes, being a vehicle for caricature which served to render innocuous the fascinating but dangerous culture of the blacks."[8] In short, blackface minstrelsy answered a need in white culture to sort out these mixed feelings toward blacks and also get in touch with what black culture had to offer, but in a way that kept the attractive otherness of black culture at a distance.[9]

Eric Lott, in his impressive study of minstrelsy entitled *Love and Theft,* also underlines the ambivalence of the white audience's meeting with blackness, and how the minstrel show took the form of a simultaneous drawing up and crossing of racial boundaries. According to Lott, the minstrel show displayed a mixed erotic economy of celebration and exploitation, and minstrelsy was often an attempt, within a context of cross-racial desire, to repress through ridicule the real white interest in black cultural practices. According to Lott, this made blackface minstrelsy a sign less of absolute white power and control than panic, anxiety, terror, and pleasure. He writes, "The minstrel show was less the incarnation of an age-old racism than an emergent social semantic figure highly responsive to the emotional demands and troubled fantasies of its audiences."[10]

As Edward Said has argued with regard to the Orient, such primitivist representations of an othered culture by the dominant culture often have consequences also for the othered culture's understanding of itself. As he states in *Orientalism,* "Like any set of durable ideas, Orientalist notions influenced the people who were called Oriental as well as those called Occidental, European, or Western; in short, Orientalism is better grasped as a set of constraints upon and limitations of thought than it is simply a positive doctrine."[11] This mechanism is also at work in the primitivist representation of black culture, which has influenced black self-representation in certain ways. In some cases it has been adopted without mediation or even comment. In other cases it has been inverted or reproduced with a double message. This may have been the case when, in the last decades of the nineteenth century, black artists entered the minstrel stage, many of them "blacked up" and acting out the same stereotypes as the white minstrels of the previous decades. Surprisingly, blackface minstrelsy by black performers was extremely popular with not only white but black audiences too. So how could this be?

According to Small, there may be several reasons for black artists blacking up. First of all, the minstrel stage was one of the few opportunities for a black performer to earn a living. Second, it meant a chance to display one's theatrical and musical skills. Third, and most important in this context, blackface minstrelsy may be interpreted as an example of an old strategy used by the abused: to take the abusive label, invert its meaning, and wear it as a badge of pride. Small claims that the black minstrel probably had much more to say to the black audience than to the white. And he was probably able to do so, for, as Small reminds us, both the black minstrel and the black audiences were descendants of slaves who had been communicating clandestinely for generations: "And so it was that minstrelsy, which had been a way of affirming the inferiority of black people, became for those same people an avenue of advancement and helped in the creation of a language of self-presentation which was not without importance in the struggle for recognition as people. But ... there was a price; the minstrel image has haunted blacks ever since."[12]

The double voice of the black minstrel, as well as the ambivalent response of its white audience, suggests preconditions for the exchange between black music and a mixed audience, and it is no less topical today. The outcome of this double-voiced strategy is, however, twofold. On the one hand, it is a form of black power in which black agency links up with white passivity, a situation that may be used by black artists for their own benefit. On the other hand, it is yet another case of black people affirming the role of the exotic other. As such, the double-voiced utterance is both a means of uniqueness and a confirmation of the status quo. Seen from the outside, it affirms the stereotype; seen from the inside, it comments upon it in a process of self-parody or self-reflection.

A parallel situation from contemporary music arises in rap and the black concept of "badness," which signifies a certain way of behavior, a style and attitude, as Cornel West explains:

> For most young black men, power is acquired by stylizing their bodies over space and time in such a way that their bodies reflect their uniqueness and provoke fear in others. To be "bad" is good not simply because it subverts the language of the dominant white culture but also because it imposes a unique kind of order for young black men on their own distinctive chaos and solicits an attention that makes others pull back with some trepidation. This young black male style is a form of self-identification and resistance in a hostile culture.[13]

Badness is both a means of uniqueness and a confirmation of the primitivist representation of black culture. As such, it is attractive to, but out of reach for, whites (and, we should add, black women, who instead suffer from this form of black power).[14] This source of power, however, can also be considered an internalization of the otherness of black culture, one put forward by the dominant white culture. Particularly if we take into consideration the profound inequalities in discursive and economic power, badness may appear to be another example of an oppressed culture adopting the oppressor's representation of itself.

Why, then, is this primitivist representation relevant to a study of funk?

The primitivist account of black culture in our recent history, as wild, irresponsible, closer to nature, out of control—but also more sexually potent—unavoidably influences contemporary relations between blacks and whites on all levels. It does not always sound as baldly colonial as Hegel's quotations, but it is still there in its more or less subtle disguise as an imagined counterpart in the process of Western self-definition: a dream of otherness. This is certainly also the case in the field of music. It is striking how black music has been placed in opposition to European high art musical traditions in the West. In contrast with Western art music's traditional focus on form, harmony, and thematic development, African music, for example, has been identified mainly with rhythm. This has no doubt influenced the study of African music, both regarding what music is chosen and what aspects of it are examined. In short, studies of rhythm, in particular West African drumming, seem to be privileged over vocal traditions and other African music that is more focused on melody and chords, and this selection of music is probably biased according to musical aspects that are constitutive of the music's otherness.

This was addressed by Kofi Agawu in an article entitled "The Invention of 'African Rhythm'" (1995). In a rather harsh critique, Agawu questions the validity of the account of African music given by both Western and African scholars within this field, especially its focus on the complexities of African rhythm. This construction is, according to Agawu, maintained by three errors; the first concerning the claim that African music should constitute a homogenous whole: "The continued use of the phrase 'African music' when one's authority is an African village/town, or region reproduces the metonymic fallacy—the part representing the whole—faced by most writers on Africa."[15] The second error he calls "the retreat from comparison": although the claim about the complexities of African rhythm presupposes, a comparative framework, it rarely leads to explicit comparison. He continues: "For such comparisons to have force, we need to do more than casually allude to the other term in the binary framework."[16] The third error has to do with the lack of a critical evaluation of African musical practice, both with regard to whether a performance is good or not and whether informants are reliable.[17]

From Agawu's Foucaultian informed perspective, the construction of the notion "African rhythm" is at the center of a whole discourse that has been—and still is—extremely powerful within the field of black music studies:

> Note that this notion has been promulgated by both Western and African scholars … It is therefore not simply a case of westerners (mis)representing African music—although given the political and economic realities that have shaped the construction of the library of African music, and given the blatant asymmetries of power that the colonial encounter has produced, there are solid grounds for indulging in the politics of blame. What we have, rather, are the views of a group of scholars operating within a field of discourse, an intellectual space defined by Euro-American traditions of ordering knowledge. It is difficult to overestimate the determining influence of this scholarly tradition on the representation of African music.[18]

In *Lying Up a Nation: Race and Black Music* (2003), Ronald Radano extends Agawu's critique, arguing that the emphasis on rhythm as the primary defining quality of black music is a modern idea, deeply linked with what he calls "the dialectics of modern racial ideology." According to Radano, the idea emerged in the beginning of the twentieth century in response to a specific historical circumstance, namely the increasing presence of African American popular music in the public sphere. Radano identifies this linking of race and rhythm as a meeting or crossroads of two conceptions of blackness that he names descent and displacement. *Descent* is the search for the origins of black rhythm. Radano, interestingly, traces this line back to theories of cultural and racial difference in early comparative musicology, pointing out how the idea of rhythm as a more natural, more original—that is, a more primitive—form of human behavior took shape as part of the overall processes of "ostensive self-definition by negation" presented above.[19] As we know, rhythm has been placed at the center of the identity of black culture in subsequent discourses, and if we adopt Radano's perspective, this may appear to be an instance of unmediated appropriation of the first position's (white comparative musicology) representation of an othered culture (black music). I will return to a discussion of this toward the end of this chapter.

In addition to this search for origin along the temporal-historical axis, Radano identifies a spatial axis, a conception of blackness as *displacement, or* more precisely as "sounds out of-place." As African Americans began to move about the American territory in the postbellum era, they inevitably challenged the boundaries that had once constrained them both physically and socially. As a consequence, black music appeared in public more frequently, becoming, in his words, "a potent blackness 'on the loose,"[20] He writes: "In black musical production, then, we recognize the emergence of a formidable social expression inextricably related to the creation of American modernism. Its potency derives from its articulation of a radically new conception of racial otherness growing from the spatial dimensions of the crossroads as it intersects temporal affiliations north and south." While earlier conceptions of otherness linked the identity of 'the other' to a certain place, which according to an ethnocentric point of view was conceived of as homogenous and with absolute properties, this new understanding of black music "defined the essential nature of blackness by exceeding place in ways that anticipated other fractured dimensions of modernist art and culture."[21]

According to Radano, this made the new black music and its ragged rhythm uncanny, a magical force that was thought to infect anybody—or rather any *body*—that came in contact with it. In line with this, when "hot rhythm" peaked with the music of the "jazz age" of the 1920s, it was considered almost an epidemical threat. As one contemporary writer put it, hot rhythm could "get into the blood of some of our young folks, and I might add older folks, too."[22]

The parallel to the discourse on rock 'n' roll in the 1950s is indeed striking, and within the Anglo-American field of pop and rock in the 1960s and 1970s we find the same double notion: on one hand the romantic primitivist understanding of black music as origin and nature, and on the other hand the intertwined conception of hot rhythm. On the positive side, we have the communal feeling of the rock concert or the dance floor, and the ideal of honesty in musical expression; on the negative side, we have the aspects of rock culture that are perceived as "dirty"—irresponsibility, sexual freedom, pleasure seeking in the moment—all commonly linked with rock's roots in black musical culture.

A twenty-five-year-old text by Simon Frith may serve as an example of how important the primitivist account of black music has been for rock: "Whereas Western dance forms control body movements and sexuality itself with formal rhythms and innocuous tunes, black music expresses the body, hence sexuality, with a directly physical beat and an intense, emotional sound—the sound and beat are felt rather than interpreted via a set of conventions. Black musicians work, indeed, with a highly developed aesthetic of public sexuality."[23] Frith's quotation also seems to describe black music as closer to nature. Significant qualities of the music are understood as unmediated bodily expression and as ineligible for conventional processing and interpretation on the reception side. In short, the artifact nature of black music is denied and the body is reduced to the sexual body alone.[24]

The longing for the "other side" of typical Western values, for keeping a certain distance from the mainstream, is central to the entire history of popular music in the West from the 1950s onward.[25] In line with this, Robert Pattison has interpreted the whole field of rock as a rebellion against rationality and order—the official super-ego of the West, as he calls it. To quote the title of his book, rock is "the triumph of vulgarity."[26] The perceived "black" aspects of popular music, especially its rhythm and its distorted sounds, have been central means for realizing rock's subversive power, as well as its anti-Western values. These aspects have, in short, worked as a carrier of the otherness sought after in this music. In the words of Radano and Bohlman, "The imagic power of 'blackness' appears as a dislocated, fragmentary hypertext of post–World War II American popular sound."[27]

As a genre focused on rhythm or groove, funk has been perceived almost as blackness in its purest form. This musical difference from the "official" musical tradition of the West, art music, has made funk an especially effective means for living out the other side of Western culture. It is, thus, not very surprising that funk has been described as "body music" within the West, and more than this, as the bodily experience par excellence: sexual pleasure. It has been interpreted as a distillation of repetitive rhythm, the aspect of rock commonly regarded as most closely related to sex.

To interrogate this reductive understanding of funk is not to deny this music's striking physical appeal: funk is designed to move the body; it is dance music. Rather, we may begin to introduce a more nuanced understanding of the appeal of funk and the complexities of its grooves. Moreover, the flip side of the primitivist understanding of black music is that the spiritual aspects of the funk experience seem to have completely vanished. It is my claim that these spiritual aspects are as important as its bodily aspects to the white Western fan's fascination with funk and the state of being it offers. Most likely, as I will argue toward the end of this book, they are inseparable.

Black is Beautiful!—Black Music and Black Struggle

Within American academia, we find a discourse on African American music that is far from the body-and-sex discourse of rock. Historically, it points back to the vital period of black political struggle in the 1960s, when aesthetic aspects of black music were often subordinated to political aims, or, as Henry Louis Gates Jr. writes: "One repeated concern of the Black Aesthetic movement was the nature and function of black literature vis-à-vis the larger political struggle for Black Power. How useful was our literature to be in this centuries-old political struggle, and exactly how was our literature to be useful?"[28]

This program for the Black Arts Movement is highly present in the seminal 1972 anthology *The Black Aesthetic*. In his introduction, Addison Gayle Jr. writes: "The question for the black critic today is not how beautiful a melody, a play, a poem, or a novel, but how much more beautiful has the poem, melody, or novel made the life of a single black man? How far has the work gone in transforming an American Negro into an African-American or black man?"[29]

A main task for the Black Aesthetic Movement was, as one white critic described it, "the act of creation of the self in the face of the self's historic denial by our society."[30] Although this must be said to be a constant aspect of black culture and black political struggle in the United States, the 1960s were characterized by a sharpening of the effort against the white mainstream. A policy of explicit anti-integrationism articulated a rather harsh critique of the black middle class that was ready to fit into the American mainstream. In this era, "American" in fact comes close to meaning the opposite of black: to be American is to be anti-black, or, in the words of Gayle: "The serious black artist of today is at war with the American society as few have been throughout American history."[31] Later he adds, "To be an American is to be opposed to humankind, against the dignity of the individual, and against the striving in man for compassion and tenderness: to be an American is to lose one's humanity."[32]

The backdrop for this confrontational line was no doubt partly the American intervention in Vietnam. However, the double moral standards of liberal white America, as well as an increasing understanding of how the liberal ideology in many respects failed to change the conditions of black America—it often worked instead as a vehicle of repressive tolerance[33]—were also important. According to Gayle, revealing the white liberals as "the modern-day plantation owners they are" should be a primary target for African American critics. The liberal's ideology, he writes, is "a cosmology that allows him to pose as humanitarian on the one hand, while he sets about defining the black man's limitations on the other."[34]

In line with this, one point central to the Black Aesthetic Movement was the encouragement of the black artist to give up working with the white public in mind. The price for becoming an American was too high, Gayle says, because it seemed to mean giving up one's own identity. Or, in Hoyt W. Fuller's words, "[The] black writer has wasted much time and talent ... seeking an identity that can only do violence to his sense of self."[35] The true black artist should rather speak honestly and avoid pretending or adjusting his mannerisms to the mainstream white audience. According to Gayle, the black artist has simply "given up the futile practice of speaking to whites, and has begun to speak to his brothers."[36]

As a result, the principles for a genuinely black aesthetic were worked out in the different fields of art. Among these, music seemed to have a privileged position. First, it was a cultural expression that presented itself as less "infected" by the Anglo-American West, at least when compared to writing, which was the primary mode of expression for many of the articulate participants in the Black Aesthetic Movement. In the field of writing, it seemed much more complicated to cut off black practice from Western practice. Many black writers were themselves fully aware of the subtleties and complexities characterizing the relation between the white canon and black literature, and they struggled with the dual nature of their heritage. In the domain of music, however, it seemed as if the black tradition were more unequivocally black. At least the terrain was easier to map, because the demarcation line was more striking. In his introduction to an essay on black aesthetics in music, for example, Jimmy Stewart does not hesitate to state that "There have always been two musical traditions: the musical tradition or aesthetic of white people in the West, and the musical tradition of Black people in this country."[37]

Today, such a clear-cut separation is more difficult to maintain; the overlaps and intermingling are striking. Moreover, decades of deconstruction and postcolonial thought have brought about insights into how identity is always part of a relational framework. Nevertheless, even though one might not hold on to an essentialist position, it is not difficult to understand what Stewart means. There are differences that make it easy to distinguish between white and black musical traditions, not least , regarding the *approach* to music making. One might, in short, say that black musicking has a different creative focus; it is a *performing art* in the deepest sense. Or, in Stewart's words, "the imperishability of creation is not in what is created, is not in the art product, is *not in the thing* as it exists as an object, *but in the procedure* of its becoming what it is."[38]

As a consequence, in the Black Aesthetic Movement's attempts to identify an especially black literary aesthetics, writing partly took music as a model: "The writers are deliberately striving to invest their work with the distinctive styles and rhythms and colors of the ghetto, with those peculiar qualities which, for example, characterize the music of a John Coltrane or a Charlie Parker or a Ray Charles."[39]

A key theme within the Black Aesthetic Movement was its link to African culture. As a performing art, music is a form of cultural heritage that may be transmitted independent of material resources. It was, therefore, well suited to rebut the claim that an enslaved people was a people of lost culture.[40] Together with storytelling and other oral literary practices, approaches to music making were examples of cultural resources that had traveled from one continent to another with the people and their collective memory, and the approaches could later be applied to the instruments of the new world. This could, then, be linked to the fact that the black treatment of instruments—the piano or the voice, for example—is very different from the Western art music tradition's treatment, and it could further be used as evidence for the existence of a particularly black aesthetic linked with African musical practices. In Stewart's words,

The instruments didn't come with free lessons and all, like you get at Wurlitzer ... It was a matter of being left to our own resources to determine how the music was going to be produced on those instruments. This ... meant that we had to impose on borrowed instruments an aesthetic convention that we obviously possessed even before we acquired them … It indicates that a Black aesthetic existed, and that this aesthetic has always governed what we have produced.[41]

While the political aspects of this debate peaked in the late 1960s, it has remained very influential in American scholarship to this day. As Gates writes, "The impetus of the Black Arts movement of the sixties, the literary and aesthetic wing of the Black Power movement, served two functions to which academic critics of the seventies and eighties are heir: the resurrection of 'lost' black texts, and the concomitant need to define the principles of criticism upon which a 'genuinely black' aesthetic could be posited."[42] In line with this, musicological attempts at defining a genuinely black aesthetic have been focused on the African influence on black American music, and on the common approach to musicking, claiming that it is the approaches, rather than the actual sounds that these approaches make, that unite the different black musical traditions.[43] Or, as composer and musicologist Oily Wilson states, "The common core of this Africanness consists of the way of doing something, not simply something that is done."[44] According to Wilson, this influence can be summed up as follows:

- a tendency to create musical structures in which rhythmic clash or disagreement of accents is the ideal;
- a tendency to approach singing or the playing of any instrument in a percussive manner;
- a weakness for a kaleidoscopic range of dramatically contrasting qualities of sound;
- a tendency toward a high density of events within a relatively short time frame; and
- a tendency to create musical forms with antiphonal or call-and- response musical structures.

Furthermore, importance is placed on the tendency to incorporate physical motion as an integral part of the music-making process, and on the social setting: music is a social activity where everybody, in a sense, participates on an improvisatory basis, although within a clearly defined and shared framework.[45]

Given the favorable position of jazz and other African American popular styles with regard to both their aesthetic quality and their popularity, music has been a powerful way of focusing a specific black identity within the larger American society. Music has, moreover, worked as a convincing link to the African past. Not least, much funk fits easily into the characteristics listed by Wilson above, and James Brown's funk in particular is often used to substantiate the linking of African and African American music.[46] In his book on black musical styles from 1950 to 1990, Guthrie P. Ramsey Jr. points to James Brown's production of the 1960s as extremely important for the new nationalism or black consciousness in the same period. According to Ramsey, the 1960s and 1970s should be regarded as the second phase of what he calls "a grand narrative of progress" named

"Afro-modernism." This story is connected to the new urbanity of African American communities and the significant sociopolitical progress in black America in the first half of the twentieth century.[47] In this second phase of Afro-modernism, the results of migration patterns in the first part of the century coincides with mass media texts, which African Americans living all over the United States would believe spoke to and about them as a group. According to Ramsey, James Brown epitomized this moment: "James Brown ruled the private and public spaces of black Chicago. You heard him constantly on the radio, at the block party, in roller rinks, homes, clubs, and stores. Everywhere."[48] There were several factors that contributed to this. First, as mentioned previously, his musical language, "the *spontaneity-within-the-pocket* funk approach" that he developed in this period, attracted black cultural nationalists interested in the link to an African past.[49] Second, his lyrics—both his political use of the word "black" and his emphasis on social justice and racial uplift—and his oral style of vocal delivery, which evoked a seemingly on-the-spot communication with an imagined community, combined with his own personal history to make him a reliable spokesman for black communities.

The relation between the music of James Brown, the politicized discourse of the Black Arts Movement, and the specific historical situation of African Americans in the United States in this period illustrates how music, discourse, and sociopolitical circumstances intertwine. In fact, Ramsey's account of the importance of James Brown for this era reminds us of the reciprocal relation of music and social and cultural matters. Contrary to what was often the case in the "older school" of cultural studies and subculture theory, where music was assumed to mirror underlying social structures and relations, the formative role of music in *shaping* such cultural and social matters must also be taken into account. It is exactly when we come to this relation between music and sociocultural identity that we find a severe difference between the discourses discussed in this chapter.

As scholars G. Born and D. Hesmondhalgh point out, music may be used in sociocultural processes in different ways. While it is worth recalling, especially in the context of this study, that music may well be used to *transcend* a certain sociocultural identity, music is also, as the discourse surrounding the funk grooves of the 1960s and 1970s in black America shows, a very effective means of affirming and delimiting the boundaries too: "Against prevailing views that music is primarily a means for the imagining of emergent and labile identities, we stress that music is equally at times a medium for marking and reinforcing the boundaries of existing sociocultural categories and groups."[50] To point out this fact is not to subscribe to an essentialist position, nor to fall back on an old static model of homology. Rather, it is a reminder of the fact that, in Ramsey's words, "All this talk of fluidity, indeed the idea of ethnicity as process and not a static existence, does not prevent our understanding how people experience group identity from a reified, though contested, 'center.'"[51] Keeping this in mind and recalling as well the formative role of music in these processes, both on an individual and a collective level, we may approach the task of understanding how funk, as Western music "with a distinct difference," as Ramsey puts it, came to play different roles in the two different social worlds that meet in the subject matter of this book.[52] Before moving on to the analyses in parts II and III, however, a few comments on this difference, and the related focus on funk as grooves, need to be made.

A Common Source of Otherness?

Both the Black Arts Movement of the 1960s and the African retention arguments put forward by African American musicologists are examples of how important music has been in the process of shaping an African American history and identity in the United States. Within these discourses the features of black music are not seen as part of an interracial relation but rather in isolation from, and sometimes even in opposition to, white culture. In *Lying Up a Nation,* Radano criticizes the essentializing tendency of scholarly research on black music in general, although he credits the major contributions these scholars and writers have made in making the black tradition visible in academic institutions and writings. In Radano's view, the power of black music to enforce the collective "we" of blackness in these works comes forward as a black musical metaphysics emerging from America's own racial imagination, one that responds to the assimilationist intentions of erasure:

> In political terms, the metaphysical claims of black music that became emblematic of the Black Arts Movement challenged a vulnerable white supremacy that could no longer explain away the power and appeal of black musical achievement. As enabling as these racial essentialisms may have been, however, they also constrained the comprehension of black music's more fundamental insurgencies, particularly with reference to the undermining of racial categories.[53]

Radano's claim is that the importance of black music for the black identity project has led to a politics that betrays the underlying interracial relations' role in the understanding of the conceived essence of black music.[54] One consequence of such a politics is that one overlooks the fact that the discourses on blackness discussed in this chapter, although differing severely in important aspects, share some fundamental features. They both rely on the notion of black rhythm as a core characteristic of black music. Moreover, they both separate themselves from the mainstream, understanding blackness as difference. Radano's work shows how the results of the European processes of self-definition by way of negation in the nineteenth century may have blended into the Afro-centric discourse on black music in the United States in the following century, forming "a sturdy basis for defining and redefining difference across the twentieth century."[55] According to Radano, this historic moment, which is characterized by the shift in public perception that reinvented black music as rhythm, represents no less than "a veritable watershed in the formation of black modern music."[56] It was from this common ground that black rhythm spread across the Western world, infiltrating the very core of the experience of being modern on both sides of the color line.

In general, the hybrid character of funk and other black American music, on the production and the reception sides, seems to be under- emphasized in the ethnomusicological discourse on black music. Radano's rendering of how the story of black rhythm as the main identifying feature of black music came to be as part of an interracial relation of black and white is thus both important and convincing. Moreover, it suggests a view of black music that recognizes the significance of blackness and black music for both blacks and whites. In this book, the aim of which is to investigate the meeting of black dance music and a white Northern European audience in the 1970s, such an interracial matrix for understanding black music in fact becomes no less than a fundamental premise.

Funk is commonly regarded as black rhythm music par excellence. As such, funk has served as a consummate example of the blackness of black music. In line with the critique above, one might ask if the focus on rhythm in the study of funk, and in this book, betrays a more correct—in the sense of free of racial inclinations—approach to funk. In my view, however, there are many reasons for keeping a focus on rhythm in the study of funk. First, and this is presumably in great part due to the circumstances focused upon by Radano, the *reception* of funk, on both sides of the color line, has been extremely focused on rhythm. Put differently, the ideological grounding of certain tendencies in the historical reception of funk cannot change the *effect* of black rhythm on its audience as it once was, there and then. Even though one might have wished that the reception turned out to be less inclined to racial categories, the fact that it was may not be revised.

Second, despite the aforementioned ideological construction's disproportionate influence upon the perception of black musicking, rhythm is an important aspect of it. To completely avoid discussing black rhythm when dealing with black music would be to throw out the baby with the bathwater. After the "watershed" described by Radano, black music has to a great extent developed as rhythm music, because the ideology constraining black music to rhythm has influenced its production, especially as commercial distribution has become more and more important. This is also a point made by Radano: "As black performers entered into more public circumstances controlled by white authority of taste, they were compelled to work within the parameters defining the nature of race music. In this, they did not simply perform black music but produced those particular expressions that affirmed racial difference within a broad system of relations and according to a structural logic that was unmistakably ideological."[57] In line with this, it is possible to believe that African American musicians have continued to develop and generate forms that highlight musical blackness, though for the pleasure of an interracial audience. This probably holds true for many popular black forms, like swing, rhythm and blues, bebop, cool, soul, funk, and more. And as West reminds us, this structural logic of racial origin is still at work in our time in what is probably the most widespread and influential contemporary manifestation of blackness: rap.

There is also a final, and perhaps more pragmatic, reason for sticking to a focus on groove in this situation: there is a striking lack of studies of rhythm and groove in musicology, including popular music studies. And as would hopefully be clear by now, this lack is not a coincidence. Rather, it is in itself a product of a racially inclined musicological tradition, which, as Radano suggests, may also be the common ground of the otherness of *both* discourses of blackness presented and discussed in this chapter. As a fulfillment of a black aesthetic on several levels, including its emphasis on performance in general and performing with "style" in particular, funk may serve as a perfect starting point for correcting this imbalance in musicological focus and interest.

II   A Brand New Bag

Analytical Investigations

Despite some telling descriptions of the turn toward funk by James Brown and his band, there are few attempts in the musicological literature to actually trace these changes in songs. A confrontation with the early funk of James Brown as sounding music would probably disturb the clarity of the picture that is typically presented:

> Brown would sing a semi-improvised, loosely organized melody that wandered while the band riffed rhythmically on a single chord, the horns tersely punctuating Brown's declamatory phrases. With no chord changes and precious little melodic variety to sustain listener's interest, rhythm became everything. Brown and his musicians and arrangers began to treat every instrument and voice in the group as if each were a drum. The horns played single-note bursts that were often sprung against the downbeats. The bass lines were broken up into choppy two- or three-note patterns, a procedure common in Latin music since the Forties but unusual in R&B. Brown's rhythm guitarist choked his guitar strings against the instrument's neck so hard that his playing began to sound like a jagged tin can being scraped with a pocketknife. Only occasionally were the horns, organ or backing vocalists allowed to provide a harmonic continuum by holding a chord.
>
> The chugging push-pull of the Brown band's "Brand New Bag" was the wave of the future.[1]

In this text from *The Rolling Stone Illustrated History of Rock and Roll*, we get the impression of a total change from previous musical styles and of all of the features of the new style working comfortably together.

Certainly, many of the songs from this period—from "Papa's Got a Brand New Bag" in 1965 to the more fleshed-out funk tunes of the early 1970s—are more or less funk. They are, however, always something else as well. It is usually different aspects of different songs that point toward the "new style": all of the features listed above—semi-improvised vocals, one-chord "harmony," implied polyrhythm, the rhythmic riffing of the horn section and the guitar, the fragmentation of the bass line, and an overall percussive approach—are relevant, but they are seldom, if ever, present at the same time. The transition from rhythm and blues to funk, the former represented by tunes like "Papa's Got a Brand New Bag" and "I Got You (I Feel Good)" (1965), the latter by "Cold Sweat" (1967), is in many ways rather vague, either because the new features to some extent were already there or the older ones remained present.

Notes: Two Discourses on Blackness

1. Radano and Bohlman 2000: 32.
2. Hegel 1980 (1830): 177.
3. Ibid.: *176–177.*
4. See Snead 1984: 63.
5. White 1972: 5.
6. Gran 2000: 47.
7. See Marshall Berrnan's *All That Is Solid Melts into Air* for an interesting discussion of how modernity's own discourse on modern life has always been both affirmative and critical, often at the same time: "Our nineteenth-century thinkers [Marx and Nietzsche] were simultaneously enthusiast and enemies of modern life, wrestling inexhaustibly with its ambiguities and contradictions'[7] (Berman 1982: 24).
8. Small 1987: 154.
9. The ridicule of blacks also served as a protection against having to deal with the terrible conditions under which many people actually lived. Hoyt W. Fuller puts it this way: "The facts of Negro life accuse white people … the white viewer must either relegate it to the realm of the subhuman, thereby justifying an attitude of indifference, or else the white viewer must confront the imputation of guilt against him. And no man who considers himself human wishes to admit complicity on crimes against the human spirit" (Fuller 1972: 6).
10. Lott 1993: 6.
11. Said 1978: 42.
12. Small 1987: 152.
13. West 1994: 128.
14. West points out that the situation is different for black women because the dominant ideal of female beauty is different: "The ideal of female beauty in this country [the United States] puts a premium on lightness and softness mythically associated with white women and downplays the rich stylistic manners associated with black women … This means that black women are subject to more multi layered bombardments of racist assaults than black men, in addition to the sexist assaults they receive from black men. Needless to say, most black men … simply recycle this vulgar operation along the axis of lighter hues that results in darker black women bearing more of the brunt than their already devalued lighter sisters" (West 1994: 130).
15. Agawu 1995: 384–85.
16. Ibid.: 385.
17. Ibid.: 386.

18. Ibid.: 383.
19. Radano 2003: 247–55.
20. Ibid.: 255.
21. Ibid.: 258.
22. Alan M. Kraut in the *New York Times,* February 12, 1922, quoted in Radano 2003: 237.
23. Frith 1983: 19.
24. In a more recent book, *Performing Rites* (1996), Frith takes exception to the primitivism of the rock discourse on blackness and relates it to the mind-body split of Western thought: "There is, indeed, a long history in Romanticism of defining black culture, specifically African culture, as the body, the other of bourgeois mind" (127). In the chapter "Rhythm: Race, Sex, and the Body," his overall agenda is to loosen the close tie between rhythm and sex, which he sees as an ideological construction: "The equation of rhythm and sex is a product of high cultural ideology rather than of African popular musical practice" (141). Here, Frith reveals the traditional essentialism regarding the nature of blackness to be racist and focuses on blackness as socially and historically constructed.
25. Jazz was also perceived as subversive to the dominant values of establishment culture. In the words of Lawrence Levine, "Jazz was seen by many contemporaries as a cultural form independent of a number of the basic central beliefs of bourgeois society, free of its repressions, in rebellion against many of its grosser stereotypes'" (Levine 1978: 293).
26. See Pattison 1987.
27. Radano and Bohlman 2000: 33.
28. Gates 1987: xxv–xxvi.
29. Gayle 1972: xxii.
30. Richard Gilman, quoted in Gayle 1972: xv.
31. Gayle 1972: xvii.
32. Ibid.: xxii.
33. See Marcuse 1969.
34. Gayle 1972: xix.
35. Fuller 1972: 7.
36. Gayle 1972: xxi. The female black subject seems to be almost as absent in the Black Aesthetic Movement as the black subject is within American society as a whole (judging by Gayle and his male co-writers).
37. Stewart 1972: 77.
38. Ibid.: 80, emphasis added.
39. Fuller 1972: 9.
40. In the so-called Herskovits-Frazier debate, E. F. Frazier responded to Melville Herskovits's pioneering study of Africanisms in African American culture, *The Myth of the Negro Past* (first published in 1941), by arguing that slavery was so devastating in America that it destroyed all African elements among black Americans. Herskovits, for his part, had emphasized the continuity of West African carryovers in African American culture. For a short presentation of the Herskovits-Frazier debate and the study of African cultural survival in North America, see Holloway's introduction to the anthology *Africanisms in American Culture* (Holloway 1990: ix–xxi).
41. Stewart 1972: 81.
42. Gates 1987: xxv.

43. See, for example, P. K. Maultsby, ''Africanisms in African-American Music'' (Maultsby 1990), and O. Wilson, "The Significance of the Relationship between Afro-American Music and West African Music" (Wilson 1974).
44. Wilson 1974: 20.
45. Wilson 1983: 3.
46. Wilson, for example, turns to James Brown's "Super Bad" to demonstrate reminiscences of African cross-rhythms in African American music (Wilson 1974:12–13).
47. Ramsey 2003: 27–28.
48. Ibid.: 149.
49. Ibid.: 153.
50. Born and Hesmondhalgh 2000: 32.
51. Ramsey 2003: 38.
52. Ibid.: 19.
53. Radano 2003: 35.
54. To me it remains a bit unclear whether Radano himself believes in the power of black music as such, or whether he ascribes to the view that the power of black music may be fully accounted for at the level of discourse. If the latter, he may be accused of a form of reductionism that sometimes goes together with a certain misconception of the poststructuralist insistence on the constitutive character of discourse, as expressed, for example, in the slogan *Il n'y a pas dehors le texte*. With this utterance, French philosopher Jacques Derrida reminds us of the fact that all experiences are "always already" inscribed in discourse, in the sense that there is no inter- subjective or social experience as such. This is sometimes misconstrued as a denial—at the level of the individual—of all experiential modes other than the textual. In this study, even though I also ascribe to a nonessentialist view on the issue of cultural identity, I remain open to the importance and power of nondiscursive modes of experience.
55. Radano 2003: 276.
56. Ibid.: 272.
57. Ibid.: 271.

Notes: A Brand New Bag

1. Palmer 1992:167–68.
2. In the liner notes to *Star Time,* producer Jerry Wexler, who was then working with Aretha Franklin and other soul stars for Atlantic Records, says, "'Cold Sweat' deeply affected the musicians I knew … It just freaked them out. For a time, no one could get a handle on what to do next" (White and Weinger 1991: 31).
3. Schematically the standard form of pop/rock may be summed up as ABABC(A)B form, where A is the verse, B the chorus, and C the bridge or interlude. The chorus at the end is often repeated and/or faded out. Social theorist Max Weber's description of the nature of ideal-type concepts and their significance for the social sciences was worked out in his writings on the methodology of the social sciences. See Weber 1949. The most correct label, at least in terms of the literature in question, would probably be "West African rhythm," but because all of these texts use African rhythm or even African music (often in opposition to another ideal type, namely European music), I will also use these labels when I discuss these works.
4. Weber 1949: 90.

♪ Why Punk

Background Comparisons with Previous Art Movements; Some Defining Characteristics of Punk

By Craig O'Hara

"In a mechanical and depersonalized world man has an indefinable sense of loss; a sense that life. … has become impoverished, that men are somehow 'deracinate and disinherited,' that society and human nature alike have been atomized, and hence mutilated, above all that men have been separated from whatever might give meaning to their work and their lives." (Charles Taylor as quoted in *Man Alone* edited by Eric and Mary Josephson, Dell Publishing, New York, 1962–11).

There is a current feeling in modern society of an alienation so powerful and widespread that it has become commonplace and accepted. Some trace its roots to the beginnings of the Industrial Revolution when the work place became a second home for young and old alike. It does not take a Marxist or a learned sociologist to realize the role of mass production and maximum efficiency in creating alienation. Any rivethead, phone salesperson, or warehouseman could tell us this. The peculiar part is that man has been the one who created, agreed to, and accepted these feelings as normal. Perhaps in the late 20th century we cannot remember a time without such feelings and that we are now merely inheriting the negative structures which cause alienation. Few can argue with the idea that "Western man (and Eastern as well) has become mechanized, routinized, made comfortable as an object; but in the profound sense displaced and thrown off balance as a subjective creator and power" (ibid, 10).

Human beings act as if they have nothing in common with each other. It is as if we have all been brought here to function for ourselves in a way that does not include others. Many philosophers, sociologists, and theologians have attempted to show the ridiculousness of the atomistic, alienated lifestyles we have chosen. While the intellectual community has often shown the ability to see the 'big picture' of how things really are, this insight has mostly been kept to themselves in academic publications and confined to institutions of higher education. The elitism and monetary cost of the Ivory Towers insure that the number of people entering who suffer under the oppression the professors are so eager to study will remain few.

Repeatedly, however, a group of the alienated will recognize what is happening to themselves. This realizarior can be based on an active rejection either of or by the mainstream society. These groups can either reject the alienation they see before them or can be unwillingly alienated from the mainstream. Blacks, homosexuals, HIV+, the lower classes, etc., all have been brought together by either the realization of hierarchies or forced together by an actively destructive, authority-backed power. It is important to note that the realization of one's own group, or self, being an out-group does not entail the realization of other out-groups suffering under the same treatment. People have too often woken up to see the details of their own suffering while still remaining ignorant to the suffering of others.

Some out-groups greatly desire to be a part of the mainstream while others do not. Nevertheless, "all such out-groups face a certain degree of isolation from society; they are in the community but not of it. As a result, they tend to form more or less distinct 'subcultures' of their own" (ibid, 35). These subcultures appear to have members who are much less alienated from their own being and are often seen trying to reclaim their subjective powers. Members of subcultures, regardless of how oppressed, have often succeeded in finding a solidarity and understanding amongst themselves that is lacking in mainstream society. Members seem to regain a sense of themselves and each other that had been previously lost, forgotten, or stolen. This is seen in the emergence of support groups based on shared experiences, beliefs, sex or race. What subcultures can succeed in doing is "to imbue their members with some sense of higher purpose" (ibid, 51). This higher purpose is not always positive, as in cases such as the KKK or other hate group subcultures, but is an important component to have in any movement desiring to make changes in the status quo.

The subculture of Rock and Roll music has been an unsteady and complicated one to define. It seems idealistic and unlikely that Rock music (having started a number of years before Elvis Presley and continuing in its many forms today) has had any higher purpose than to entertain.

Rebellious youths have been drawn to its changing forms for four decades, but as a whole it has been merely another part of the ever growing entertainment industry. Early Rock and Roll vaguely addressed the racial barriers and inequalities of the fifties, but it was not until the late sixties that distinct politics were carried in Rock music. It was at this time that Rock showed its power and the subculture became a counter-culture.

A look back on the radicals of the 6G's, and I don't mean the hippies who were content to wear flowers and beg for change in San Francisco, shows their passion for Rock music and the integral link Rock'n'Roll played in their politics. From the Black Panthers falling in love with Bob Dylan in Oakland, CA to White Panther John Sinclair and his MC5 brothers calling for armed revolution in Michigan, these folks all recognized and appreciated the power of Rock music as the people's music. Prior to death and sell outs, 60's radicals Jerry Rubin and Abbie Hoffman along with countless others, channeled Rock'n'Roll to create an enormous anti-government movement made up of young dissatisfied freaks.

Unfortunately, whatever good this music served by giving praises to freedom and disdain for social hypocrisy, it met the same fate as all earlier and later forms of popular Rock: commercial dilution/creative exhaustion, co-option and takeover by mainstream forces Mark Andersen, Washington Peace Letter, Nov. 1991, 1). Rock music became "either commodified, mainstream music promoted and packaged by corporate giants, or ritual, shallow hedonism" (ibid).

An exception to Rock and Roll's predictable mainstream politics and actions has been the movement called Punk Rock, or simply Punk. The time and birthplace of the Punk movement is debatable. Either the New York scene of the late sixties/early seventies or the British Punks of 1975–76 can be given the honor. For our purposes, neither one deserves a long investigation as the specific politics and genuine forming of a movement was not until the late seventies. In general it is though that the New Yorkers invented the musical style while the British popularized the political attitude and colorful appearances. A quick look at the background of the English scene will show the circumstances in which modern Punk was born.

Tricia Henry has written a very good book which documents the beginnings of the Punk movement I in New York and its subsequent rise in England. While the book is good, it ignores everything done since 1980, when she considers Punk to have died. Several books of this kind have been written (all concentrating on the largest of all Punk bands, the Sex Pistols) and most lack a great deal of information, as they were done by writers who were not part of the movement, but outside interpreters. Henry is, however, correct and thorough on the subject at hand.

"For the large number of people on welfare—or "the dole," as it is known in Great Britain—especially young people, the outlook for bettering their lot in life seemed bleak. In this atmosphere, when the English were exposed to the seminal Punk Rock influences of the New York scene, the irony, pessimism, and amateur style of the music took on overt social and political implications, and British Punk became as self-consciously proletarian as it was aesthetic" (Tricia Henry, Break All Rules!, University Microfilms, Ann Arbor, Mi, 1989, p.8).

It is true that unemployment and poor social conditions provoke angry feelings of alienation and frustration. It is also true that these feelings can be expressed in many ways. Crime has been the most popular response in recent times, but at this place and time the hoodlums began playing guitars as well as committing petty crimes of frustration. "To ignore the obvious connections between the Punk phenomenon and economic and social inequalities in Great Britain would be to deny the validity of the philosophical underpinnings of the movement. Punk in Britain was essentially a movement consisting of underprivileged working-class white youths. Many of them felt their social situation deeply and used the medium of Punk to express their dissatisfaction" (ibid, 67).

The purpose of saying this is to give a basis for where the Punks are coming from and why they hold the ideas they do. It would be a lie, however, to say that these original Punks had well-developed social and political theories. They may have been against all the standard 'isms', but were more apt to spit and swear than to explain their feelings to the mainstream public. "These were Punks, not social activists, and their message was bleak. The Sex Pistols' music was an outburst of hatred and despair. Face life as we see it, they cried—frustrating, meaningless, and ugly. Scream it out with us … "There's no future!'" (ibid, 66).

The goal of these Punks was to express their rage in a harsh and original way. The most hated thing in the world was someone who was a willing conformist. Many Punk bands have built their platforms or messages with the advocacy and admittance of non-conformity. Conformity is rejected on every front possible in order to seek the truth or sometimes merely to shock people. What is so wrong with conformity? The noted sociologist Elliot Aronson defines conformity as the following: "a change in a person's behavior or opinions as a result of real or imagined pressure from a person or group of people" (Elliot Aronson, The Social Animal, Freeman and Company, San Francisco, 1972, 16). The real or imagined pressure that Punks reject is not only the physical kind or the interest to be accepted, but the kind of conformity "that results from the observation of others for the purpose of gaining information about **proper** behavior …" (ibid, 25).

Punks question conformity not only by looking and sounding different (which has debatable importance), but by questioning the prevailing modes of thought. Questions about things that others take for granted related to work, race, sex, and our own selves are not asked by the conformist whose ideas are determined by those around her. The nonconformist does not rely on others to determine her own reality.

The questioning of conformity involves the questioning of authority as well. Punks do not have a great deal of respect for authority of any kind, as will be noted in the section on anarchy. In general, forced authority has been looked at as a great evil causing agent. From the German Nazis in World War II, to the subjects of Stanley Milgram's shock experiments, to today's police force, it has been proven that unjustified obedience to authority has resulted in mass acceptance of harmful actions.

By acting as anti-authoritarian nonconformists, Punks are not usually treated very well by those people whose commands to conform are rejected. Our society, well practiced at doublethink and scapegoat imagery, has used language to create a negative image of those who pursue nonconformist means. "For 'individualist' or 'nonconformist,' we can substitute 'deviant;' for 'conformist' we can substitute 'team player.'" (ibid, 14). This is exactly what modern society has done and its negative portrayal of the Punk movement will be seen in the section on Punk's media misrepresentation.

We have seen that nonconformists may be praised by historians or idolized in films or literature long after the fact of their nonconformity. As for their own time, the non-conformist is labeled a rebel, a deviant, or a troublemaker by the status quo she is going against. Corporate music and fashion magazines that banned or ridiculed Punk for the last twenty years now hail many bands as "ground breakers" or talented originators. Corporate music executives once disgusted by Punk are now signing young bands left and right in an effort to make money off the "cutting edge," nonconformist sounds.

While mass acceptance may be tempting and even lucrative for some, this quote by Dick Lucas of the English bands **Subhumans** and Citizen Fish sums up the feelings many Punks have towards society and mainstream culture:

> "I have never come to terms with the idea that I am 'part of society' and should construct my actions to suit the prevailing moods of conformity, acceptance and achievement. Closed by the rigorous mind training of school and media, the mass mentality of Western culture revolves around upholding the past to attempt to secure the future, whilst suffering the present as beyond its control, 'safe' in the hands of government who feed the present to the masses as a product of technological/material/industrial progress." (Dick Lucas, Threat By Example, edited by Martin Sprouse, Pressure Drop Press, San Francisco, 1989, 13).-

Dick is not .alone in his thinking. Hundreds of thousands of Punk fans feel the same way. With this attitude in mind, I will attempt to show what Punk is, how it has been portrayed by the media, and some of the specifics of the philosophy.

> "The distinguished Soviet psychologist Pavel Semenov once observed that man satisfies his hunger for knowledge in two ways: (1) he observes his environment and tries to organize the unknown in a sensible and meaningful way (this is science); and (2) he reorganizes the known environment in order to create something new (this is art)" (**Aronson,** 269).

Under this definition Punk can be defined as an art form. Punk is much more than this, as it involves particular theories and politics, but when trying to understand what Punk is, comparisons to previous art movements are helpful. Early Punks (perhaps quite unknowingly) used many of the same revolutionary tactics employed by members of early avant-garde art movements: .unusual fashions, the blurring of boundaries between art and everyday life, juxtapositions of seemingly disparate objects and behaviors, intentional provocation of the audience, use of untrained performers, and drastic reorganization (or disorganization) of accepted performance styles and procedures.

The most frequently mentioned comparison between Punk and a known art movement is with Dada. "Dada, generally placed between 1916 and 1922, gained notoriety in France shortly after World War I for vigorously rejecting all previous existing social and aesthetic values" (Henry, 3). There have been at least three studies that I know of where Punk has been likened to a modern day version of Dada. The comparison is valid though I would guess that Punks would generally show a distaste for Dadaist art. Both are subversive but thankfully Punk appears to be less absurd and abstract about its subversiveness.

A movement to which early Punks expressed greater similarities was the Futurist movement. Futurism was a movement launched in 1909 by Filippo Marinetti with his "Foundation and Manifesto of Futurism," published in the large-circulation Paris daily, Le Figaro. "Like other movements in the historical avant-garde, it was an interdisciplinary movement which included visual art, literature and performance. It was dedicated to the rejection of traditional art forms, non-naturalist expression, and audience involvement" (Henry, 2). This audience involvement is an important link between the art and Punk movements as both have attempted to break down the standard barriers present in the performer/viewer relationship.

"As part of the Punk policy of provocation, performers were known to include in their performances behavior such as vomiting on stage, spitting at the audience, and displaying wounds that were the result of self-mutilation having cut and bruised themselves with objects such as broken bottles, fish hooks and knives. The audiences role often included throwing 'permanently' affixed seating, beer bottles, glasses, and anything else that made itself available at the performers" (Henry, 4).

This interaction was actively pursued in the early years of Punk, but there is a very large separation becoming more apparent. As the audiences get larger and larger, concerts are becoming more entertainment than interaction oriented. Small gig halls are still hosting interactive settings but larger venues are echoing typical Rock 'n' Roll concerts. Also the performance characteristics of Punks as specified above have been extremely toned down. When these do occur, they are usually thought of as acts of unoriginal shock value or simply yearning for the "good old days" of Punk when there were no politics other than expressing rage.

Also influencing the later Punk movement was the type of dress the Futurists chose. Futurists meant to take their anti-art message to the streets by wearing outrageous clothes, earrings, and make-up. This was later duplicated by the fashion-oriented Punks of Kings Road in London.

An important difference is to remember that Punk has evolved past the 'shock tactics' of colored hair and dog: collars to have a fairly cohesive philosophy with little or nothing to do with one particular style of dress. While useful at the time, and still fun today, shocking people with appearances has taken- a back seat to shocking people with ideas.

These short comparisons (again, longer ones have been done) of Punk to avant-garde art movements show that Punk was not unique in its expression, or even methods, of rebellion. What needs to be done is an accurate update of what the Punk scene is and has to say in today's world.

From this point forward, I will be using sources from the Punk scene almost exclusively for information. Thousands of fanzines (magazines put out by Punks for and about Punks) have been written expressing the writers' views of what Punk is, its politics, its best music, and the writers' purpose for communication. By using these as sources I will aim to produce an accurate picture of the philosophy of modern Punk.

"To start with, I'll tell you what I think Punk isn't—it isn't a fashion, a certain style of dress, a passing 'phase' of knee-jerk rebellion against your parents, the latest 'cool' trend or even a particular form of style or music, really—it is an idea that guides and motivates your life. The Punk community that exists, exists to support and realize that idea through music, art, "fanzines and other expressions of personal creativity. And what is this idea? Think for yourself, be yourself, don't just take what society gives you, create your own rules, live your own life." (Mark Andersen, *Positive Force* handout, 1985).

There have been many observers and participants in the Punk scene that have not noticed any meaningful underlying purpose. Young people are traditionally known to go through a phase of rebellion which manifests itself against parents, school, and authority in general. Punk has incorrectly been labeled as simply one of these phases in which the rebellious person tries to show that she is different from her peers. It is true that the traditional styles of dress and music of Punk Rock are often offensive and shocking to the mainstream public, but it is misleading to think of Punk as an appearance oriented movement. Mindless, temporary rebellion can be very fun, but is not very effective or useful. Punks have evolved far enough to favor substance over style, a fact almost always ignored or twisted in media representations. It is not enough for a person to look different from the mainstream, there is an important emphasis on consciously becoming one's own self.

When people who want only to be unique or different from the rest of society adopt the Punk look, they succeed in appearing different from the norm. This is a fairly meaningless step. For someone to attempt individuality and become themselves "requires an honest, often -painful look inside yourself, asking tough questions like: Who am I? What do I want from life? What should I want? What should I do? Ultimately, this process will, no doubt, make you refuse to conform to many of society's rules and expectations.." (ibid). It should be stressed that answering these questions requires further questioning of *why* do you want something, *what* are the reasons behind your desires. This process is aimed at making a person aware of himself and his own identity. In this respect the person becomes different from others. From the realization of one's own nonconformity comes the realization that society was not set up to accommodate a civilization of individuals. "Instead it is designed to accommodate some non-existent 'normal' individual and force others to fit into that mold with the end result being institutionalized dehumanization" (ibid).

Rebellion is one of the few undeniable characteristics of Punk. It is implicit in the meaning of Punk and its music and lyrics. Whether a person sticks it out long enough to learn important personal realizations or not, "everyone who gets involved in Punk is usually prompted by some form of rebellion, be it against parents, authorities, or the whole system itself" (Steve Beaumont, letter in <u>Maximum</u> Rock N Roll #53, Oct., 1987). Young people "reach the age where something clicks inside them and they feel they want to do things themselves. Kids that are fed up with conditions around them—be it socially, musically, or whatever" (Al Flipside, "What's Changed in Ten Years," <u>Flipside</u> #48, Feb.

1986). For those who become associated with the movement (and they need not be young people), this initial rebellion turns into a force for education and personal change.

The most important (and perhaps most radical) thing for the Punks to do is take on responsibility. This goes first for themselves and how they order and live their personal lives, then extends to include others. -What sort of responsibilities are these exactly? … "To use our mind, to treat people with respect, not to judge on outward appearances, to support others in their struggle to have the right to 'be themselves,' even to help bring positive change to our world" (Mark Andersen).

Not all **Punks** agree on how to support others or bring about change—outside of their own circle, but there are agreed upon necessities. As Punk is now comprised of a clear majority of middle and service class whites instead of inner city working class whites or minorities, an important action has been to reject their own privileged places in society.. "We are the inheritors of the white supremacist, patriarchal, capitalist world order. A prime position as defenders of the capital of the ruling class and the overseers of the underclass has been set aside for us by our parents, our upbringing, our culture, our history, and yet we have the moral gumption to reject it. As Punks we reject our inherited race and class positions because we know they are bullshit." (Joel, columnist for the Punk-anarchist fanzine Profane Existence #13, Feb. 1992). If Punks were born into this world to be the sons and daughters of America, they have instead become orphans of a fucked up society.

So what is Punk? The following three definitions of Punk must be mentioned, as they are all relevant opinions and are all true:

Punk is a youth trend. "I'll tell you what Punk is—a bunch of kids with funny haircuts talking pseudo-political bullshit and spouting liberal philosophies they know little or nothing about" (Russell Ward, letter in MRR #103, Dec. 1991).

Punk is gut rebellion and change. "Hardcore: a bleached-blonde defiant sixteen-year-old living alone in a downtown hotel; sleazy but on her own. Hardcore: the S.S.I. recipient being paid off by the government to stay out of trouble and renting a rehearsal studio with his monthly check. Hardcore: the corporate flunky who quits his job to manage a band of acned adolescents" (Peter Belsito and Bob Davis, Hardcore California, Last Gasp Publishing, San Francisco, 1984, 7).

Punk is a formidable voice of opposition. "We have created our own music, our own lifestyle, our own community, and our own culture. … We are building a movement based on love, taking actions in hope that some day peace may finally be achieved. We may stumble in our efforts, but we still struggle to carry on. Freedom is something we can create every day; it is up to all of us to make it happen" (Profane Existence #4, June 1990).

While the third serves as the ideal to the other two, the first is the one most commonly presented in the media. As will be shown, this is the least accurate but the most popular image of Punk.

♪ Rebellion and Girldom

By Jacqueline Warwick

The Shangri-Las were a group of suburbanites from Queens who began singing together when they met at public high school in 1963. Although the group was officially a quartet, right from the beginning it was common for only three singers to participate in many performances and recording sessions, usually Mary Ann and Margie Ganser and Mary Weiss, whose older sister Betty was also a group member. Likewise, publicity shots for the group throughout its career sometimes show all four singers, sometimes only Mary Weiss and the Gansers, and sometimes one of the Gansers and the two Weiss sisters. Mary Weiss, who sang lead on all the best-known recordings, provides continuity through the various incarnations of the group, and the most typical publicity shots of the Shangri-Las depict her flanked by the Gansers, who cultivated their resemblance with identical hairstyles and a tendency to pose in mirror image to one another. The balanced effect is a pleasing one, clearly identifying Mary Weiss as a leader supported by matching bookends. In performance, of course, this arrangement changed so that the Gansers stood together, slightly apart from the lead singer, in order better to hear one another as they provided backing harmonies.

The Shangri-Las' ethnic backgrounds are significant, for they are the first group examined in my study who were not (at least in part) African American; both the Weiss sisters and the Ganser twins were raised in Roman Catholic families of European descent, and all four singers grew up in difficult economic circumstances in a working-class Long Island suburb. Like the Chantels, discussed in Chapter 1, the Gansers as young girls learned to sing harmony by participating in school choirs led by nuns, and the Weiss sisters sang in a church choir.

In their early publicity shots, which coincided with the peak of the main girl group craze in 1963, the Shangri-Las present an image of demure suburban girlhood, with tidy upswept hairstyles, knee-length skirts, and friendly smiles. This was not a style that they liked, and their appearance would undergo a radical transformation in response to the enormous success of their song "Leader of the Pack" in late 1964. Since this song narrated the experience of a girl whose boyfriend is a notorious bad boy, the group and their new label, Red Bird, shrewdly reinvented the Shangri-Las as tough, "don't mess with me" rebel girls.[1] The Shangri-Las' whiteness afforded them greater freedom to play with this version of girl identity than was available to groups like the Ronettes, as we have seen. Nevertheless, the slacks, white shirts, and vests that the singers chose to wear were generally considered provocative, and Mary Weiss recalls raising eyebrows by shopping for the pants she preferred in men's clothing stores.[2]

By contemporary standards, it may be difficult to understand the Shangri-Las' image as genuinely dangerous and subversive; the juxtaposition of their fresh faces and sulky pouts is reminiscent of a fluffy kitten puffing itself up with rage—it seems there is no real threat, and so the anger is adorable. Certainly, the singers' 1965 roles as spokespersons in radio "Good Taste Tips" sponsored by the makers of the soft -drink 7-Up (to say nothing of commercials for Revlon and Breck shampoo) presented them urging girl listeners to uphold conventional middle-class gender roles. In one of these announcements, for example, Mary Weiss recommends that girls who are "smart" let their dates know they expect doors to be held open and chairs pulled out for them: "He'll love it and think you are a lady, and in return it will flatter his masculine ego."[3] In spite of this prim advice, the Shangri-Las were generally perceived as tough and rebellious, an important instance of white girls adopting a defiant stance in a society that was still more inclined to associating unladylike, "bad girl" behavior with non-white teens.

Indeed, as I noted in Chapter 8, "Leader of the Pack," surely the group's most notorious song, was actually banned in Britain because of the dark themes in its content. It begins with spoken dialogue in unpolished Long Island accents between identical twins Marge and Mary Ganser and lead singer Mary Weiss[4] in some unspecified female space, probably the "Ladies' Room" that is so often the site of important female conversations and girl talk. Over a descent of stark octaves in the piano on C, then A, G, and F, and the rhythmic pattern of the girl group beat sounding slowly and portentously in the bass drum (as opposed to the snare drum that normally presents it), Weiss hums to herself and adopts a nonchalant tone when the twins ask her about her mysterious and dangerous boyfriend, Jimmy, but then literally bursts into song as she describes how they met and what he represents to her. The timeline of events in the song is ambiguous; are we to understand that the tragedy of Jimmy's death is something that has occurred before the beginning of the song (in which case, it is difficult to imagine that the Ganser sisters have not already heard about the ghastly accident)? Or should the listener believe, rather, that the song begins and ends at different points in the story, so that the opening discussion sets the stage for the dramatic events that will ensue? Either way, the whiny quality of Weiss's voice, strained near the top of her vocal range, perfectly evokes the slightly smug, spoiled girl who enjoys impressing her friends with the drama and status her glamorous, dangerous, rebel boyfriend confers on her. The backup singers respond, alternately begging for more information and retreating to wordless lines as she drifts into spoken reminiscence during a middle eight section in the related minor key.

A different outcome to the tragedy of the scenario in "Leader of the Pack" is imagined in the Shangri-Las' 1965 release "Out in the Streets" (which never entered the Top Forty). In this song, the narrator recognizes that her rebel boyfriend has reformed his wild ways in order to be considered respectable enough to date her. The backing vocalists sing softly about how he has turned away from his gang of friends and rejected his life in the street, and Mary Weiss acknowledges that he has made this sacrifice for her sake. Sorrowfully, she notes that he does not smile anymore and accepts that she must prove her love for him by releasing him from their relationship and letting him return to what we assume is his natural state of being. The song supports the view that love that defies class barriers is doomed, but, unlike "Leader of the Pack," it ends with all characters alive and well, if chastened by the futility of love across social boundaries. Both of these songs, then, make clear that the girl's affections are transgressive, that loving a boy from the wrong side of the tracks is a serious offense against the norms of propriety.

"Out in the Streets," like "Leader of the Pack" and most Shangri-Las recordings, was produced by George "Shadow" Morton, who earned his nickname because of his tendency to appear and disappear without warning. Morton was a former high school classmate of well-known songwriter Ellie Greenwich's, and he traded on this connection in bringing the Shangri-Las to the Red Bird record label. Morton's production style involved using echo and reverberation on a scale comparable to Phil Spector, and he also used sound effects to heighten dramatic impact; in the case of "Leader of the Pack," he imported the sounds of a motorcycle revving its engine and even simulated the sounds of a crash for the tragic climax. Morton's use of sound effects was a departure from Spector's style, as Spector preferred to create drama through musical suggestion rather than direct quotations of specific sounds (his 1964 record for the Ronettes, "Walking in the Rain," is exceptional in that it features the sound of rain falling).

In "Leader of the Pack," as in other songs by the Shangri-Las, the girl's rebellion against middle-class norms takes the form of partnering a boy who is conspicuously bad. Note that, as in songs discussed in Part 1, "the Boy" in "Leader of the Pack" and "Out in the Streets" is constituted for us only through Weiss's description of him; she and the Gansers exist in a sort of girldom, where "Jimmy's" only function is to give them something to talk about. This procedure of constructing a shadowy male figure whose purpose is simply to heighten the drama between the more interesting female characters is a strategy common to soap opera writing, as Bonnie Dow and other feminist television critics have noted, taking up an idea proposed by Dorothy Smith.[5] Drawing on Gayle Rubin's important work on the "traffic in women," Patricia Juliana Smith identifies this strategy as fetishizing the boyfriend into "the Apparitional Boy, a simulacrum … the object of the female fantasy gaze, the token of exchange among girls."[6] Thanks to Morton's strategic use of sound effects, the lyrics to "Leader of the Pack" never have to spell out that Jimmy is a motorcyclist, presenting an elegant economy even in the midst of angst-ridden, high melodrama.

For melodrama is undoubtedly the most apt term I could use to describe the œuvre of the Shangri-Las. Even their first release with Red Bird, 1964's "Remember (Walkin' in the Sand)" relates the anguish of a girl recalling a romance that ended against her will, and the intensity of her stormy emotions is heightened by the sound of waves crashing on the beach and a veritable army of seagulls crying overhead. Much of their repertoire presents apocalyptic narratives of teenage love and rebellion leading to death; in addition to "Leader of the Pack," this motif also generates "Give Us Your Blessings" (in which a teenage couple is killed in a car crash while trying to elope) and "I Can Never Go Home Anymore" (in which a girl's mother dies, broken-hearted over her daughter's failure to conform to conventional family life), both from 1965. By the time the group had recorded their last single with Red Bird, 1966's "Past, Present and Future," they had earned the moniker "myrmidons of melodrama," and this final song consists solely of a portentous spoken monologue about suffering in love and trepidation about future romances over a piano part borrowing heavily from the well-known first movement of Beethoven's "Moonlight" Sonata (only Mary Weiss's voice is heard in this recording). From the cryptic clues given in the lyrics, the listener can construe that romance with a rebel has led to heartbreak and anguish, but it is clear that the girl's melancholy has actually added to her allure with other suitors, and that the attractions of other bad boys may—despite her protestations—eventually tempt her out of her grief.

Bad Boys and Rebel Girls

The theme of romance with irresistible, forbidden boys is not unique to the Shangri-Las, though. Among the many girl group songs celebrating rebel boyfriends, the Girls' "Chico's Girl" remains a cult favorite despite the fact that it made no chart impact when released in 1966, perhaps a few years too late to benefit fully from popular interest in girl group records. The song was written by the songwriting team of Barry Mann and Cynthia Weil (who also wrote material for the Shangri-Las), recorded by a quartet of sisters named Sandoval in Los Angeles, and later revived by comedienne Bernadette Peters on ' her eponymous 1980 album; it is the Girls' original version, however, that is included in the four-CD box set *The Brill Building Sounds* a showcase of the best recordings of this generation of songwriters and producers.[7] The song features a terse, arpeggiated bass line that serves as an ostinato underpinning sulky, half-spoken vocals and a dramatic instrumentation that includes castanets, maracas, horns, and distorted electric guitar. The story line should by now be familiar; Chico is a rebel (and advertises himself as such on the back of his jacket) who grew up in the toughest part of town, but he has a tender side that he reveals only to the narrator, Chico's girl. The soloist fairly spits out lyrics justifying Chico's gang lifestyle—"his neighborhood's a jungle, so he travels with a pack"—but she adopts a sweeter vocal timbre to rhapsodize about the secret, precious vulnerability that he allows her alone to see, and her melody is supported by high-pitched vocals from the backing singers that lean toward a choral sound.

Use of the name Chico, rather than the more generic and customary Jimmy or Johnny, signals clearly that the rebel in this case is Hispanic. The unremarkable name of the group, the Girls, meanwhile, together with the singers' unaccented American pronunciation, obscured any questions about the Sandoval sisters' ethnic background for those who interacted with them only through recordings. The Latin feel to the song, generated largely through percussion instruments such as maracas and guiro (or at least, a sharp, crisp, rattling sound that suggests a guiro or castanets), was not in itself unusual among songs written and produced by Brill Building songwriters at that time, as Ken Emerson demonstrates in *Always Magic in the Air: Hoe Bomp and Brilliance of the Brill Building Era.* Songs such as the Drifters' ""This Magic Moment" and "Sweets for My Sweet," Sam Cooke's "Everybody Likes to Cha Cha Cha" and Ben E. King's "Spanish Harlem," as well as the Ronettes' "Be My Baby" and the Crystals' "Uptown" (both discussed in Chapter 9) are among well-known songs of the early 1960s that gestured toward the enormous contemporary popularity of the mambo, the cha cha, and other Latin dance styles among non-Latin audiences, sometimes with explicitly Latin themes in the lyrics, but equally often without.[8] Considering "Chico's Girl" in the context of a vogue for Latin elements in pop music, it is possible to see that many listeners would not have assumed the singers themselves were Hispanic; the name of the song's hero makes Chico the only indisputably Latin character of the piece. The song thus offered the possibility of imagining the thrills and dangers of cross-racial romance for middle-class white teens who listened to the record a year before the controversial 1967 film *Guess Who's Coming to Dinner* tackled the topic of interracial marriage for more adult audiences.

Sociologist Donna Gaines reports that in suburban communities with middle-class values in the 1960s, teenage romance with the wrong boy "could ruin a teenage girl's chance at a good life. He could cost her her respectability, and the relationship could tarnish the class aspirations of an entire community."[9] The phenomenon of the American "juvenile delinquent" was of great public concern during the 1950s and 60s, and discourse surrounding "bad girls" differed significantly from the perceptions of male teens in trouble; the cases of girls going bad were particularly horrifying because they were generally understood to stem from a lack of fatherly authority. Indeed, Rachel Devlin provides evidence that because juvenile delinquency was so determinedly cast as a male problem, girls who transgressed legal and social codes at the time were treated informally and discreetly by police and other authorities who sought to minimize embarrassment for the parents of offending girls. While bad boys were more easily understood as individuals, responsible for their wrongdoings, bad girls at mid-century were seen as evidence of inadequate patriarchal control, and they threatened an entire social order.[10] Taking up with a bad boy was often understood as a girl's first step on a slippery slope away from father's loving control and toward a life of adolescent—and eventually adult—disrepute.

Thus, the subversions presented in girl group songs like "Leader of the Pack," "Out in the Streets," and "Chico's Girl" are real and should be taken seriously. Of course, the ideology of rock rebelliousness treats the comfort and security that steady relationships offer with profound ambivalence. Simon Reynolds and Joy Press observe that for legendary 1960s rock rebel Jim Morrison, for example, "women constituted his 'Soul Kitchen,' a nourishing hearth that provided a brief resting-place before he hit the road again."[11] As I noted in Chapter 1, Reynolds and Press identify "The Road" as male territory, and the rebellious wanderer hero as a male who resists the suffocating embrace of female domesticity. By contrast with this "authentic" and worthwhile kind of subversiveness, rock ideology has typically failed to see rebellion in girls' songs about being in love with a misunderstood rebel. Yet even when the girls in these songs seem to do little more than offer comfort and unwavering devotion to their rebel boyfriends, demonstrating conventional female behavior and loyalty, the mere fact of being a rebel's girlfriend entailed real risks and represented a dangerous, exciting fantasy marketed to girls.

Furthermore, the girls narrating the 1962 hit "He's a Rebel" (credited to the Crystals, but recorded by Darlene Love and the Blossoms) not only brag about a dangerous boyfriend, but they also go so far as to imply behavior on the protagonist's own part that is significantly more provocative than the stance of Chico's girl, who effaces herself entirely except to declare love and support to her rebel boyfriend. The girl in "He's a Rebel" sings the praise of a boy who will "never, never be any good" but nevertheless makes her proud when he holds her hand, precisely because he is bold and stands apart from the crowd. A buoyant groove centered in the bass drum lends confidence to Darlene Love's solo vocals, which begin deep in her range (with an F-sharp below the staff) then ascend more than an octave to trumpet her feelings of love alongside the full, gospel-fired singing, of the other Blossoms. In the song's middle eight section. Love interrupts a saxophone solo to assert that she herself will reject respectable behavior to join her rebel boyfriend: "If they don't like him that way, they won't like me after today!" The girl in this song draws courage from her boyfriend's independence, and their relationship inspires her to dismiss the criticisms of those who condemn unorthodox behavior and actually to embrace nonconformity herself; her choices meet with unambiguous approval from the backing vocalists singing with her. From this song—which was significantly more popular than either "Out in the Streets" or "Chico's Girl," reaching the number-one position in 1962—it was only a small step to songs in which girls gleefully reported actual participation in inappropriate behavior.

The Shangri-Las' 1964 "Give Him a Great Big Kiss," for example, presents the account of a bold girl who dares to invade the male sphere and claim her boyfriend by kissing him in front of his friends, and the musical language is upbeat and infectious. The song begins with Mary Weiss's spoken "When I say I'm in love, you'd best believe I'm in love, L-U-V!" setting the tone for a sassy and delightful declaration of adolescent love on the part of a confident girl. Rhythmically energetic percussive forces soon come to the fore, with a horn section and piano providing syncopated R&B-styled riffs over a harmonic foundation that alternates jauntily between the home key and its relative minor. At various points in the song, the backing vocalists collude with the horns to provide a fanfare-like riff that descends low into their range on the syllables "da da da," a light-hearted and amusing effect contributing to a cheerful mood; toward the end of the recording, they echo this riff on an "oo" vowel, at a higher, more conventional position in the female vocal range. At the crucial chorus of the song, all instruments except percussion drop out, focusing the listener's attention on the Shangri-Las singing in unison with repeated, even eighth notes accompanied by steady handclaps: "I'm gonna walk right up to him, give him a great big kiss! MWAH!"

It is significant that this statement is sung by *all* the Shangri-Las, even though there are no individual vocal parts; the song is about one girl's romance with one boy, but the performance makes it clear that this is a fantasy all girls can share. The unison singing of this line thus supports the idea that group membership could embolden girls to express their desires and needs. Once again, the recipient of the girl's love is a bad boy, with dirty fingernails, ever-present sunglasses, and tight pants; although an affinity for motorcycles and gangs is not made explicit, the hero's similarity to "Jimmy" in "Leader of the Pack" makes this a possibility. This song, then, portrays a dangerous hoodlum positioned carefully in the street, and it celebrates the self-assured bravado of a girl, whom we can imagine marching uninvited up to her beloved in full view of his gang of friends (and hers, as the backing vocals attest) in order to mark her turf with a noisy, possessive kiss.

Other examples of girls transgressing propriety to take the lead in romantic relationships occur with the Marvelettes' 1962 "Beechwood 4-5789," in which the protagonist gently but firmly teaches a boy how to woo her and ask for her phone number; with the Shirelles' 1960 "Tonight's the Night," in which a girl breathlessly anticipates a romantic evening with a boy; and with the Chiffons' 1963 hit "He's So Fine," in which a gang of girls plots to win the affections of a particularly fine specimen of boy. This latter song introduced the vocables phrase "doo lang doo lang doo lang" into the lexicon of girl talk discussed in Chapter 2, and it is also famous for subconsciously inspiring George Harrison's first solo hit, "My Sweet Lord," in 1970.[12] The Chiffons began as a trio of thirteen- and fourteen-year-old girls who met their manager, Ronnie Mack, when he came scouting for talent at their Bronx high school. After some minor successes, the group—now bolstered with a fourth' singer, Sylvia Peterson—recorded Mack's "He's So Fine," a song he had been trying to sell to more established acts for some time. With lead singer Judy Craig (now sixteen) declaring "I don't know how I'm gonna do it, but I'm gonna make him mine" and itemizing the boy's charms to her appreciative backing vocalists, the song made it clear that girls were perfectly capable of taking an aggressive lead in romance. The bold stance of "He's So Fine" garnered enough enthusiasm to earn it the number-one position on both the pop and R&B charts in early 1963.

Given the pressures of demure feminine behavior in a culture of respectable containment that I analyzed in Part 4, it is hardly surprising that songs like these represented exciting possibilities for the girls who listened to them. I do not want to suggest naively that these tiny insurrections signaled equality between teenage girls and boys—it has not escaped my attention that all of these bold statements revolve around heterosexual romance and that having the validation of some kind of boyfriend is the necessary prerequisite for rebellion. However, against the backdrop of an association of girls with domestic, closed spaces and an emphasis on passive, meek behavior with only the nicest boys, so strong in communities with middle-class values, it is clear that songs about outcast boyfriends, and songs wherein girls took the initiative to act on their own desires, must be understood as resistant to the rigid boundaries that confined girls.

Moreover, if breaking with the rules of home only in order to become the devoted consort in another patriarchal relationship seems a partial liberation at best, the girl group repertoire also includes songs that positioned girls standing apart from the confines of conventional heterosexual relationships. In most cases, the narratives of these songs take the end of a romance as their point of departure, portraying girls who venture outside the domestic sphere because of grief or—in the Angels' 1963 "My Boyfriend's Back"—outrage. While disappointment in romance is, in songs like this, presented as the most acceptable (perhaps the only acceptable) cause for girls' disruptive behavior, the fact remains that these songs depict girls going out into the world to try and resolve injury or injustice unfairly meted out by boys.

In the Angels' "My Boyfriend's Back," the dangerous boyfriend is invoked to restore a girl's reputation. Listeners witness a girl bursting into male territory to scold a boy who has been gossiping about her; she triumphantly reports that her boyfriend is back and that the hour of her vengeance is nigh, and backing voices quickly confirm her self-righteousness. The spoken introduction to the song indicates that the girl has been a victim of circumstances not unlike those that befell the biblical Susanna—a boy has taken advantage of her boyfriend's absence to make advances and, finding himself rebuffed, has spread malicious rumors about her infidelity.

Although the song purports to be about the beating the boyfriend will shortly bestow on the gossiping boy, and thus might suggest that only he has the power and authority to right the wrongs perpetrated, it is the strength of the girls' indignation and fury that dominates. Lead singer Peggy Santiglia and backing singers the Allbut sisters, Barbara and Phyllis, have all perfected the slightly nasal, whiny vocal sound of petulant teenage girls, even though all three singers were in their early twenties and were experienced vocalists who had performed in Broadway musicals and numerous recording sessions—Barbara Allbut studied vocal performance formally at the prestigious Juilliard School of Music until her career as an Angel demanded her full attention.[13] The main melodic figure used in this song is built around small, descending intervals of a fourth and a second, and it closely resembles the kind of sing-song whine used in childish taunting, further fostering a connection to young people and immature communication methods. Finally, the handclaps heard prominently throughout the song enact a variation of the girl group beat, helping to erase any doubt that this record should be considered part of the genre in spite of the middle-class and adult appearance of the singers.

Furthermore, in the last charting single of an eight-year career, 1968's "Destination: Anywhere," the Marvelettes presented the narrative of a girl who ventures alone into the world in flight from heartbreak. While the song can hardly be described as cheerful it conveys determination and courage on the part of the girl, who stubbornly insists on a train ticket to "anywhere" in. spite of the ticket agent's dismay. The girl's dogged efforts to get away from her painful circumstances, and her willingness to trust to fate in choosing a place to make a fresh start, evoke the romantic figure of the lone, wanderer hero who broods over mysterious injuries as he roams a melancholy landscape; such a character is encountered in (among other sources) the Band's song "The Weight," released in the same year as "Destination: Anywhere." When the Marvelettes adopted the stance of an aloof, brooding, and, above all, *masculine* archetype, they challenged assumptions about conventional gender roles and appropriate options for "nice" girls, suggesting that they too were capable of striding off alone into the sunset.

In "I'd Much Rather Be with the Girls," Donna Lynn articulates a tart response to a boy who has abandoned her, by rhapsodizing over the pleasures of going out with girlfriends. Backed by other female singers who confirm her statements, fourteen-year-old Lynn draws on her background as a Broadway singer/actress to produce an assertive, chest-dominated "belting" vocal sound that lends credibility to her stance. The song was written by Keith Richards and Rolling Stones manager Andrew Loog Oldham as "I'd Much Rather Be with the Boys," but the band decided not to release it themselves, perhaps because the unabashed celebration of homosociality seemed too risky for a group determined to assert their identity as sexually dangerous bad boys. In any case, the songwriters sold it instead to Mancunian beat band the Toggery Five.[14] The group was modestly successful with the song, and Donna Lynn subsequently transformed it into a girl's stirring declaration of independence, at once hearkening back to the Shirelles' unrepentant dismissal of a disappointing boy in their 1958 debut "I Met Him on a Sunday" (discussed in Chapter 2) and also anticipating the Spice Girls' cheeky 1996 celebration of girls' friendships, "Wannabe."

NOTES

1. John J. Grecco, "Out in the Streets: The Story of the ShangriLas," http:// www.redbirdent.com/slasl.htm, accessed October 1, 2005.
2. Miriam Linna, "Good Bad but not Evil," http://www.nortonrecords. com/index2.html, accessed June 23, 2006.
3. *The ShangriLas: Myrmidons of Melodrama*, "Good Taste Tip from Mary Weiss," (FKR Productions). RPM Records RPM 136, 1994.
4. Although Betty Weiss did not even participate in this recording, the Gansers address the protagonist (Mary Weiss) as "Betty" in this song.
5. See Bonnie J. Dow, *Prime-Time Feminism: Television, Media Culture, and the Women's Movement Since 1970* (Philadelphia: University of Pennsylvania Press, 1996); and Dorothy E. Smith, "Women's Perspective as a Radical Critique of Sociology," reprinted in *Feminism and Methodology*, ed. Sandra Harding (Oxford: Oxford University Press, 1997), 84–96. Originally a conference paper for the American Academy for the Advancement of Science (Pacific Division), Eugene, Oregon, 1972.

6. Patricia Juliana Smith, "Ask Any Girl: Compulsory Heterosexuality and Girl Group Culture," in *Reading Rock and Roll: Authenticity, Appropriation, Aesthetics,* eds. Kevin J. H. Dettmar and William Richey (New York: Columbia University Press, 1999), 107.

7. The track is also included, happily, in the Rhino Records 2005 box set *One Kiss Can Lead to Another: Girl Group Sounds Lost & Found.* Rhino Records R2 74645.

8. Ken Emerson, "It Was Just Jewish Latin," in *Always Magic in the Air: The Bomp and the Brilliance of the Brill Building Era* (New York: Viking, 2005), 121–40.

9. Donna Gaines, "Girl Groups: A Ballad of Codependency," in *Trouble Girls: The Rolling Stone Book of Women in Rock,* ed. Barbara O'Dair (New York: Random House, 1997), 103–16.

10. Rachel Devlin, "Female Juvenile Delinquency and the Problem of Sexual Authority in America, 1945–1965," in *Delinquents and Debutantes: Twentieth-Century American Girls' Cultures,* ed. Sherrie A. Inness (New York: New York University Press, 1998), 83–108.

11. Simon Reynolds and Joy Press, *The Sex Revolts: Gender, Rebellion and Rock'n'Roll* (Cambridge, Mass.: Harvard University Press, 1995), 45.

12. When the Chiffons' record label sued Harrison for closely imitating the melody, harmonic framework, and texture of "He's So Fine," the former Beatle was found guilty of "subconscious plagiarism." Considering Harrison's close relationship to girl groups in the early days of his career—the Beatles had performed many girl group songs, and Harrison had dated one of the Ronettes—as well as the fact that "My Sweet Lord" was produced by Phil Spector, it is surprising that no one involved in making his record noticed the striking similarity to the Chiffons. The girl group underscored their moral victory by releasing a cover version of "My Sweet Lord" in 1975. Jay Warner, *The Da Capo Book of American Singing Groups,* (New York: Da Capo Press, 1992), 344.

13. Warner, *The Da Capo Book of American Singing Groups,* 325.

14. Sheila Burgel, liner notes to *One Kiss Can Lead to Another: Girl Group Sounds, Lost and Found,* Rhino Records R2 74645, 54, 2005. The Rolling Stones did record the song in 1965, and it is included on the 1975 album *Metamorphosis,* a compilation of outtakes and other unreleased material.

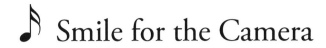

♪ Smile for the Camera

By Gillian A. Garr

"I may be dressing like the typical bimbo, but I'm in charge … people don't think of me as a person who's not in charge of my career or my life. And isn't that what feminism is all about? Aren't I in charge of my life, doing the things I want to do, making my own decisions?"

MADONNA, on ABC's Nightline, December 3, 1990

The performer—female or male—who turned out to be the most skillful at capitalizing on the potential of video, especially its capacity to comment on and challenge conventional perceptions of sex and sexuality, was undoubtedly Madonna. Madonna dove headfirst into the arena of sexuality, cultivating the image of a modern-day Marilyn Monroe in one of her many incarnations—though aside from looks, there were few other similarities between the two. Whereas Monroe's sexuality had only increased her vulnerability and insecurity, sexuality represented the core of Madonna's strength. Her initial street urchin look, with torn jeans, lingerie worn as "outer wear," dangling jewelry, a belt buckle that read "Boy Toy," and bare midriff (an appearance as rag-tag as Lauper's thrift-store chic, though Lauper was seen as the friendly "good" girl while Madonna embodied the raunchy "bad" girl) was adopted by "Madonna Wannabes" across the country. The mainstream press wasted no time taking pot shots at her appearance ("Around her famous navel the MTVenus packed a little mound of tummy blub," noted *Entertainment Weekly*), and feminists were either drawn to or repelled by the image of a woman in power who had resorted to her sexuality to get that power and was now influencing an army of pre-teens to do the same.

To female artists trying to escape being regarded as sexual objects first and performers second, Madonna's tactics were seen as reactionary and regressive. "The thing about her that people think is so great is that she's made it in a man's world and is now a multi-million dollar corporation," said Exene Cervenka in *Option*. "So she's successful and that's supposed to be great for women. But what made her successful was keeping her pants unzipped." Karen, Finley also expressed the problems some women had in admiring Madonna's undeniable strength, while feeling uncomfortable with what they perceived as her underlying message. "I think she's really powerful and I like her," says Finley, "but I find her politics extremely offensive. She really doesn't know how to present herself publicly unless she is presenting herself as being sexually desirable. And record companies love that."

For her part, Madonna claimed to take her role less seriously, "I never "set out to be a role model for girls or women," she said in *Cosmopolitan,* answering charges about her "regressive" image by saying, "They didn't get the joke. The whole point is that I'm *not* anybody's toy. People take everything so literally." She also pointed out the double standard she felt lay behind the attacks on her utilization of sexuality in her work. "When someone like Prince, Elvis or Jagger does the same thing, they are being honest, sensual human beings," she told *Newsweek* in a 1985 article on "Rock's New Women" (which featured Cyndi Lauper on the cover). "But when I do it: 'Oh, please. Madonna, you're setting the women's movement back a million years.'"

Born Madonna Louise Veronica Ciccone in 1958 in Bay City, Michigan, Madonna grew up in a family of five brothers and two sisters. She began performing at a young age and later appeared in plays while attending Catholic school. She persuaded her father to let her study dance instead of the piano, and eventually set herself up as a dance instructor to the neighborhood children. After high school she won a dance scholarship to the University of Michigan, but left for New York in 1978, training first at Alvin Ailey's American Dance Center, and later with the Center's co-founder, Pearl Lang, in Lang's own dance company. But she felt the opportunities in the dance world were limited, and landed a job in a disco revue in Paris, singing backup for French singer Patrick Hernandez and so impressing the producers they wrote her a specialty number, "She's a Real Disco Queen."

Back in New York, Madonna began performing with bands, starting out as a drummer in a group called the Breakfast Club in 1979. But she soon stepped out from behind the drums as a singer, fronting her own bands. In the early '80s, one of her bands signed a management contract, but musical differences soon arose between Madonna and the rest of the group, leading to an eventual split. Madonna then began writing and recording more dance-oriented material with Stephen Bray, a friend from college, and hanging out at the Danceteria club, where Karen Finley was waitressing. She eventually met DJ Mark Kamins, who played a demo of her first single, "Everybody," at the club, and, noting the favorable response, helped Madonna get a record deal with Sire Records.

"Everybody," produced by Kamins, was released in April, 1982 and proved to be a strong dance club favorite, as did her follow-up 12-inch single "Burning Up"/"Physical Attraction," though neither appeared on the Top 40 charts. In 1983 Madonna released her self-titled debut album, which also became a dance club favorite but had little impact in the charts until the release of the single "Holiday" toward the end of the year. By early '84, the single peaked at number 16, followed in the spring and fall by two Top 10 hits,

"Borderline" and "Lucky Star"; the album itself reached number 8 and sold over nine million copies, its success delaying the release of *Like a Virgin* until 1985.

If 1984 had provided Madonna with a solid introduction to the pop mainstream, her accomplishments in 1985 solidified that success and firmly established the performer as a full-fledged pop star. *Like a Virgin* became her first number 1 album (all of Madonna's LPs have reached the Top 10, except for an album of single remixes, which reached number 14), along with four Top 5 single hits, including the title track, which reached number 1, and went on to sell eleven million copies. Produced by Chic's Nile Rodgers, *Like a Virgin* was a more polished effort than its predecessor and featured five songs written or co-written by Madonna. She also branched out into film (having made her debut in the low-budget soft core film *A Certain Sacrifice* in 1980): her role in Susan Seidelman's *Desperately Seeking Susan* received good reviews even from critics who were not Madonna fans, and her appearance in *Vision Quest* resulted in another number 1, "Crazy for You." She also embarked on her first concert tour, which was unsurprisingly an instant sellout.

The excitement and attention Madonna's work elicited was matched by incessant coverage in the media (including a *Time* cover story in 1985), which found the performer's heady mix of sexuality and success both irresistible and saleable. Whereas sex had always been a part of rock, few understood how to use it as an instrument of provocation as well as Madonna, who appeared to delight in her ability to use her. sexuality to extract what she wanted from men, disposing of them … with efficiency when finished—as vividly illustrated in the video for "Material Girl," where Madonna accepts jewels from a chorus line of adoring men, along with their wallets and money, and then kicks them down the stairs. It was a stance traditionally taken by men, rather than women, and Madonna's co-opting of the pose flew in the face of both conservatives, who found such tactics "obscene" when carried out by a woman, and some feminists, who found Madonna's apparent celebration of female duplicity offensive. Madonna freely admitted to the commercial potential of her public image and again contended that people on both sides of the debate missed the underlying irony. "I know the aspect of my personality, being the vixen, the heart-breaker and the incredibly provocative girl is a very marketable image," she told *People*. "But it's not insincere. You just can't take it seriously."

But if the characterizations she presented in videos and onstage were delivered with a wink, Madonna's ambitions regarding her work were deadly serious, an aspect of her personality that was at first overlooked in favor of topics the media found more worthy of investigation, such as the publication of nude photos taken of Madonna before her recording success or the state of her turbulent "marriage to actor Sean Penn (married in 1985, the couple divorced in '89). Donna Russo, vice president of publicity at Warner Bros., was among those who admired Madonna's handling of her own career. "She's very much a businesswoman," says Russo. "She's incredibly disciplined, she knows exactly what she's doing, exactly where she's headed, she knows exactly how she likes things. She keeps track of all her money, she keeps track of all her business deals. No one's going to rob Madonna! She's a perfectionist of the first order. And I admire that, because it's so hard to be that disciplined. It's like she's been in a Buddhist temple in her past life or something."

With the release of *True Blue* in 1986, Madonna began co-producing her work. More pop-oriented than its predecessors, *True Blue* hit the top of the charts, produced five Top 5 singles, and sold seventeen million copies. In 1989 Madonna released her most accomplished album yet, *Like a Prayer*. Along with such jubilant numbers as "Express Yourself," "Keep It Together," and a collaboration with Prince on the track "Love Song," the album (which again topped the charts) also took an autobiographical look at Madonna's life—her troubled marriage, her mother's death, and her relationship with her father. She followed up this ambitious project with *I'm Breathless: Songs From and Inspired by the Film Dick Tracy*, a film in which she also starred. *Breathless*, which reached number 2 on the charts, also revealed how far her voice had developed from her early dance rock days, as she tackled material ranging from Broadway composer Stephen Sondheim's intricate work to her own tribute to nightclub *poseurs*, "Vogue" (a number 1 hit). In 1992, Madonna announced the formation of her own entertainment company, Maverick, in partnership with Time Warner, in a deal that was reported to advance her as much as sixty million dollars. As her career progressed, Madonna would continue to use her media platform to confront attitudes regarding sexuality, a topic that would take on entirely different meanings in light of the AIDS epidemic.

While Madonna's rise put the solo female singer firmly in the spotlight (launching a series of solo female singers—including Debbie Gibson and Tiffany, among others—into the pop marketplace) other female performers were presenting updated versions of tried and true roles for women in rock and finding substantial success: Joan Jett resumed her "tough chick" role as a solo artist, the Bangles emerged as the latest all-female band, and Whitney Houston found long-lasting success as rock's new diva. A key difference between these performers and their predecessors was the degree of involvement they had in the creation of their music, a situation that was becoming the norm for a growing number of female artists in the rock mainstream. Most were writing their own material; some, like Joan Jett, Cyndi Lauper, and Madonna, also began producing their records. Even Whitney Houston, primarily regarded as a singer, moved into production on her third album, 1991's *I'm Your Baby Tonight*.

♪ Thrashing All Around

Rhythm, the Body, and the Genre of Thrash Metal

By Glenn T. Pillsbury

> What is this crap? The guitars sound like rusty chainsaws and the singer barks like he wants to be let outside to chase a cat. This band has a big underground buzz, but they're not going anywhere. I'll stake my entire reputation on that.
>
> **—Jeff Gilbert, early reviewer of Metallica's *Kill Em All*, 1984**

For the New Jersey music promotion and shopkeeping team of Jon and Marsha Zazula the arrival of San Francisco–based Metallica in April 1983 may have indeed been the answer to a prayer, even if most of the rest of America had not exactly felt the need to appeal to the divine on behalf of homegrown heavy metal. The Zazula's record shop and flea market, Rock & Roll Heaven, had acquired a copy of Metallica's 1982 demo *No Life 'Til Leather* via the tape-trading network of the underground metal scene. Eager to expand their promotion interests, the Zazulas contacted 18-year-old drummer Lars Ulrich, wired $1,500 to him and three other young men in California, and then prayed, once more, that the band would actually make it 3,000 miles across the country without killing themselves or each other. Gigs in the New York–New Jersey area had been booked already and the band (which had recently added Cliff Burton on bass) did make it. Barely. In particular, tensions between Metallica's two guitarists, James Hetfield and Dave Mustaine, had reached an alcohol-fueled breaking point on the cross-country trek, and after only two shows on the East Coast, Mustaine was officially kicked out, sent back west to California on a Greyhound bus. At the same time Kirk Hammett, recently drafted out of another San Francisco metal band called Exodus, was quickly making his own trip east to audition as Metallica's new lead guitar player. Hammett's first gig took place exactly one week after Mustaine's last. Following two more shows, and with the band's lineup apparently settled, the Zazulas then took the biggest financial risk of their lives by bankrolling the recording of Metallica's first album, *Kill 'Em All* (in May 1983) and then forming Megaforce Records in order to manage the band and promote the album.

In the received history of thrash metal, the Zazula's gamble paid off exceptionally well for Metallica. For the Zazulas, the episode also turned out to be one of the high points of their professional activities in American metal. The two groups would part company in mid-1984, following the Megaforce release of Metallica's second album, *Ride the Lightning*. At that point the Zazula's promotion efforts proved to be so successful that Michael Alago, head of Artists & Repertoire for Elektra Records, lured away Metallica.[2] Unable to compete with the broad marketing reach of Elektra (or those of the band's new management company, Q-Prime), Megaforce stood little chance of retaining any business association with Metallica. In the face of sticking with a financially troubled independent label (even with the close personal ties that went along with it), the band consciously decided to make a move into the burgeoning major-label metal market and tap into resources that would enable its commercial visibility to expand far beyond its already impressive underground status.[3] Metallica's decision was ultimately a business one, and would be its most significant career decision until the preproduction for the *Metallica* album at the end of the decade aimed, in part, to give their music a broader commercial appeal. For not the last time, moreover, accusations of "selling out" accompanied the label and management decision.

The intense commercial activity surrounding Metallica during 1983 and 1984 offers an illuminating nexus in the discussion of popular music and identity. Intertwined are the emotional impact of heavy and powerful music played to an enthusiastic audience and the desires of a range of individuals to capitalize on that enthusiasm for mutual monetary gain. Moreover, the arrangement with Elektra promised to give the band an unusual amount of authority over the artistic content being released in their name.[4] In other words, Elektra would not force the band to change its writing and recording habits by insisting on a company-chosen producer or company-hired songwriting help. At the same time, the arrangement enabled Metallica to appear as though it was separate from the industrial machinations that seemed to create pop metal bands, even though their relationship with Elektra—also home of Motley Crüe and Dokken, two of the most successful pop metal bands during the 1980s—meant the band was ensconced in it to some degree.[5]

The Genre of Thrash Metal

Formed in late 1981, Metallica emerged as perhaps the single most important group of a heavy metal underground during the 1980s, a musical style variously labeled "thrash metal," "speed metal," and (later in the decade) even "death metal." Based on their reworkings of British metal groups such as Diamond Head, Iron Maiden, and Motörhead, Metallica is usually credited with inventing the thrash metal genre during 1982 and throughout 1983, a process that culminated commercially with the release of *Kill 'Em All* in July 1983.

Throughout the 1980s many thrash metal groups followed, taking the sounds of *Kill 'Em All* as an important model and developing the particular aesthetic of shock and intensity that parents' groups would eventually understand as genuine celebrations of violence, mayhem, and Satan worship.

However, when we study the history of genres, we can best look for beginnings rather than origins, as different conversations wherein people come and go, where certain things jump out of previous conversations to be re-articulated in others. Within those conversations the details and […] In the case of the thrash metal genre, then, […] and say that Metallica drew on the multisectional song structures of New Wave of British Heavy Metal (NWOBHM) groups such as Diamond Head and Venom, foregrounding the speed, the particular harmonic language emphasizing tritones and flatted seconds, dark, fantastic lyrical imagery, and the celebration of a metal musical-cultural identity quite opposed to the glam metal scene in Los Angeles.[8] Throughout the 1980s, numerous bands joined the conversation, notably Mega-deth, Slayer, and Anthrax, and each offered further reconfigurations. For instance, Slayer placed less emphasis on the notion of multisection song structures in favor of even more breathtaking speed, even more shocking lyrics, and wildly chaotic guitar solos, while Megadeth's early music focused largely on Dave Mustaine's lead guitar skills.

Moreover, 1983 might be thought of as the origins of a thrash metal "school" simply because some of the most successful bands associated with the style released their first albums that year.[9] In the intersection of commerce and creativity, and due to the necessity of historically situated individuals for the production of musical meaning, the application of the thrash metal label to the 1983 albums represents the distillation of broad notions of musical identity into a linguistic expression. The large-scale commercial infrastructures of the record label system are of course not the sole means by which generic conventions are expanded to new participants, but neither is the label system insignificant in that regard. The understanding of Metallica (or Slayer, or the other 1983 bands) as representative of something called thrash metal took place after *Kill 'Em All* had come out.

By many accounts, thrash metal was not a term used to describe the 1983 bunch before they had connected with record labels, nor did the bands use it in their own promotion efforts.[10] Indeed, Metallica's 1982 business card used the term "power metal" to describe the band, but even that label did not amount to much importance. Accounts of early 1980s metal musicians and fans consistently acknowledge the appearance of the term thrash metal as occurring after they had heard the 1983 bands on purchased recordings and read about them in metal fanzines and other publications. It was in this way that the institutionalization of thrash metal and its application to Metallica's music largely took place. Such a sociolinguistic pattern was not unique to thrash metal, but it does help illustrate part of the dynamic interplay between musical expression and cultural meaning. Thus, while 1983 makes for a tidy origin for thrash metal, it overlooks the complexities of individual identities as well as the complex processes by which meanings are incorporated into new situations. Why, though, is the term thrash metal attached specifically to the

1983 moment? If sheer speed represented the most obvious and remarkable characteristic of the music, what was the difference between up-tempo metal from the late 1970s (for instance) and up-tempo metal from 1983 onwards? When does speedy metal not automatically constitute a distinct generic type called thrash metal? Where do the beginnings lie, and what kinds of utterances and subject positions become reconstituted in order to mark the beginning of a different set of conversations?

The primary musical difference lies in the consistent treatment of tempo in a rhythmically intense manner and as a distinctly aggressive musical element. The speed of thrash metal in the early 1980s was also a reconfiguration of the sonic transgression from two other sources: American hardcore punk bands such as Black Flag, Dead Kennedys, Misfits, and TSOL; and the British metal bands Venom and Motorhead. The relationship between American hardcore and thrash metal was complex, but a large degree of aesthetic influence projected outward from hardcore toward metal in the first half of the 1980s. Indeed, thrash metal giants Slayer and Anthrax (as well as Metal Church) were organized in 1982 by guitarists who had begun their performance careers in otherwise unsuccessful hardcore bands. The frenetic pace of hardcore, driven by loud rock instrumentation and a high-pitched distorted vocal style, stood as perhaps the most direct sonic link between the two styles. Thrash metal also drew on a similar suburban working class audience that characterized the hardcore scenes in Orange County, CA and San Francisco. Moreover, it imported hardcore's mosh pits and its image of independent Do It Yourself (DIY) values.[11] Still, though they shared a common interest in presenting extreme transgression, individual musicians could also be (and were) adamant about either a hardcore or metal identity. Thus, thrash metal's ultimate musical divergence from hardcore involved a conscious move to write more musically involved songs, as well as to embrace some amount of individual virtuosity. Frenetic tempi, according to the early thrash aesthetic, occupied only one element (to be sure, a significant one) of the ideal musical picture.

Lyrically, too, thrash metal musicians were much less ardent in their politics than most hardcore bands, preferring instead to derive their images of power from other sources. To thrash fans and musicians, hardcore seemed too preachy, too concerned about getting a "message" across (and usually a Leftist one at that), and perhaps too real. Dead Kennedys's "California Über Alles" (1980), for instance, opens with the lines "I am Governor Jerry Brown / My aura smiles and never frowns / Soon I will be President …" and exemplifies the potential for a kind of seriocomic critique largely jettisoned by thrash (even while the underlying harmonic language of these lyrics, with its rhythmic articulation of the tonic chord and reliance on a quasi-Phrygian tension in the riff, could comfortably be found a few years later in thrash metal[12]). Thrash metal ultimately came to present a politics of its own, indeed one that shared some common sociological roots and inquiries with hardcore. As will be discussed in Chapter 3, thrash metal lyrics later in the decade would question injustices related to industrial capitalism, warfare, the environment, as well as the issue of social control. But thrash metal's initial answers to questions of broader social relevance rarely revolved around music as the means for political commentary or direct sociopolitical change, Instead, thrash metal focused on the elevation of the individual, rather than a united underclass of "kids" (represented by bands), as the agent of social struggle. Indeed, its notable reliance on imagery drawn from fantasy and the occult provided the palette for thrash metal's representation of the triumph of the individual.

A British model for the aggressive speed of American thrash metal came from the particular punk/metal approach of Iron Maiden between 1979 and 1981, in particular the band's first two albums, *Iron Maiden* and *Killers,* featuring lead singer Paul Di'Anno. Di'Anno styled himself squarely between the contemporary idealized endpoints of metal and punk: he sported short spiky hair, but wore leather pants; he could sing with a punk shriek in songs such as "Sanctuary" and "Running Free," but also made an effort to "sing" during the band's less intense, more esoteric songs (e.g., "Strange World" and "Remember Tomorrow" from *Iron Maiden).* Nevertheless, Iron Maiden's use of two lead guitarists, who both played solos on most songs, and the technical ability of its bassist and group leader, Steve Harris, worked to secure its identity as a metal band. Harris, who professed very little respect for punks and punk music, also insisted upon an emphatic assertion of Iron Maiden's metal identity. Indeed, as Waksman explores, Iron Maiden ultimately offered another competing claim for heavy metal against both the constructed chaos of Venom and the pop sound of Def Leppard.

Yet, as a genre and a broader category of musical identity and experience, thrash metal should be thought of as more than just fast songs. As I mentioned previously, tempo in thrash metal was a consistent (though not necessarily constant), aggressive presence in the music. Earlier metal songs, such as Judas Priest's "Exciter" (the opening track to the 1978 album *Stained Class)* featured a fast tempo, intense texture, and rapid rifling across a dramatic structure, but they also lacked the particular component of confrontational aggression provided by either hardcore or Venom. Singer Rob Halford's voice was far too trained (in a classical sense), and usually far too beautiful for his vocals to have been considered transgressive in the way Chronos' vocals for Venom (or Motörhead's Kilmister) were. Additionally, within the oeuvre of Judas Priest the musical style of "Exciter" did not represent the band in a general way, competing as it did with delicate ballads like "Before the Dawn" and "Last Rose of Summer," or the mid-tempo hard rock of "Living After Midnight" and "Sinner."[15] As such, "Exciter" may have foregrounded tempo, but in doing so it did not also fundamentally redirect the band's overall musical aesthetic.[16]

Fast songs contribute to a range of possible subject positions, and tempo gains much of its significance from its relationship from song to song. Metallica's approach to aggressive speed differed noticeably from its contemporaries in the Los Angeles heavy metal scene, and the band's first recording, included on the first *Metal Massacre* compilation (1982), illustrates how surrounding context can inform the reception of musical style. The album features songs by nine metal bands with Metallica's "Hit the Lights" positioned last on the album.[17] While "Hit the Lights" has a fast tempo (160 bpm), other songs on the album also have sections of up-tempo rapid riffing such as "Live for the Whip" by Bitch. However, on this album there is a clear difference between fast and up-tempo in that

"Hit the Lights" makes *fast* the main point by consistently presenting the idea of fast as distinctly aggressive. In other songs on the compilation fast might also signal intensity, but sections of lesser intensity also seem to negate that sense of drive. "Live for the Whip" begins with a very fast, active riff marked by solid sixteenth notes in the guitar, but the energy falls away completely during the much slower whole-note feel of the song's verse sections (the drumbeat, in particular, falls off considerably). Thrash metal songs might also use tempo as a rhetorical tool to distinguish and characterize individual sections in songs, but never at the level of the whole note.

In "Hit the Lights," on the other hand, Metallica's aesthetic foregrounds consistent speed as a sign of consistent aggression and power.[18] The difference can be heard in the kind of rhythmic atmosphere created by the main riff, as repeated sixteenth-notes in the guitar and the continuous rapid snare hits on offbeat eighth-notes make the song feel twice as fast. The song's lyrics celebrate a heavy metal identity, and, [...] it is one of a number of thrash metal songs from the 1983 period that are about thrash metal itself. Hetfield's short opening shriek that coincides with the introduction of the full band texture is also crucial for making the fast tempo sound aggressive: his short, high-pitched, distorted vocalization coming across as a blast of transgressive energy. Indeed, initial vocalizations such as this became a significant stylistic marker for early thrash metal, appearing on the opening tracks of the debut albums by Slayer, Megadeth, and Anthrax. In each instance the shriek launches the proper introduction of the songs and thus serves as both a structural demarcation and a moment of controlled chaos.[19]

FIGURE 8.2
THE FAMILY WELLNESS HOUSE

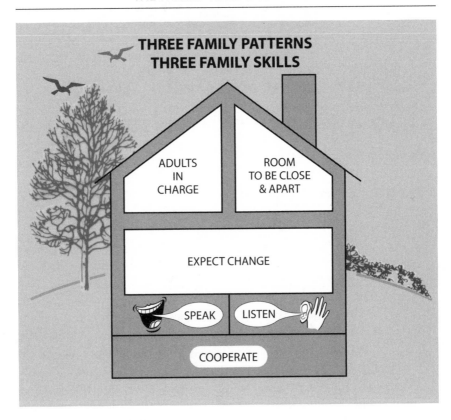

Epilogue

How to Survive and Thrive as a Mental Health Professional

Lo mas que lloras, lo menos que orinas.
[The more you cry, the less you pee.]

George Doub

JUST AS A healthy person must balance being an individual with connecting with others, and room to be close with room to be apart, so too the mental health professional must balance caring for self with caring for others. To do one and not the other is like caring for the body but not attending to the soul. To help others is a transcendent experience. Although the work can be extremely difficult and draining, it can also be incredibly satisfying. This positive outcome will only be achieved if we learn to live life fully, to thrive and not merely survive. To care for others over the long haul, clinicians must be equally fervent in caring for self.

George Doub, the cofounder of the Family Wellness model, died at 70 years of age doing two of the things he loved most: helping others and being around trees. Despite his chronological age, George had the vigor of a 40-year-old, the impishness and rebelliousness of a 14-year-old, and the playfulness of a 4-year-old. Although George had long ago graduated to the adults' table, he preferred being at the kids' table. George modeled, to those fortunate enough to be around him, how to help others, how to enjoy life, and how to be playful.

George frequently provided in-service training for social workers who worked with children damaged by severe physical abuse, sexual abuse, and neglect. In the midst of one such training, George invited the participants to connect with their own childhood experiences. One social worker started crying uncontrollably. The other seasoned clinicians were unsure about how to handle this very powerful and delicate situation involving one of their peers. George suddenly announced that it was okay to cry because, as he wryly observed, "The more you cry, the less you pee!" Such was George's ability to be both deep and irreverent, often at the same time.

The Family Wellness model provides a framework that psychotherapists and other mental health practitioners can adapt to varying theoretical orientations in a way that is practical and useful, both for the clinician and for the people whom we serve. This model assumes the best in people, recognizes the worst in people, and seeks to point all toward strength by building on what is already working in their lives, even in the worst of situations. Practitioners of the model catch people doing something right and celebrate those efforts.

The desire to help others is an altruistic instinct. Altruism is helping others without an expectation of receiving anything in return. At one level, it is writing a million-dollar check and asking for the gift to be anonymous. At another level, it is doing something kind and not expecting to be recognized for the kindness. People who give something or do something and want everyone to know about it have already received what they wanted. There is no additional reward. However, those who give and do it in secret receive the greatest possible reward: the satisfaction of being good stewards of what has been entrusted to them.

Therapists do amazingly good work for individuals and for society. They help those who have lost their way, those who were never on the way, or those who are simply way out there. Although therapists are generally compensated for their efforts, they usually provide their services in private, behind closed doors. Clinicians seldom get accolades, yet they generally feel a true sense of humanitarianism because of the nature of their work. Some therapists, however, continuously help others and forget to care for themselves. When that happens, the therapist's resources diminish.

When people have limited resources, they are less able to help others. Therapists, nevertheless, give because that is what they do. When therapists give out of emptiness rather than fullness, they sometimes become bitter, resentful, and angry. Such situations invite personal and professional burnout. The more therapists can achieve self-care and accept care from others, the more resources they will have to care for others.

You may have heard of the Beatitudes, which are written in the New Testament Gospel of Matthew. These observations and promises start with the word "blessed" (or the more modern word "happy"). I would suggest following "C" attitudes as a means for mental health professionals to care for themselves so that they have the resources to help others.

1. Be compassionate. Mental health professionals are a self-selected group of people who love the sometimes unlovable, who seek to understand the unknowable, and who desire to help the helpless and hopeless. It is love and concern for our fellow sojourners that bring many into the profession. The demonstration of compassion and respect for our clients produces the mirror that allows individuals to see themselves in a new way. Show that same compassion toward yourself. Forgive yourself when necessary, and see yourself for who you really are: a hero who passionately champions the well-being of others.

2. Be curious. You want to know what makes people tick. Wonder, also, about how a heavy airplane can stay suspended in air, how electricity comes to your home through wires, how computers work, why homegrown tomatoes taste better than those from the grocery store, and how musicians hear symphonies in their heads. That curiosity provides the never-ending source of delight in learning new things and being amazed by the familiar.

3. Be creative. There are many ways to get a job done. Clinicians sometimes get into patterns of problem-solving based on what we learned in school or from an admired supervisor. The familiar is good, yet we sometimes need to use new lenses through which to see ourselves and our work. I hope that your exploration into how the Family Wellness model works has helped you to find at least a few new tools for your work or has helped to sharpen the tools you already possessed. Creative endeavors in our work and in our play will keep us fresh throughout our journey.

4. Be careful. This book has emphasized the importance of a sound assessment even under circumstances that require quick decision making. Our assessment process should never be so quick that it becomes impulsive. We must be careful to weigh and evaluate all of the best available information before coming to any conclusion.

Decisions made on limited information should be so qualified. Being careful is the mark of a seasoned clinician.

5. Be carefree. Sometimes, clinicians are so careful that they develop paralysis by analysis. There is a time and place to be wild enough to make informed leaps of faith. Allowing ourselves to think outside of the box can free us to consider any and all options. At times, seasoned clinicians become rigid and unable to devise new hypotheses because these ideas seem out of step with our particular theoretical orientation. The ability to set orthodoxy aside, if only briefly, can free the thought process to consider all options. The clinician who can seem wild and crazy (as opposed to actually being wild and crazy) can enjoy the profession over the long haul.

6. Be contagious. Infect everyone around you with the love that brought you into the profession. Work so hard that people wonder how you do everything you do. At the same time, catch the passion that others have for what they do. Listen and learn what others have to teach you. Learn so much that you ooze passion and wisdom. Play hard—so hard that people wonder what's wrong with you.

7. Be cool. Learn to play the saxophone, play boccie (Italian lawn bowling), paint landscapes, or whatever else you always wanted to do.

8. Be courageous. Recognize no limits. Challenge authority. Embrace your passions. Continue to learn when others know it all. Continue to work when others are tired or retired. Continue to help when others only help themselves. Being a mental health professional is not for wimps.

9. Be crazy. Not literally (licensing boards frown on that). Just sort of. Think, feel, and live outside the box. Outrageous thought, ludicrous behavior, reverence, irreverence, spontaneity. Whatever you call it, have fun!

The legacy that George Doub left was a way of thinking and a way of being. He exemplified the best of what it is to be a mental health professional. He lived the "C" attitudes. Virginia Morgan Scott, who has earned the right to rest on her accomplishments, continues to recognize no limits. She teaches social workers in South Korea, conducts senior women's support groups, and captures the beauty of the world she sees through her love of photography. Her curiosity and fascination with life and the people who are our fellow sojourners keeps her as committed to growth as ever.

A popular bumper sticker of another era read: "He who dies with the most toys wins!" Psychotherapists will likely not be in that winner's circle. For one thing, most clinicians do not have that many toys (child therapists excluded). For another thing, therapists simply question the meaning of winning. Finally, therapists do not actually die. Instead, they simply reinterpret the context.

For us, surviving the therapeutic life is to run the course well. Work hard, play hard, live well. Upon death, the epithet is not usually, "He wished he had worked more." Make time for the people that matter in your life. Spend time with them. Balance love, work, and play. Give to yourself so that you have more to give to others.

To laugh often and much; to win the respect of intelligent people and the affection of children; to earn the appreciation of honest critics and endure the betrayal of false friends; to appreciate beauty; to find the best in others; to leave the world a bit better, whether by a healthy child, a garden patch or a redeemed social condition; to know even one life has breathed easier because you have lived. This is to have succeeded.

Ralph Waldo Emerson

References

Ainsworth, M. (1973). The development of infant-mother attachment. In B. M. Caldwell & H. N. Ricciuti (Eds.), *Review of child development research* (Vol. 3). Chicago: University of Chicago Press.

Ainsworth, M. (1985). Patterns of infant-mother attachments: Antecedents and effects on development. *Bulletin of the New York Academy of Medicine, 61,* 771–791.

Ainsworth, M. D. (1989). Attachment beyond infancy. *American Psychologist, 44,* 709–716.

Ainsworth, M., Blehar, M. C., Waters, E., & Wall, S. (1978). *Patterns of attachment: A psychological study of the strange situation.* Hillsdale, NJ: Erlbaum.

Alexander, F., & French, T. (1946). *Psychoanalystic therapy: Principles and applications.* New York: Ronald Press.

American Psychiatric Association. (2000). *Diagnostic and statistical manual of mental disorders* (4th ed., text rev.). Washington, DC: American Psychiatric Association.

Belsky, J., Campbell, S. B., Cohn, J. F., & Moore, G. (1996). Instability of infant-parent attachment security. *Developmental Psychology, 32,* 921–924.

Benenson, J. F. (1993). Greater preference among females than males for dyadic interaction in early childhood. *Child Development, 64,* 544–555.

Bowlby, J. (1969). *Attachment and loss: vol. 1. Attachment.* New York: Basic Books.

Bowlby, J. (1973). *Attachment and loss: vol. 2. Separation, anxiety, and anger.* New York: Basic Books.

Bowlby, J. (1988). *A secure base: Parent-child attachment and healthy human development.* New York: Basic Books.

Brems, C. (2002). *A comprehensive guide to child psychotherapy,* (2nd ed.). Boston: Allyn and Bacon.

Bretherton, I. (1990). Open communication and internal working models: Their role in the development of attachment relationships. In R. Dienstbier & R. A. Thompson (Eds.), *Nebraska symposium on motivation 1988: Vol. 36. Socioemotional development* (pp. 57–113). Lincoln: University of Nebraska Press.

Bukowski, W. M., Gauze, C., Hoza, B., & Newcomb, A. F. (1993). Differences and consistency between same-sex and other-sex peer relationships during early adolescence. *Developmental Psychology, 29,* 255–263.

Carlson, J., & Lewis, J. (2002). *Counseling the adolescent* (4th ed.). Denver: Love.

Carter, B., & McGoldrick, M. (1989). *The changing family life cycle: A framework for family therapy* (2nd ed.). Boston: Allyn and Bacon.

Cloud, H., & Townsend, J. (1992). *Boundaries: When to say yes, when to say no, to take control of your life.* Grand Rapids, MI: Zondervan.

Corey, G. (1996). *Theory and practice of counseling and psychotherapy.* Pacific Grove, CA: Brooks/Cole.

Corsini, R. J., & Wedding, D. (1995). *Current psychotherapies* (5th ed.). Itasca, IL: F. E. Peacock.

Cox, M. J., Owen, M. T., Henderson, V. K., & Margand, N. A. (1992). Prediction of infant-father and infant-mother attachment. *Developmental Psychology, 28,* 474–483.

DeAngelis, T. (1997). When children don't bond with parents. *APA Monitor, 28,* 10–12.

Eckerman, C. O., & Didow, S. M. (1996). Nonverbal imitation and toddlers' mastery of verbal means of achieving coordinated action. *Developmental Psychology, 32,* 141–152.

Eder, R. A. (1989). The emergent personologist: The structure and content of 3 1/2-, 5 1/2-, and 7 1/2-year-olds' concepts of themselves and other persons. *Child Development, 60,* 1218–1228.

Eder, R. A., Gerlach, S. G., & Perlmutter, M. (1987). In search of children's selves: Development of the specific and general components of the self-concept. *Child Development, 58,* 1044–1050.

Erikson, E. H. (1963). *Childhood and society* (2nd ed.). New York: Norton.

Family Wellness Associates. (2012). *Family wellness instructor manual.* Salida, CA: Author.

Fonagy, P., Moran, G., Edgcumbe, R., Kennedy, H., & Target, M. (1993). The roles of mental representations and mental processes in therapeutic action. *Psychoanalytic Study of the Child, 48,* 9–48.

Greenspan, S. I. (2003). *The clinical interview of the child* (3rd ed.). Washington, DC: American Psychiatric Publishing.

Guidano, V. (1991). *The self in process: Toward a post-rationalist cognitive therapy.* New York: Guilford.

Gumbiner, J. (2003). *Adolescent assessment.* Hoboken, NJ: John Wiley.

Gurman, A. S., & Jacobson, N. S. (2002). *Clinical handbook of couple therapy* (3rd ed.). New York: Guilford.

Isabella, R. A., & Belsky, J. (1991). Interactional synchrony and the origins of infant-mother attachment: A replication study. *Child Development, 62,* 373–384.

Jacobs, T. (1990). The corrective emotional experience: Its place in current technique. *Psychoanalytic Inquiry 10,* 433–545.

Jones, S. L., & Butman, R. E. (1991). *Modern psychotherapies: A comprehensive Christian appraisal.* Downers Grove, IL: InterVarsity Press.

Kerr, M. E., & Bowen, M. (1988). *Family evaluation: An approach based on Bowen theory.* New York: Norton.

Landreth, G. L. (1991): *Play therapy: The art of the relationship.* Bristol, PA: Accelerated Development.

Lanyado, M., & Horne, A. (2000). *The handbook of child and adolescent psychotherapy: Psychoanalytic approaches.* New York: Routledge.

Levenson, H. (1995). *Time-limited dynamic psychotherapy: A guide to clinical practice.* New York: Basic Books.

Miller, G. (2005). *Learning the language of addiction counseling* (2nd ed.). Hoboken, NJ: John Wiley.

Minuchin, S. (1974). *Families and family therapy.* Cambridge, MA: Harvard University Press.

Mitchell, S. (1988). *Relational concepts in psychoanalysis.* Cambridge, MA: Harvard University Press.

Morris, R. J., & Kratochwill, T. R. (1998). *The practice of child therapy* (3rd ed.). Needham Heights, MA: Allyn and Bacon.

Mullahy, P. (1952). *The contributions of Harry Stack Sullivan.* New York: Hermitage House.

Newman, B. M., & Newman, P. R. (1999). *Development through life: A psychosocial approach* (7th ed.). Belmont, CA: Wadsworth.

Olson, D. H., Olson-Sigg, A., & Larson, P. J. (2008). *The couple checkup.* Nashville: Thomas Nelson.

Park, K. A., & Waters, E. (1989). Security of attachment and preschool friendships. *Child Development, 60,* 1076–1081.

Pelham, B. W., & Swann, W. B. (1989). From self-conceptions to self-worth: On the sources and structures of global self-esteem. *Journal of Personality and Social Psychology, 57,* 672–680.

Rempel, J. K., Holmes, J. G., & Zanna, M. P. (1985). Trust in close relationships. *Journal of Personality and Social Psychology, 49,* 95–112.

Scott, V., Doub, G., & Runnels, P. (1999). *Raising a loving family.* Holbrook, MA: Adams Media.

Schacht, T. E., Binder, J. L., & Strupp, H. H. (1984). The dynamic focus. In H. H. Strupp & J. L. Binder, *Psychotherapy in a new key: A guide to time-limited dynamic psychotherapy.* New York: Basic Books.

Shapiro, J. L. (1995). *The measure of a man: Becoming the father you wish your father had been.* New York: Berkley.

Sullivan, H. (1953). *The interpersonal theory of psychiatry.* New York: Norton.

Tracy, R. L., & Ainsworth, M. (1981). Maternal affectionate behavior and infant-mother attachment patterns. *Child Development, 52,* 1341–1343.

van Ijzendoorn, M. H., Goldberg, S., Kroonenberg, P. M., & Frenkel, O. J. (1992). The relative effects of maternal and child problems on the quality of attachment: A meta-analysis of attachment in clinical samples. *Child Development, 63,* 840–858.

Vaughn, B., Egeland, B., Stroufe, L. A., & Waters, E. (1979). Individual differences in infant-mother attachment at 12 and 18 months: Stability and change in families under stress. *Child Development, 50,* 971–975.

Volling, B. L., Youngblade, L. M., & Belsky, J. (1997). Young children's social relationships with siblings and friends. *American Journal of Orthopsychiatry, 67,* 102–111.

Webster's encyclopedic unabridged dictionary of the English language. (2001). New York: Random House.

Weiss, J. (1993). *How psychotherapy works: Process and technique.* New York: Guilford.

Yalom, I. D., & Leszcz, M. (2005). *The theory and practice of group psychotherapy* (5th ed.). New York: Basic Books.

Index

[Page numbers followed by *f* or *t* refer to figures or tables, respectively.]

Index

[Page numbers followed by *f* or *t* refer to figures or tables, respectively.]

treatment planning (*continued*)
  romantic intimacy issues, 62–65
  self-sense assessment for, 22
trust
  clinical assessment and, 178–79
  in interpersonal relationship, 48, 67,
    181
  in therapeutic relationship, 101–2

violent or dangerous behavior, assessment of, 7–8

"We" sentences, 138–39
wimps, 114, 120–21

Yalom, Irving D., 42
"You" sentences, 106, 113, 119, 141